Benjamin Britten

His Life and Operas

by the same author

STRAVINSKY: THE COMPOSER AND HIS WORKS
TIPPETT AND HIS OPERAS
A HISTORY OF ENGLISH OPERA

BENJAMIN BRITTEN

His Life and Operas

by
ERIC WALTER WHITE

Second Edition, 1983
Edited by John Evans

UNIVERSITY OF CALIFORNIA PRESS
Berkeley and Los Angeles

This edition first published in 1983
by the University of California Press
Berkeley and Los Angeles, California

Printed in Great Britain

Library of Congress Cataloging in Publication Data

White, Eric Walter, 1905–
Benjamin Britten, his life and operas.

"Short bibliography": p.
Includes index.
1. Britten, Benjamin, 1913–1976. 2. Composers—England—Biography. I. Title.
ML410.B853W4 1982 782.1′092′4[B] 82–10882
ISBN 0–520–04893–8
ISBN 0–520–04894–6 (pbk.)

To Bettina Hürlimann-Kiepenheuer

Contents

Illustrations

ILLUSTRATIONS

ILLUSTRATIONS

Preface to the Second Edition, 1983

When at the end of the Second World War our contacts with Europe were being renewed, it was pleasant to find that our European friends wanted to find out what had been happening in Great Britain during the same period, and in particular what new manifestations there had been in the world of the arts. Sometime in 1945 my friends Martin Hürlimann, founder of the Atlantis publishing house in Zurich, and his wife Bettina, came over to London from Switzerland, and I took them to Sadler's Wells Theatre because I thought they would be interested in *Peter Grimes*, a new English opera that had recently been written by one of our most promising young composers, Benjamin Britten. I was particularly impressed by their enthusiastic reaction to this novelty because I felt it came from members of an audience that was familiar with the main stream of European culture and could therefore be accepted as a reliable judgement.

Within a few weeks of the first performance of *Peter Grimes* so many music and opera critics had turned up in London from different parts of the world that it was clear that in a comparatively short space of time the opera had earned itself a place in the international operatic repertory and Britten had been accepted as an important composer in that field. I was delighted. As an amateur of opera myself, and of English opera in particular, I welcomed this blossoming of native talent and its world-wide recognition.

On their return to Zurich the Hürlimanns wrote me a letter, confirming their interest in *Peter Grimes* and offering me a contract for a short book on Benjamin Britten to be published (in German) in their series of Atlantis Musikbücher. This invitation I accepted with pleasure as soon as I could be assured of the approval of Britten himself. This was quickly forthcoming; and henceforward whenever I consulted Britten on any of his music I could be certain of receiving a detailed and most considerate reply; but this did not alter the fact that the responsibility for the final text of these writings was mine alone.

Benjamin Britten: eine Skizze von Leben und Werk was published in Zurich in November 1948 in a German translation by Bettina and Martin Hürlimann; and the English edition was published a few days later by

Boosey & Hawkes in London. The text included separate essays on *Peter Grimes*, *The Rape of Lucretia* and *Albert Herring*. This proved so useful that in 1954 it was decided to bring it up to date by including chapters on *Paul Bunyan*, *The Beggar's Opera*, *The Little Sweep*, *Billy Budd* and *Gloriana*. A further revision and enlargement took place in 1970, when the book, now lavishly illustrated, was published by Faber and Faber in association with Boosey & Hawkes. New chapters were added on *The Turn of the Screw*, *Noye's Fludde*, *A Midsummer Night's Dream*, *Curlew River*, *The Burning Fiery Furnace* and *The Prodigal Son*.

I am deeply grateful to John Evans, Research Scholar to The Britten Estate, who has undertaken the editorial responsibility for the present edition. He has incorporated my new chapters on *Owen Wingrave* and *Death in Venice*, has updated the bibliography and list of published works, and has revised the text, where recent scholarship has shed new light on aspects of Britten's career.

Acknowledgements are also due to a number of other individuals who have assisted me in my researches for the earlier editions—W. H. Auden, Prince Ludwig of Hesse and the Rhine, Elizabeth Mayer and William Plomer (all now, sadly, deceased); and Henry Boys, Eric Crozier, Imogen Holst, Iris Lemare, Donald Mitchell, Peter Pears, Myfanwy Piper and Basil Wright. I am grateful to The Britten Estate, Boosey & Hawkes and Faber Music for permission to quote music examples from copyright material.

These little essays on the operas lay no claims to offer musical analyses in depth. Their aim has been simply to try to answer some of the more obvious questions an astute listener is likely to ask.

Those of us who took part in the renaissance of English music which occurred during Britten's lifetime realized that we were lucky enough to have been involved in an important moment of music history. When comes such another Golden Age?

E. W. W.

Part One
LIFE

A page from Britten's manuscript full score of 'L'Enfance' from *Quatre Chansons Françaises* (1928)

I
Early Works and Training

Edward Benjamin Britten was born at Lowestoft, Suffolk, on St Cecilia's Day (22 November) 1913, the youngest of four children. His father was a dental surgeon, and his mother a keen amateur singer, who acted for some years as secretary of the Lowestoft Choral Society. The Britten family lived in a house directly facing the North Sea.

Music was an early love of his. He started to compose at the age of five. He had piano lessons from Miss Ethel Astle, a local teacher, when he was eight, and started viola lessons with Mrs Audrey Alston of Norwich about two years later.

There were other activities too. Some years afterwards when he was accorded the freedom of his home town, he recalled his appearance on the stage of the Sparrow's Nest as 'a very small boy, dressed in skin-coloured tights, with madly curly hair, trying desperately to remember the lines spoken by Tom the water-baby, sitting on the lap of Mrs Do-as-you-would-be-done-by'* played on this occasion by his mother. It seems appropriate that this musician should have shown such an early interest in the stage.

His activity as a juvenile composer was phenomenal. He himself has described these early efforts as follows:† 'I remember the first time I tried, the result looked rather like the Forth Bridge, in other words hundreds of dots all over the page connected by long lines all joined together in beautiful curves. I am afraid it was the pattern on the paper which I was interested in and when I asked my mother to play it, her look of horror upset me considerably. My next efforts were much more conscious of *sound.* I had started playing the piano and wrote elaborate tone poems usually lasting about twenty seconds, inspired by terrific events in my home life such as the departure of my father for London, the appearance in my life of a new girl friend or even a wreck at sea. My later efforts luckily got away from these emotional inspirations and I began to write sonatas and quartets which were not connected in any direct way with life . . . At school I somehow managed

* From Benjamin Britten's speech at Lowestoft, 28 July 1951.

† From *The Composer and the Listener*, a broadcast talk by Benjamin Britten, 7 November 1946.

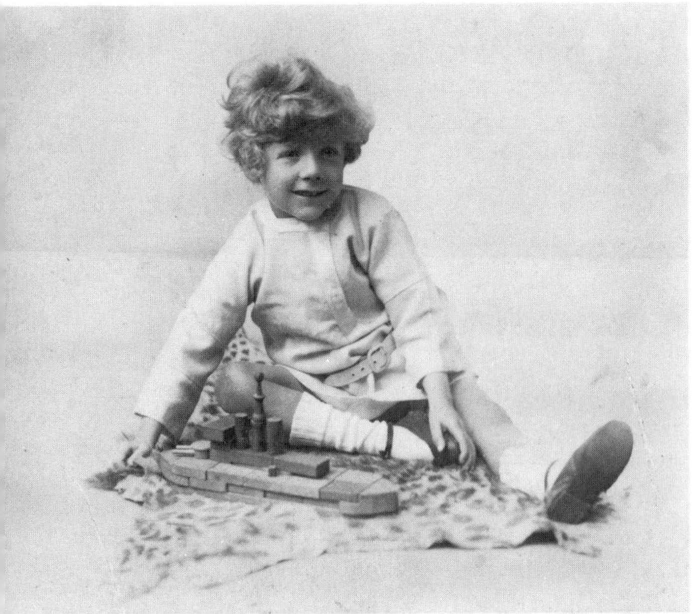

(*Left*) Benjamin Britten aged four (*Right*) Britten aged about seven

Britten with his family and friends at Lowestoft

to be able to fit in a great deal of writing with the extremely busy life that everyone leads at school . . . I wrote symphony after symphony, song after song, a tone poem called Chaos and Cosmos, although I fear I was not sure what these terms really mean.' By the time he left his preparatory school, South Lodge, at the age of fourteen to enter Gresham's School, Holt, he had already written ten piano sonatas, six string quartets, three suites for piano, an oratorio, and dozens of songs. Some of his piano music and three of the songs were arranged later for string orchestra in the *Simple Symphony* (1934). Other songs (*e.g.* the collection *Tit for Tat*) have been published in the course of time. There is no doubt that these early compositions provide convincing evidence of his musical precocity.

As a child he heard little music outside his home, with the exception of the local choral society concerts, some occasional chamber music concerts, and the Norfolk and Norwich Triennial Festival. At the 1924 Festival, he was present when Frank Bridge conducted his suite *The Sea* and, in his own words,* 'was knocked sideways'. Three years later when Bridge came to the 1927 Festival, his viola teacher, Audrey Alston, took her young pupil to meet the composer. 'We got on splendidly' Britten wrote years later,† 'and I spent the next morning with him going over some of my music . . . From that moment I used to go regularly to him, staying with him in Eastbourne or in London, in the holidays from my prep school. Even though I was barely in my teens, this was immensely serious and professional study; and the lessons were mammoth. I remember one that started at half past ten, and at tea-time Mrs Bridge came in and said, "Really, Frank, you must give the boy a break." Often I used to end these marathons in tears; not that he was beastly to me, but the concentrated strain was too much for me . . . This strictness was the product of nothing but professionalism. Bridge insisted on the absolutely clear relationship of what was in my mind to what was on the paper. I used to get sent to the other side of the room; Bridge would play what I'd written and demand if it was what I'd really meant . . . He taught me to think and feel through the instruments I was writing for.' This discipline was especially salutary to a person of Britten's phenomenal facility and fluency.

He spent two years at Gresham's School, Holt (from September 1928 to July 1930). During that period his interest in music was as intensive as ever—to the surprise of some of the other boys when they caught him reading orchestral scores in bed!‡ He was taking piano lessons from Harold Samuel in London, and his composition lessons with Frank Bridge

* From 'Britten Looking Back' by Benjamin Britten. *Sunday Telegraph*, 17 November 1963.

† Ibid.

‡ *Cf.* Benjamin Britten's speech on receiving an honorary degree at the University of Hull, 1962, reprinted in the *London Magazine*, October 1963.

Britten with Frank and Ethel Bridge, *c.* 1930

continued during the holidays. When he left school at the age of nearly seventeen, the die was cast and he had made up his mind to make music his career. In this he was backed by his parents; but there were a number of people who couldn't take such a decision seriously. There has always been a section of the population in this country that is suspicious of the arts and finds it difficult to accept the view that they can offer a talented young man a respectable livelihood. In later years he recalled how, at a tennis party at Lowestoft in the summer of 1930, he was asked by some people what career he intended to choose. When he told them he meant to be a composer, they were amazed. 'Yes, but what else?' they asked.* Clearly they looked on music as a spare-time occupation.

But if Britten thought that his troubles were over when he entered for an open scholarship in composition at the Royal College of Music, London, he was much mistaken. His examiners on that occasion were John Ireland, S. P. Waddington, and Ralph Vaughan Williams; and, according to Ireland,† the other two adjudicators were at first against making the award at all, one of them going so far as to say 'What is an English public school boy doing writing music of this kind?' But eventually Ireland managed to convince them, and the award was made.

His period at the College was an unhappy and frustrating one. As he himself said,‡ 'when you are immensely full of energy and ideas, you don't want to waste your time being taken through elementary exercises in dictation'. Although he was still composing reams of music, opportunities for performance inside the College were very restricted. When he failed to get two choral psalms of his performed, Frank Bridge tried to intervene, saying it was important for a young composer to hear what he'd written, 'because without aural experience it was difficult to link notes and sounds'. Vaughan Williams claimed that the singers weren't up to scratch, to which Bridge retorted that it was up to the College to have a sufficiently good chorus and he ought to use his influence. Only one of Britten's works was played at the College during the whole of the time he was a student; and that was his *Sinfonietta* (op. 1) for ten instruments, which was included in the programme of a chamber music concert on 16 March 1933, more than two months after it had received its first performance elsewhere. A String Quartet in D major (composed in 1931) was given a 'play through' by the Stratton Quartet, but it had to wait until 1975 for its first performance.

During the three years he remained at the College he worked under John Ireland for composition and Arthur Benjamin for piano. He won the Ernest Farrar Prize for composition and passed the examination for the Associateship of the College as a solo pianist in 1933. The importance of this period resided mainly in the fact that he now had better opportunities for hearing

* From *British Composers in Interview*, by Murray Schafer. Faber, 1963.

† Ibid.

‡ Ibid.

music, especially contemporary music, making friends with other musicians, and generally broadening his intellectual horizon. Among the classics, the strongest influences on his work were Mozart and Schubert, rather than Beethoven and Brahms; his love of Purcell was a later growth. His feeling for melody and lyricism led him to find in Mahler a congenial spirit. He was convinced that in compositions like *Des Knaben Wunderhorn* and the *Kindertotenlieder*, Mahler had expressed the idea behind the music with such success as to achieve real perfection of musical form. Among contemporary composers, he particularly admired the works of Stravinsky, Schoenberg and Berg. He tried (in vain) to get the score of *Pierrot Lunaire* bought for the library at the College. He was deeply impressed by the concert performance of *Wozzeck* that Sir Adrian Boult conducted at the Queen's Hall on 14 March 1934; so when he was given a small travelling scholarship on leaving the College, it was natural that he should express a wish to go to Vienna that autumn to study with Berg. But the College was consulted, and difficulties arose. Britten says,* 'I think, but can't be sure, that the Director, Sir Hugh Allen, put a spoke in the wheel. At any rate, when I said at home during the holidays, "I *am* going to study with Berg, aren't I?" the answer was a firm "No, dear." Pressed, my mother said, "He's not a good influence," which I suspected came from Allen. There was at that time an almost moral prejudice against serial music . . . I think also that there was some confusion in my parents' minds—thinking that "not a good influence" meant morally, not musically. They had been disturbed by traits of rebelliousness and unconventionality, which I had shown in my later school days.'

Outside the College, he pursued the possibility of getting his music performed, with varying degrees of success. M. Montagu-Nathan, when acting as secretary of the Camargo Society, met him at a party in 1932 and, finding he had written a ballet score, prevailed on him to submit it. Whether the manuscript was ever read by Edwin Evans, the Society's chairman, or by Constant Lambert, its conductor, is not clear; but in the course of time the score was returned to the composer and nothing more was heard of it.†

More fruitful was his contact with the Macnaghten-Lemare concerts of new music given at the Ballet Club Theatre (later known as the Mercury Theatre). It was here that the public heard his music for the first time. A *Phantasy for String Quintet* in one movement (posthumously published) and Three Two-Part Songs for female voices to words by Walter de la Mare were given at the concert on 12 December 1932; and the performance was reviewed by *The Times*, *Musical Times* and *Music Lover*. The notice by 'C.D.' in *Music Lover* particularly riled the young composer. 'C.D.' praised the three part-songs as being 'good from one who, I believe, is only 19; even

* From 'Britten Looking Back', op. cit.

† 'A Lost Opportunity' by M. Montagu-Nathan. *Radio Times*, 31 July 1953.

though they were reminiscent in a quite peculiar degree of Walton's latest songs which were heard recently elsewhere'. The Walton songs referred to were the Three Songs from *Façade* which had been performed for the first time at the Wigmore Hall on 10 October 1932. Twenty years later, recalling this first contact with his critics, Britten wrote: 'I was about 17 and three part-songs of mine had been given at a London theatre concert. They were written as a student's exercise, with the voice parts in strict canon. The first was amiably grotesque, the second atmospheric in a cool way, the third lumpily "folky". The only written criticism of this performance damned them entirely—as being obvious copies of Walton's three *Façade* Songs. Now anyone who is interested can see for himself that this is silly nonsense. The Walton Songs are brilliant and sophisticated in the extreme—mine could scarcely have been more childlike and naïve, with not a trace of parody throughout. It is easy to imagine the damping effect of this first notice on a young composer. I was furious and dismayed because I could see there was not a word of truth in it. I was also considerably discouraged.'*

On 31 January 1933, came the *Sinfonietta* which had been written the previous summer; and the programme of the concert on 11 December 1933 included Two Part-Songs for Mixed Choir and another unpublished work, entitled *Alla Quartetto Serioso—'Go play, boy, play'*. A programme note stated: 'This Quartet is not yet finished. There will be five movements in all, the three movements that are ready being the first, second, and fifth, viz. 1. Alla Marcia, 2. Alla Valse (the dance), 5. Alla Burlesca (ragging).'

In 1934, the year in which Holst, Delius and Elgar died, Britten came of age. He had left the College the previous year and was starting the difficult business of earning his living by composing. In addition to the works mentioned above, he had already written the *Phantasy Quartet* for oboe, violin, viola and cello, and a set of choral variations for mixed voices unaccompanied entitled *A Boy was Born*. During the year he was to add the *Simple Symphony*, a piano suite entitled *Holiday Diary*, a suite for violin and piano, and also a collection of twelve children's songs for voice and piano, *Friday Afternoons*, written for a boys' school at Prestatyn, where his brother was headmaster. None of these works had long to wait for performance. The *Phantasy Quartet* was first played by Leon Goossens and the International String Quartet in London, and also at the 1934 ISCM Festival at Florence (5 April). *A Boy was Born* was broadcast by the BBC on 23 February 1934; and when it was given its first public performance at the Macnaghten-Lemare concert of 17 December 1934, it received a glowing review from A. H. Fox-Strangways in the *Observer*.† ['The music] has one mark of mastery' he wrote, 'endless invention and facility. [The composer] takes what he wants, and does not trouble about what other people have

* From 'Variations on a Critical Theme'. *Opera*, March 1952.

† Afterwards reprinted in *Music Observed*, Methuen, 1936.

thought well to take. He rivets attention from the first note onwards: without knowing in the least what is coming, one feels instinctively that this is music it behoves one to listen to and each successive moment strengthens that feeling.'

Not all the critics were as enthusiastic as Fox-Strangways. On several occasions 'J.A.W.' complained in the *Daily Telegraph* that 'the solving of technical problems' seemed to 'occupy the composer's mind to the exclusion of musical ideas'; and William McNaught wrote: 'This young spark is good company for as long as his persiflage remains fresh, which is not very long. To do him justice, his *Sinfonietta* closed down in good time.'

Fortunately this was the period when John Grierson had collected some remarkably talented persons to work on documentary films for the GPO Film Unit; and Britten joined the group in 1935. In the five years 1935–9 he produced incidental music for some thirty documentary films by the GPO Film Unit, two documentary films by other units, and one feature film, *Love from a Stranger* (Trafalgar Films), directed by Rowland V. Lee.

He entered into this work with great zest and seems to have enjoyed its special conditions and restrictions. Some years later, when recalling this period of his life, he said:* 'I had to work quickly, to force myself to work when I didn't want to and to get used to working in all kinds of circumstances. The film company I was working for was not a big commercial one, it was a documentary company and had very little money. I had to write scores not for large orchestras but for six or seven instruments, and to make these instruments make all the effects that each film demanded. I also had to be very ingenious and try to imitate, not necessarily by musical instruments, but in the studio, the natural sounds of every-day life. I well remember the mess we made in the studio one day when trying to fit an appropriate sound to shots of a large ship unloading in a dock. We had pails of water which we slopped everywhere, drain pipes with coal slipping down them, model railways, whistles and every kind of paraphernalia we could think of.' In a short time he built up a considerable reputation in this specialized field. In 1936, shortly after the release of *Coal Face*, a pictorial survey of the coal industry in Great Britain, directed by Grierson with music by Britten, Kurt London wrote:† 'It is astonishing to observe how, with the most scanty material, using only a piano and a speaking chorus, he can make us dispense gladly with realistic sounds. This stylization makes a much stronger impression than a normal musical accompaniment.'

As soon as it was realized that this young composer had a flair for occasional and incidental music, commissions for theatre and radio as well as further film work followed. Britten was prepared to oblige with every type of music, light or serious; and the successful undertaking of these commissions

* From *The Composer and the Listener*, op. cit.

† *Film Music* by Kurt London, Faber and Faber, 1936.

showed that he was a reliable business man, who could work quickly and to time, and make the best of the limitations of the particular medium he was writing for and of the resources (however modest) that had been placed at his disposal. These virtues always stood him in good stead. He was often able to complete the greater part of the composition of a new work in his mind so that (as was the case with Mozart) the act of committing it to paper became an almost mechanical process which could be carried out at high speed. There was the added advantage that this enabled him to plan his musical life in advance so that he knew with reasonable certainty when he would be free to compose and by what date he could promise delivery of a new work. Reliability, expeditiousness and an unfailing capacity for hard work: these are formidable assets for an artist to have. When they are allied to an instinctive talent of no mean order, the result is bound to be phenomenal.

II
Collaboration with W. H. Auden

Four years before Britten entered Gresham's School, Holt, W. H. Auden, one of the older boys at the same school, published his first poem, *Woods in Rain*,* a set of octosyllabic couplets in the conventional Georgian style. In 1926 he became co-editor of *Oxford Poetry*; and his undergraduate poems, which had wide currency at the University, showed him at that time to be under the influence of masters like Rainer Maria Rilke and T. S. Eliot. By 1930, when his *Poems* were published by Faber and Faber, he had found his distinctive style.

Poems has rightly been hailed as a landmark of modern poetry. It is also a prophetic book, alive with a premonition of the doom that was so soon to bring disaster to the world. These thirty poems are imbued with a sense of struggle: war between classes, between parties, between members—war between life and death. But there is never any doubt what action has to be taken:

. . . never serious misgiving
Occurred to anyone,
Since there could be no question of living
If we did not win.†

In fact, more important still, the danger is seen to be actual not potential, and the poet analyses the new technique of total warfare with uncanny skill.

This is the dragon's day, the devourer's;
Orders are given to the enemy for a time
With underground proliferation of mould,
With constant whisper and the casual question,
To haunt the poisoned in his shunned house,
To destroy the efflorescence of the flesh,
The intricate play of the mind, to enforce

* Published in *Public School Verse*, Vol. IV, 1923–4 (Heinemann), where the author's name was misprinted 'W. H. Arden'.

† *Poems* XII.

Conformity with the orthodox bone,
*With organized fear, the articulated skeleton.**

The political awareness of Auden and of several of his contemporary poet friends, including C. Day Lewis, Louis MacNeice and Stephen Spender, was directed during the next few years to the struggle against Fascism in its various manifestations; and their attention was naturally focused on the battleground in Spain, for (as Auden wrote)

. . . the time is short, and
History to the defeated
May say Alas but cannot help nor pardon.†

Auden was not content, however, merely to write and publish poems. He looked towards stage and screen as being possibly more persuasive pulpits than the printed page. Remembering the didactic force of Bertolt Brecht's 'epic' drama, examples of which (like *Die Dreigroschenoper* and *Mahagonny*) he had seen performed in Germany at the beginning of the thirties, he began to experiment with social and political charades of his own, cast in the form of verse masques or plays. In *The Dance of Death*, which was published in 1933 and produced two years later by the Group Theatre at the Westminster Theatre, London, he aimed at presenting 'a picture of the decline of a class, of how its members dream of a new life, but secretly desire for the old, for there is death in them'. In 1935 he wrote his first full-length verse play, *The Dog beneath the Skin, or Where is Francis?* in collaboration with Christopher Isherwood. As its alternative title implies, it is a quest drama—a search for an heir—and it was produced by the Group Theatre at the Westminster Theatre in January 1936.

Meanwhile, his desire to work for the cinema had led him to approach the GPO Film Unit and ask his friend Basil Wright whether there was any way he could be employed in documentary films. Grierson was delighted to enlist his help; and he was forthwith engaged to write scripts for two films, *Coal Face* and *Night Mail*, that the Unit had in production. As Britten had been commissioned to provide the music for both films, it was necessary to arrange a meeting between the two collaborators. This took place on 5 July 1935, when Basil Wright drove Britten down to Colwall, near Malvern, where Auden was working as a master at a boys' preparatory school called 'The Downs'.

'*Coal Face*' (wrote Basil Wright)‡ 'was a pure experiment with the sound track. Its success as a film was not great, but without it the big success of *Night Mail* could not have been achieved. In *Coal Face* (which was devised and made by Cavalcanti), Auden and Britten used for the first time the

* *Poems* XVI.
† From *Spain*, 1937, reprinted in *Another Time*, Faber and Faber, 1940.
‡ From an unpublished letter to E. W. White dated 1 April 1948.

spoken voice reciting from official reports of mine disasters and from lists of coal-mining job-names—in rhythm, sometimes unaccompanied, and sometimes with percussion. *Coal Face* also contained the first musical setting by Britten of words by Auden: the poem beginning "*Oh lurcher-loving collier, black as night*" which was specially written for the film and set for female voices.' It was in *Coal Face*, too, that he had the ingenious idea of accompanying a train going through a tunnel and approaching nearer and nearer by reversing the sound track of a recorded cymbal clash. For *Night Mail*, Britten wrote a special instrumental score; and Basil Wright recalled how when 'the closing music of the film turned out to be too long, he made some fantastically ingenious excisions from the sound track itself'. After *Night Mail*, there was some talk of another film with which Auden and Britten were to be jointly concerned—an elaborate experiment about the negro in Western civilization, *Negroes* or *God's Chillun*—but it was never released. The only other films they were engaged on together were *Calendar of the Year* (1936) and *The Way to the Sea* (1937), the latter being a Strand Film Company documentary which described the electrification of the Portsmouth railway line, and for which Auden wrote a special end-commentary.

On 25 November 1935 Britten signed a contract with the firm of Boosey & Hawkes, the music publishers. Shortly afterwards when the miniature score of his *Sinfonietta* was published, he had a copy specially bound and, on the day it came back from the binders, showed it to Auden who, being on the point of leaving for Spain, wrote in pencil on the flyleaf his poem beginning—

*It's farewell to the drawing-room's civilised cry**

This collaboration, so auspiciously begun, soon developed outside the film world. In 1936 Britten was invited to compose a work for the Norfolk and Norwich Triennial Festival and asked Auden to devise a libretto. Auden chose man's relations to animals as his subject, selecting three poems to illustrate animals as pests, pets and prey—the first an anonymous prayer for deliverance from rats, the second an anonymous dirge on the death of a monkey entitled *Messalina*, the third *Hawking for the Partridge* by T. Ravenscroft—and framed them with an original prologue and epilogue of his own. The title of this symphonic cycle for high voice and orchestra was derived from the opening of the epilogue:†

Our hunting fathers told the story
Of the sadness of the creatures,

* This poem was first printed in *The Listener*, 7 February 1937, under the title 'Song for the New Year', and reprinted in *Another Time*, 1940.

† Reprinted in *Look, Stranger!* by W. H. Auden, 1936.

Pitied the limits and the lack
Set in their finished features . . .

Auden did not completely succeed in disciplining his material, and Britten cannot have had an easy task to set it. The resulting score was in places satirical, poignant and savage. According to Scott Goddard,* *Our Hunting Fathers* on its first performance at Norwich on 25 September 1936 'amused the sophisticated, scandalized those among the gentry who caught Auden's words, and left musicians dazzled at so much talent, uneasy that it should be expended on so arid a subject, not knowing whether to consider Britten's daring style as the outcome of courage or foolhardiness'. As for Frank Bridge,† he didn't really like the work, but defended it warmly. After the first performance he gave the young composer a long talking to about the scoring, which he thought didn't work, though he approved of the approach to the individual instruments. He was severe on the last movement 'as being too edgy'; and in the end Britten revised it.

In 1937 came the first of Britten's song cycles, *On This Island.* For this he chose five lyrics by Auden, of which four came from *Look, Stranger!* and the fifth (Nocturne) was extracted from *The Dog beneath the Skin.* This selection was to have been the first of two or more collections with the common title *On This Island*: but in the event only the first set was completed. Here Britten probably showed sound judgement, for the specific gravity of these lyrics written by Auden *dans l'an trentième de son age*, with their mixture of romance, neurosis and satire, do not call for treatment on too extended a scale. When it first appeared, *On This Island* had an exciting quality of contemporaneity—it was the product of two young minds thinking along related lines and working to a common purpose—and although it has subsequently been rather overshadowed by the later song-cycles, it is never likely to lose its special attraction. Here, too, Britten benefited from Frank Bridge's criticism. It appears that the first song originally began with a downward *glissando* on the piano. As Britten said,‡ 'Bridge hated that, and said I was trying to make a side-drum or something non-tonal out of the instrument: on the piano, the gesture ought to be a musical one.' So he rewrote it as a downward D major arpeggio.

After *The Dog beneath the Skin*, two further verse plays came from Auden's collaboration with Isherwood. The Group Theatre produced *The Ascent of F6* at the Mercury Theatre, London (26 February 1937) and *On the Frontier* at the Arts Theatre, Cambridge (14 November 1938). To both of these Britten wrote incidental music scored for piano (four hands) and percussion; and in the case of *On the Frontier* he added parts for two trumpets. Other Group Theatre productions at the Westminster Theatre

* From *British Music of Our Time*, edited by A. L. Bacharach, Pelican Books, 1946.

† See 'Britten Looking Back', op. cit. ‡ Ibid.

for which Britten provided music were *Timon of Athens* (November 1935), the *Agamemnon* of Aeschylus in Louis MacNeice's translation (November 1936), and MacNeice's verse play *Out of the Picture* (December 1937).

Early in 1938 the collaboration between Auden and Britten was interrupted by a journey Auden and Isherwood made to the Far East to report on the Sino-Japanese War. At a farewell party in London for the two writers, Hedli Anderson sang three of the Cabaret Songs that Britten had composed in 1937 to words by Auden.* The only other work by Britten and Auden belonging to 1937 was *Hadrian's Wall*, a BBC radio feature.

There was a further occasion, after Auden's return from China, when they worked together. A Festival of Music for the People was organized in London 'by musicians of the progressive movement in Britain'; and for its third concert at the Queen's Hall on 5 April 1939 Britten wrote a *Ballad of Heroes* to honour men of the British Battalion, International Brigade, who had fallen in Spain. This consisted of three movements: (1) Funeral March with words by Randall Swingler; (2) Scherzo (Dance of Death) with words by Auden, and (3) Recitative and Choral with words by both Auden and Swingler. The moral of the work was contained in the Epilogue (Funeral March):

To you we speak, you numberless Englishmen,
To remind you of the greatness still among you
Created by these men who go from your towns
To fight for peace, for liberty and for you.

Britten set the text for tenor (or soprano) solo, chorus and orchestra, with three extra trumpets to be played in a gallery and (later) off; and it was conducted on this occasion by Constant Lambert. The work is pervaded by a feeling of deep bitterness, for at that moment the Spanish Civil War was over, and it seemed as if the forces of reaction were triumphing everywhere in Europe.

There is no doubt that this friendship with Auden had a great effect on Britten. It confirmed his liking for occasional quips and quiddities. It introduced him to Auden's favourite death fixation—the obsession that the illness and death of an individual symbolizes the decay and dissolution of a class—and for a period he seemed to have adopted it so wholeheartedly that it became almost a rule for his more extended compositions to include a key movement entitled Dance of Death or Funeral March. Fortunately, however, he outgrew this idea before it had time to shrivel into a fixed and meaningless cliché. But his most valuable and lasting gains were probably a fuller sense of the artist's political responsibility, a deeper appreciation of

* Britten composed a fourth Cabaret Song, entitled *Calypso*, in America in 1939; and all four songs were posthumously published by Faber Music in 1980.

the beauties of poetry, and a growing awareness of the aesthetic problems involved in the alliance of words and music. Through Auden he was introduced, not only to the poetry of some of his contemporaries, but also to that of earlier writers like Donne and Rimbaud.

For his part, Auden always found Britten a wonderful person to work with; and in later years his opera librettos for Stravinsky and Henze doubtless benefited from this collaboration.

III
American Visit

Important though Britten's collaboration with Auden undoubtedly was, it would be wrong to imply that it occupied his working life during the last years of the thirties to the exclusion of other activities. During this period a number of other works were written and performed. In London the Lemare Concerts at the Mercury Theatre continued to feature his music. A *Te Deum* written specially for Maurice Vinden and the Choir of St Mark's, North Audley Street, London, was performed at the Mercury Theatre on 27 January 1936, and provoked a rather curious review from Constant Lambert, who wrote in *The Sunday Referee*: 'Mr Britten is, I admit, rather a problem to me. One cannot but admire his extremely mature and economical methods, yet the rather drab and penitential content of his music leaves me quite unmoved. At the same time he is the most outstanding talent of his generation and I would always go to hear any first performance of his.'

1936 was the year in which he went to Barcelona, where he played his Suite for Violin and Piano with Antonio Brosa at the ISCM Festival. On this occasion he met the young composer Lennox Berkeley, who had been living in Paris for some time, and found him to be a most congenial companion. Years later Berkeley recalled how they had explored the city together.*

> Our schedule was very full. Among the various sideshows for those attending the festival was an afternoon display of folk dancing, held in a small park called Mont Juic. Ben Britten and I went there together and were much taken with some of the tunes that accompanied the dances. Ben wrote them down on old envelopes and various pieces of paper which he produced from his pockets. From these jottings we eventually constructed the orchestral Suite which we called *Mont Juic*. Only later did we discover that Mont Juic was better known as the name of the prison, but despite the risk of seeming to suggest that we had been

* 'Views from Mont Juic' by Lennox Berkeley. *Tempo*, September 1973.

lodged there during our stay in Barcelona, we decided to keep to the title.

Neither of them realized that at that moment Spain was on the brink of civil war. When Britten returned to London, his Suite for Violin and Piano was announced for performance at a Lemare Concert on 1 February 1937, but was withdrawn on account of his mother's death the day before. (His father had died a few years previously.)

In 1937 he obtained his first popular success with the *Variations on a Theme of Frank Bridge*. He accepted an invitation in May of that year to write a new work for the Boyd Neel String Orchestra to play at the Salzburg Festival on 27 August; and Boyd Neel recalled* that in ten days' time he appeared 'with the complete work sketched out. In another four weeks it was fully scored for strings as it stands today, but for the addition of one bar'. The theme he chose came from the second of Frank Bridge's *Three Idylls* for string quartet (1911), and he wrote variations on it, entitled March, Romance, Aria Italiana, Bourrée Classique, Wiener Waltzer, Moto Perpetuo, Funeral March, Chant, and Fugue and Finale, which reveal to the full his resource and skill in dealing with a string orchestra. When some years later he was cross-examined about his preference for this medium, he replied:† 'I am attracted by the many features of the strings. For instance the possibilities of elaborate *divisi*—the effect of many voices of the same kind. There is also the infinite variety of colour—the use of mutes, pizzicato, harmonics and so forth. Then again, there is the great dexterity in technique of string players. Generally speaking, I like to think of the smaller combinations of players, and I deplore the tendency of present-day audiences to expect only the luscious "tutti" effect from an orchestra.'

The work caused a sensation at Salzburg and soon gained for its composer an international reputation. Within less than two years it had been played more than fifty times in various parts of Europe and America.

Late in 1937 he acquired a converted windmill in Snape in Suffolk, a few miles inland from Aldeburgh, and one of the first works he composed there was the Piano Concerto.

The Piano Concerto in D major was first performed at a Promenade Concert at the Queen's Hall on 18 August 1938, with the composer as soloist. In its original form, it comprised four movements: I. Toccata, II. Waltz, III. Recitative and Aria, IV. March. Britten himself explained that the work 'was conceived with the idea of exploiting the various important characteristics of the piano, such as its enormous compass, its percussive quality, and its suitability for figuration; so that it is not by any means a

* 'The String Orchestra' by Boyd Neel in *Benjamin Britten: a commentary* (edited by Mitchell and Keller). Rockliff, 1952.

† 'Conversation with Benjamin Britten.' *Tempo*, February 1944.

symphony with piano, but rather a *bravura* concerto with orchestral accompaniment.' Eight years later, the third movement, which had given the impression of being a weak and rhetorical setting of an imaginary script, was withdrawn and an Impromptu (or, more accurately, an air with seven variations) substituted for it. For this new movement Britten used only material contemporary with the original work, drawing on incidental music to a BBC play *King Arthur* by T. H. White and using some of the figuration from the earlier movement.

The American composer, Aaron Copland, has described a happy visit to the Old Mill at Snape that summer.* He had with him the proofs of his school opera, *The Second Hurricane*, which he played over for Britten. In return Britten gave him a run-through of his recently completed Piano Concerto. Copland was 'immediately struck by the obvious flair for idiomatic piano writing in the Concerto, but had some reservations as to the substance of the musical materials'.

Meanwhile, the political scene in Europe was becoming increasingly sombre; and this naturally affected Britten. In 1937 he composed a *Pacifist March* to words by Ronald Duncan for the Peace Pledge Union, which had been founded by the Revd. Canon Dick Sheppard in 1934. The following year, he wrote incidental music for *Advance Democracy*, a documentary film directed by Ralph Bond in association with Basil Wright and produced by the Realist Film Unit in 1939. He also composed a part-song for unaccompanied mixed chorus with the same title and with words by Randall Swingler, but this was not used in the documentary film. It was followed by the *Ballad of Heroes* mentioned in the previous chapter. This, together with the incidental music for J. B. Priestley's play *Johnson over Jordan* and the radio adaptation of T. H. White's *The Sword in the Stone*, was the last music Britten wrote before leaving England for America.

This was a period of great depression and unrest. Rather than become helpless victims of a new Fascist or Nazi order with its attendant persecution and misery, many persons were looking for salvation to the New World and considering the possibility of emigration. A lead in this direction was given by Auden. He and Isherwood visited America early in 1939, and by the outbreak of war he had decided that only in the United States could he find the complete anonymity he needed if he was to break away from the European literary family and let his individual genius develop in full independence. Louis MacNeice quotes him as saying that 'an artist ought either to live where he has live roots or where he has no roots at all; that in England today the artist feels essentially lonely, twisted in dying roots, always in opposition to a group'.†

* From 'A Visit to Snape' by Aaron Copland. *Tribute to Benjamin Britten on his Fiftieth Birthday*, Faber, 1963.

† Letter from Louis MacNeice printed in *Horizon*, July 1940.

There were a number of reasons that led Britten also to leave England in May 1939. The darkening political situation was one. Then he was dissatisfied with the reception of his work in this country and had a growing sense of frustration as an artist, which he felt might be dissipated by a change of scene—in his own words,* he was 'muddled, fed-up and looking for work, longing to be used'. But the dominant factor was certainly Auden's personal example and his decision to become a citizen of the United States; and when Britten first reached America, it was his firm intention to do likewise.

Britten was accompanied on this voyage by his friend Peter Pears, who had been a member of the BBC Singers from 1936 to 1938 and had already toured America twice with the New English Singers. They went first to Canada and were then invited to New York to hear the first American performance of the *Variations on a Theme of Frank Bridge* by the New York Philharmonic on 21 August 1939. Eleven days later Auden was sitting in one of the dives on 52nd Street,

Uncertain and afraid
As the clever hopes expire
Of a low dishonest decade:
Waves of anger and fear
Circulate over the bright
And darkened lands of the earth,
Obsessing our private lives;
The unmentionable odour of death
Offends the September night.†

For Britten and Pears there was a certain degree of consolation in the fact that Pears had sympathetic friends who offered them the hospitality of their home on Long Island. There was even a substitute 'home from home' atmosphere, for 'when, driving out to Amityville, Britten read the nostalgic word "Suffolk" on the signpost, he was delighted to be by the sea again and in his native county, although so far from home'.‡ He stayed there for the greater part of the next two and a half years, with the exception of a few months spent with Auden in Brooklyn early in 1940 and a visit to California in 1941.

The Violin Concerto in D minor was one of the first of his works to be written in America—it was finished at St Jovite in the Province of Quebec, Canada, in September 1939 and received its first performance (28 March 1940) by the New York Philharmonic under John Barbirolli, with Antonio

* *On Receiving the First Aspen Award*, Faber, 1964.

† From *Another Time*.

‡ From 'Benjamin Britten: Another Purcell', by Phoebe Douglas. *Town and Country*, December 1947.

Brosa as soloist. Although the violin part, which was edited by Brosa himself,* calls for great virtuosity from its executant, the Concerto is by no means an extended violin solo with orchestral accompaniment, but represents a real advance on the Piano Concerto in powers of construction. Another composition belonging to this period is *Canadian Carnival* (*Kermesse Canadienne*), a light-hearted frolic for symphony orchestra.

But more important than either of these was *Les Illuminations*, which was finished at Amityville on 25 October 1939. When this song cycle for high voice and string orchestra received its first complete performance† in London on 30 January 1940, it not only confirmed the uniformly favourable impression made by the *Variations on a Theme of Frank Bridge* two years previously, but also showed Britten to be a song-writer of exceptional range and subtlety. When Rimbaud wrote the prose poems in *Les Illuminations*, he was living in London with Verlaine, spending much of his time in the East End and the docks. Remembering the prophetic Latin tag *Tu Vates eris* that Apollo had inscribed on his brow when he was a schoolboy of fourteen, Rimbaud was arrogantly confident that through the stimulus of debauch and vice he could attain the power of supernatural vision. In poems like *Métropolitain*, *Villes*, and *Parade* (the last two of which are included in Britten's song cycle) he seemed to have discovered all the monstrous significance of a modern industrial capital. Contact with the fierce alchemy of these poems quickened a new nerve in Britten's musical sensibility. The words and music fused in a sudden startling outburst of heat and energy. '*J'ai seul la clef de cette parade sauvage.*' Britten had found the key as well as Rimbaud; and the door opened on to a hitherto unknown surrealist world.

The *Diversions* for piano and orchestra were written in Maine in the summer of 1940 for the one-armed Viennese pianist, Paul Wittgenstein, who reserved the sole rights of performance until 1951. This work consisted of 'eleven straightforward and concise variations on a simple musical scheme'; and in an introductory comment to the concerto, Britten said: 'I was attracted from the start by the problems involved in writing a work for this particular medium, especially as I was well acquainted with and extremely enthusiastic about Mr Wittgenstein's skill in overcoming what appear to be insuperable difficulties. In no place in the work did I attempt to imitate a two-handed piano technique, but concentrated on exploiting and emphasizing the single line approach. I have tried to treat the problem in every aspect, as a glance at the list of movements will show: special features are trills and scales in the Recitative, widespread arpeggios in the Nocturne, agility over the keyboard in the Badinerie and Toccata, and repeated notes in the finale

* Britten later revised the solo part himself in 1958.

† 'Being Beauteous' and 'Marine' had already been performed at a Promenade concert in August 1939.

Tarantella.' The theme with its fourths shows a certain affinity with that of *The Turn of the Screw*.

The *Sinfonia da Requiem*, written about the same time, had a particularly strange history.

Having been approached through the British Council some time in 1940 and asked whether he would write a symphony for a special festivity connected with the reigning dynasty of a foreign power, Britten agreed in principle, provided it was understood no form of musical jingoism was called for. On further investigation, it appeared that the country in question was Japan and the festivity the 2,600th anniversary of the foundation of the Mikado's dynasty in 660 B.C. by Jimmu Tenno, and that other composers in France, Germany, Italy and Hungary had received similar commissions. In due course, the outline of a *Sinfonia da Requiem* in three movements—*Lacrymosa*, *Dies Irae*, and *Requiem Aeternam*—was submitted to the Japanese authorities and approved. Britten felt that this work, which is permeated with a sense of the terror and ghastliness of war, would not be inappropriate to the occasion in view of the Sino-Japanese conflict. He was wrong, however; and about six months after the completed score had been handed over, he received a furious protest through the Japanese Embassy, complaining that the Christian dogma and liturgical ceremony that lay at the basis of the work were a calculated insult to the Mikado, and rejecting the *Sinfonia* out of hand. With Auden's help he drafted a suitable reply; but shortly afterwards the Japanese attacked the Americans at Pearl Harbor, and thenceforth all communications were severed. The first performance of the *Sinfonia da Requiem* was given on 30 March 1941, by the New York Philharmonic under Barbirolli. There is no record of a performance in Tokyo, although it seems possible the work may have been put into rehearsal there sometime in 1941.

About this time Britten's interest in oriental music was stimulated by his meeting Colin McPhee; and the two musicians joined together in making gramophone records of some Balinese music which McPhee had transcribed for two pianos—an interesting anticipation of the oriental part of the score of *The Prince of the Pagodas*.

In the list of Britten's published works to which opus numbers were given, two gaps occurred between opus 15 (the Violin Concerto) and opus 18 (*Les Illuminations*). These were reserved for *Young Apollo*, a work for piano, string quartet and string orchestra written for the Canadian Broadcasting Corporation, first performed in Toronto in August 1939, but subsequently withdrawn; and a group of about half a dozen choral settings of poems of Gerard Manley Hopkins, which Britten held back from publication and performance as being not up to standard. A work for which no opus number seems to have been reserved was *Paul Bunyan*, written early in 1941. Thirty-five years later the score and text were revised and the work was given a stage performance at the Maltings Concert Hall, Snape, in the summer of 1976; and when it was finally published, it was given the opus number 17. This choral operetta, in which Britten's partnership with Auden was resumed, was put on for a week's run at the Brander Matthews Hall, Columbia University, New York, in May 1941. Their treatment of this American legend came in for some hard knocks—Britten himself wrote a few years later 'the critics damned it unmercifully, but the public seemed to find something enjoyable in the performance'.*

Britten wrote incidental music for two Columbia Workshop broadcasts while he was in America: a monologue by Auden for Dame May Whitty called *The Dark Valley*, and Auden's adaptation of D. H. Lawrence's *The Rocking Horse Winner*. He also executed various ballet commissions. *Soirées Musicales*, a suite of five movements that he had adapted from Rossini in 1935 for the use of the GPO Film Unit had already been used by Antony Tudor to accompany a ballet called *Soirée Musicale* that was produced by the London Ballet at the Palladium, London, on 26 November 1938. When in 1941 Lincoln Kirstein wanted a new ballet for the South American tour of his American Ballet, Britten composed another suite after Rossini called *Matinées Musicales*, joined this to his *Soirées Musicales* suite, and added the Overture to *La Cenerentola* as a finale. The resulting ballet was called *Divertimento*, and its choreography was composed by Balanchine. About the same time Britten made a new orchestral version of *Les Sylphides* for Ballet Presentations Inc. (Ballet Theater), New York City. There was some talk of his writing a ballet for Eugene Loring and his Dance Players to be called *The Invisible Wife*; but in the end that project came to nothing. Instead, he allowed his *Variations on a Theme of Frank Bridge* to be used by Dance Players as an accompaniment to *Jinx*, a ballet about circus people and their superstitions with choreography by Lew Christensen. This was first performed in 1942 at the National Theatre, New York.

He visited Ethel and Rae Robertson in California in the summer of 1941, and during his stay at Escondido wrote various two-piano compositions for them: the *Introduction and Rondo alla Burlesca*, the *Mazurka Elegiaca* in memory of Paderewski,† and the *Scottish Ballad* for two pianos and orchestra. At the same time he was busy on his String Quartet No. 1, which had been commissioned by that Great American patroness of music, Elizabeth Sprague Coolidge, and was performed for the first time by the Coolidge String Quartet in Los Angeles in September 1941. Later that year it won him the Library of Congress Medal for services to Chamber Music.

But, meanwhile, what had happened to his intention of seeking

* *Peter Grimes: Sadler's Wells Opera Books No.* 3.

† This was originally intended for publication in a memorial volume for Paderewski, but it was not included, as it had been mistakenly written for two pianos instead of one as specified.

naturalization as an American citizen? When the Second World War broke out in September 1939, he realized that, had he still been in England, scruples of conscience would have prevented him from becoming a combatant; but he could not help wondering whether, should he decide to return, there might be ways in which his services as a non-combatant might be useful. The progress of the war aggravated his mood of indecision. Louis MacNeice, who had numerous discussions with Auden in the autumn of 1940, wrote: 'For the expatriate there is no Categorical Imperative bidding him return—or stay. Auden, for example, working eight hours a day in New York, is getting somewhere; it might well be "wrong" for him to return. For another artist who felt he was getting nowhere it might be "right" to return.'*

In Britten's case, the mental struggle whether to stay in America or return to England was echoed by a physical illness. He suffered from an acute streptococcal infection during the whole of 1940. (It was perhaps typical of Auden that he should claim that this illness was nothing more than the physical expression of Britten's psychological indecision.) But as he recovered the following year, his course seemed crystal clear. He would not become a naturalized American, but would go back to England. His decision to return was confirmed by a strange incident that was destined to have important repercussions on his future career. During his stay in California he happened to pick up a copy of the BBC's weekly magazine, *The Listener*, for 29 May 1941, and there his eyes were caught by the opening words of an article by E. M. Forster: 'To talk about Crabbe is to talk about England.' Forster was discussing George Crabbe, the East Anglian poet of the late eighteenth and early nineteenth centuries, who had been born at Aldeburgh, not far from Lowestoft. Reading how this bleak little fishing village on the Suffolk coast 'huddles round a flint-towered church and sprawls down to the North Sea—and what a wallop the sea makes as it pounds at the shingle!' Britten realized with a twinge of homesickness that he must not only familiarize himself with Crabbe's poems (which at that time he did not know), but also get back to his native Suffolk as quickly as possible.

But it was not easy to cross the Atlantic at that stage of the war; and he and Peter Pears were kept waiting for nearly six months on the East Coast of the United States before they could obtain a passage in March 1942. The delay had certain compensations, however. It meant he was able to attend a performance of the *Sinfonia da Requiem* under Serge Koussevitzky in Boston. When in the course of conversation the conductor asked him why he had as yet written no full-scale opera, Britten, who had already been turning over in his mind the possibility of quarrying material for an opera out of Crabbe's poem *The Borough*, replied that 'the construction of a scenario,

* From 'Traveller's Return'. *Horizon*, February 1941.

discussions with a librettist, planning the musical architecture, composing preliminary sketches, and writing nearly a thousand pages of orchestral score, demanded a freedom from other work which was an economic impossibility for most young composers'.* Koussevitzky was interested in the Crabbe project and, when they met again some weeks later, announced that he had arranged for the Koussevitzky Music Foundation to put up $1,000 for the opera, which was to be dedicated to the memory of his wife, Natalie, who had recently died.

* *Peter Grimes: Sadler's Wells Opera Books No.* 3.

IV
In Wartime England

In the spring of 1942, the fortunes of Great Britain and her allies seemed to be at their nadir. Their disasters in Russia, the Far East and North Africa were only too apparent, and the pattern of recovery as yet unrevealed. Nevertheless, their faith in ultimate victory was completely unshaken.

Britten returned to a land of black-out, material privations and total mobilization. As a pacifist by conviction, he appeared before a tribunal; but in view of his conscientious objections, he was exempted from active service. He was allowed to continue with his work as a composer, and as a pianist he appeared at the special wartime concerts organized all over the country by the Council for the Encouragement of Music and the Arts (CEMA), which later grew into the Arts Council of Great Britain. Then, as always, he laid great store by his work as a musical executant. In an interview given early in 1944* he said: 'I find it valuable for my activities as a composer to see how listeners react to the music. I also enjoy rehearsals—especially if I am working with sympathetic and intelligent musicians—delving deeper and deeper into the great music of all ages, and learning a lot from it. There are some composers whose music I do not like, but performing it makes me analyse my reasons for the dislike, and so prevents it from becoming just habit or prejudice.'

He had left America on 16 March 1942, sailing in a small Swedish cargo boat, and by the time he reached England after being mewed up for more than a month in a tiny cabin next to the refrigerating plant, he had written two new choral works, the *Hymn to St Cecilia* and *A Ceremony of Carols*. In addition, he brought over from America a setting of *Seven Sonnets of Michelangelo* for tenor and piano, and a number of new works written and performed in the United States, but not yet heard in Great Britain. These were considerable assets. In wartime England, opportunities for hearing new music were all the more welcome because of their infrequency; and Britten's new compositions met with ready acceptance, partly because of their obviously attractive qualities of ease, grace and intelligibility, and

* 'Conversation with Benjamin Britten.' *Tempo*, February 1944.

partly also because it was immediately apparent that during his three years' residence in the United States his mind and music had strikingly matured.

Out of Michelangelo's seventy-seven sonnets, Britten chose numbers XVI, XXXI, XXX, LV, XXXVIII, XXXII and XXIV and set them in a fine flowing *bel canto* style. The pure and open vowels of the Renaissance Italian are adequately matched by the extended gesture of the vocal line; and each sonnet stands forth clearly, three-dimensionally, in its setting. The various songs are well contrasted with each other in tempo, mood and key.

These *Sonnets* were written in 1940 specially for Peter Pears and were an immediate success on their first performance by him with the composer at the piano (Wigmore Hall, September, 1942). The two performers had given their first concert together at Oxford in 1937; and they now decided to form a permanent tenor/pianist partnership. Furthermore, most of Britten's subsequent song-cycles, solo canticles, and also certain parts in the operas, were to be composed with Peter Pears's voice in mind, with its masterly style, clear diction, and unique vocal quality.

The *Hymn to St Cecilia* was intended to help restore the old custom of celebrating on 22 November (Britten's birthday) the feast of the patron saint of music—a custom that had been regularly observed in former centuries. Auden's invocation to the saint fully deserves to take its place among the odes of Nicholas Brady and John Dryden as set by Purcell and Handel respectively:

Blessed Cecilia, appear in visions
To all musicians, appear and inspire;
Translated Daughter, come down and startle
Composing mortals with immortal fire.

And listening mortals were certainly startled when on St Cecilia's Day, 1942, the *Hymn* was performed for the first time by the BBC Singers conducted by Leslie Woodgate. The work as a whole made an impression of simplicity, delicacy, sweetness and tranquillity—qualities that were not altogether expected from a composer who before his visit to the United States had acquired a reputation for precocious sophistication. The sweet and languid harmonies of the opening invocation, the brisk scherzo ('*I cannot grow*') with its light broken movement, the candid beauty of the soprano solo, '*O dear white children casual as birds*', and the group of gay cadenzas where the voices flamboyantly imitate violin, drum, flute and trumpet in turn—all these episodes combined to form a work that gave great pleasure and satisfaction to listeners and performers alike.

A Ceremony of Carols was first performed by the Fleet Street Choir, conducted by T. B. Lawrence, in Norwich Castle on 5 December 1942. In some ways it is a pendant to *A Boy was Born*; but whereas the earlier work was in the form of a theme followed by six variations and finale for mixed voices unaccompanied, *A Ceremony of Carols*, which was written for treble voices (generally divided into three parts with occasional solo passages) accompanied by harp, consists of a sequence of nine carols framed by a Procession and Recession with an interlude for harp solo placed about two-thirds of the way through. As with the earlier work, the words are drawn mainly from anonymous medieval carols; but there are also settings of poems by James, John and Robert Wedderburn, Robert Southwell and William Cornish.

Whereas formerly the Church was a powerful patron of the arts, in recent years the divorce between it and the artist has become unfortunately accentuated—to the detriment of both parties. It is always pleasant to find an exception—a church that recognizes the importance of the living artist and is prepared to employ him and display his work; and in the early 1940s a striking example of enlightened patronage in England was provided by the Church of St Matthew, Northampton. The commissions placed through its then incumbent, the Revd. Walter Hussey, included a statue of the Madonna and Child by Henry Moore, a mural painting of the Crucifixion by Graham Sutherland, and a Festival Cantata written by Britten to commemorate the fiftieth anniversary (on 21 September 1943) of the Church's consecration.

For this Cantata, Britten selected a number of passages from *Rejoice in the Lamb*, that strange eighteenth-century poem written by Christopher Smart, while he was in a madhouse. This work is a canticle of general praise, in which not only 'nations and languages', but also 'every creature in which is the breath of life', including the poet's favourite cat, Jeoffry, and the mouse 'a creature of great personal valour', unite in praising God and rejoicing in their service:

Hallelujah from the heart of God
And from the hand of the artist inimitable
And from the echo of the heavenly harp
In sweetness magnifical and mighty.

The music matches the thrilling visionary quality of the words.

Three years later the same church commissioned a work for organ; and Britten composed the *Prelude and Fugue on a Theme of Vittoria*.

Other commissions led to the composition of a small-scale *Te Deum* to commemorate the Centenary Festival of the Church of St Mark, Swindon (24 April 1945) and the *Prelude and Fugue* for 18-part string orchestra, written specially for the tenth anniversary of the Boyd Neel Orchestra and performed at the Wigmore Hall on 23 June 1943.

In 1944 his earlier work for strings, *Simple Symphony*, took on a new lease of life when it was used by Walter Gore (at the suggestion of David Martin) for a light essay in abstract dancing; and it was first performed in this guise by the Ballet Rambert at the Theatre Royal, Bristol (19 November 1944).

Of special importance was the *Serenade* for tenor solo, horn and string orchestra (first performed by Peter Pears and Dennis Brain with Walter Goehr and his orchestra at the Wigmore Hall on 15 October 1943). The *Serenade* was written to almost the same scale as *Les Illuminations*; but this time Britten chose an English instead of a French text, and Rimbaud's fragmentary, half-apprehended visions gave way to an exquisitely selected miniature anthology that included the Lyke Wake Dirge, lyrics by Cotton, Tennyson, Blake and Ben Jonson, and as finale a sonnet by Keats. In the words of Edward Sackville-West,* to whom the *Serenade* is dedicated: 'The subject is Night and its prestigia: the lengthening shadow, the distant bugle at sunset, the Baroque panoply of the starry sky, the heavy angels of sleep; but also the cloak of evil—the worm in the heart of the rose, the sense of sin in the heart of man. The whole sequence forms an Elegy or Nocturnal (as Donne would have called it), resuming the thoughts and images suitable to evening.' Just as *A Ceremony of Carols* was framed by a Procession and Recession, the *Serenade* has a horn solo that is played on natural harmonics as Prologue and repeated off-stage as Epilogue.

Simultaneously with his work on the *Serenade*, Britten found time to collaborate with Edward Sackville-West, who was writing a melodrama for broadcasting based on Homer's *Odyssey* and entitled *The Rescue*. In the Preamble to the published text, the author explains that he was experimenting with a form of radio-opera or radio-drama and 'in writing *The Rescue* some of the awkwardnesses incident to radio-drama were automatically removed . . . by the operatic nature of the composition, which was deliberately built upon an hypothetical structure of music'.† This meant that the composer was given many opportunities, which included passages of speech-music, instrumental solos associated with various characters, a vocal quartet of gods and goddesses, and brief transitional passages for orchestra between the scenes. Here again Britten's flair for descriptive music did not desert him. Describing the course of their collaboration, Sackville-West paid him this tribute: 'I was continually struck by the unerring instinct with which Britten hit upon the right musical backing for whatever it was I had written, or—alternatively—rose imaginatively to any occasion the script presented for quasi-independent music.' *The Rescue* was first performed by the BBC in two parts on 25 and 26 November 1943.

From this period dated his friendship with Michael Tippett, then musical director at Morley College, Lambeth. Recalling the occasion of their first meeting, Tippett wrote:‡ 'We wanted a tenor soloist for the Gibbons Verse

* 'Music: Some Aspects of the Contemporary Problem' by Edward Sackville-West. *Horizon*, June, July and August 1944.

† *The Rescue*: a melodrama for broadcasting based on Homer's Odyssey, by Edward Sackville-West. Secker & Warburg, 1945.

‡ 'Starting to know Britten' by Michael Tippett. The *London Magazine*, October 1963.

Anthem *My Beloved Spake.* Walter Bergmann, who was then chorus-master in Morley, suggested Peter Pears, recently returned from America. When Pears came to rehearsal, Britten came with him.' Tippett was so impressed by Pears and Britten as musical artists that he wrote his vocal cantata, *Boyhood's End*, for them as a duo; and this was performed by them at Morley College in June 1943. A fortnight later Tippett, who was also a conscientious objector, was sentenced to three months imprisonment in Wormwood Scrubs for failing to comply with the conditions of his exemption. While he was serving this sentence, it so happened that Pears and Britten gave a concert in the gaol. The page-turner on this occasion was John Amis, who later described* how the prison authorities were 'bamboozled into thinking that the music to be performed was so complicated that it required the expert services of Michael on the platform to help me to turn over the pages for Britten'.

Shortly after Tippett's release from prison, when Britten asked him what larger works he had written, Tippett mentioned *A Child of Our Time*, an oratorio which he had finished early in the war, but which, on the advice of Walter Goehr, he had put aside in a drawer for the time being. Britten examined the score. In one of the Spirituals he suggested 'the effect could be greatly enhanced by lifting the tenor part suddenly an octave higher†—an improvement that the composer immediately adopted. Britten's enthusiasm did much to help bring about the first performance of *A Child of Our Time* at the Adelphi Theatre, London, on 19 March 1944.

By this time Britten had found a librettist for his opera and was hard at work on the score. While still in the United States, he had thought of asking Christopher Isherwood to collaborate with him; but after his return to England it was clear the choice would have to fall on someone living in England. He already knew Montagu Slater as a poet and dramatist—in fact, he had written incidental music for two of Slater's Left Theatre productions, *Easter 1916* (1935) and *Stay Down Miner* (1936), and for his two one-act verse plays, *The Seven Ages of Man* and *Old Spain*, which were performed in the summer of 1938 as puppet plays at the Mercury Theatre, London, by the Binyon Puppets—and now he asked him to prepare a libretto, based on Crabbe's poem, *The Borough*, which would give special prominence to the character of Peter Grimes. The writing of the text, together with its revisions and corrections, took about eighteen months, and by the end of 1943 all was ready for Britten to begin the work of composition.

Before settling down to this long and arduous job, however, he wrote a special work at the request of an old friend, Lieutenant Richard Wood, who

* From 'Wartime Morley' by John Amis in *Michael Tippett*, Faber, 1965.

† From 'Starting to know Britten' by Michael Tippett, op. cit.

was in a prisoner-of-war camp at Eichstätt in Germany. It was to be written for the prisoners' musical festival early in the new year. According to Richard Wood, who organized the festival: '*The Ballad of Little Musgrave and Lady Barnard* for male voices and piano by Benjamin Britten and dedicated to the musicians of OFLAG VII B arrived just in time for us to put it into the programme at the end of the festival (which had started on 18 February 1944). Our resources and capabilities were brilliantly envisioned by the composer and the result was a little work (eight to nine minutes) of great dramatic force. The choir enjoyed singing it enormously in the end, though it was quite foreign to their style. We gave it four times.'

Britten began composing the music of *Peter Grimes* in January 1944; and the score was completed by February of the following year. The question of its production in England was naturally one that exercised his mind. Although opera in Italian had formed a regular part of London's musical diet since the beginning of the eighteenth century, opera in English had never had a real opportunity of taking root. Before the war, it was customary for some special organization or syndicate to arrange an annual eight to ten weeks' season of opera in German, Italian, and sometimes French, at Covent Garden, while it was left to a company like the Carl Rosa (founded in 1875) to tour English versions of the more popular operas through the provinces. During this period a kind of English *Volksoper* was growing up, first at the Old Vic Theatre in the Waterloo Road, London, and after 1931 at Sadler's Wells. This company presented not only operas in English, but also English operas; and before the outbreak of the war it had to its credit productions of Stanford's *The Travelling Companion*, Dame Ethel Smyth's *The Wreckers*, Holst's *Savitri* and Vaughan Williams's *Hugh the Drover* among others. Although after the onset of the German air attacks on London in September 1940 the Sadler's Wells Theatre was closed to the public and used as a rest-centre for evacuees, the opera company just managed to avoid complete disintegration. At first it toured the provinces with a scratch company of twenty-five (including the orchestra) playing simplified versions of operas like *The Marriage of Figaro* and *La Traviata*; but soon, emboldened by the eager response it evoked, it began to build up its singers, chorus and orchestra and to enlarge its repertory. At the time Britten and Pears returned to England from America, the Sadler's Wells Opera Company under the direction of Joan Cross had made the New Theatre, London, its headquarters; and in 1943 Peter Pears joined it and was soon singing leading parts in *Così fan tutte*, *La Traviata*, *The Bartered Bride* and other operas.

In February 1944, in the course of an interview, Britten said:* 'I am passionately interested in seeing a successful permanent national opera in

* 'Conversation with Benjamin Britten.' *Tempo*, February 1944.

existence—successful both artistically and materially. And it must be vital and contemporary, too, and depend less on imported "stars" than on a first-rate, young and fresh, permanent company. Sadler's Wells have made a good beginning.' A few months later, thanks largely to the enthusiastic support of the Opera Director, Joan Cross, it was agreed that *Peter Grimes* when completed should be given its first performance by the Sadler's Wells Company and that this production should mark the Company's return to its own theatre, which had now been derequisitioned. The certainty of production—and at an early date—was a fresh incentive to Britten (if one were needed) to finish the score; and, as he later admitted,* 'the qualities of the Opera Company considerably influenced both the shape and the characterization of the opera'.

Rehearsals began on tour—according to Eric Crozier† 'in a Methodist Hall in Sheffield, in a Birmingham gymnasium and in the Civic Hall at Wolverhampton. They were as thorough as circumstances could allow, with a company exhausted by much travel and busy with eight performances each week of other operas'. But, despite all difficulties, the production was ready on time; and so it came about that on 7 June 1945, a month after the capitulation of Germany, Sadler's Wells Theatre reopened with a world first performance of a new English opera. Peter Pears sang the title role; Joan Cross herself appeared as Ellen Orford; the parts of Auntie, Balstrode, Mrs Sedley and Swallow were taken by Edith Coates, Roderick Jones, Valetta Iacopi and Owen Brannigan respectively. The scenery and costumes by Kenneth Green were in an attractively realistic style; Eric Crozier produced; and the orchestra was conducted by Reginald Goodall.‡

Any apprehensions that may have been felt beforehand by the composer, by those concerned in the production, by executants or audience, were all swept away as the actual performance proceeded. The orchestra might be too small to do full justice to the interludes, the stage space too cramped for the full sweep of the action, the idiom of the music unfamiliar, the principals and chorus under-rehearsed, yet the impact of the work was so powerful that when the final chorus reached its climax and the curtain began to fall slowly, signifying not only the end of the opera but also the beginning of another day in the life of the Borough, all who were present realized that *Peter Grimes*, as well as being a masterpiece of its kind, marked the beginning of an operatic career of great promise and perhaps also the dawn of a new period when English opera would flourish in its own right.

* *Peter Grimes: Sadler's Wells Opera Books No.* 3.

† *The Rape of Lucretia* (commemorative volume) ed. Eric Crozier. The Bodley Head, 1948.

‡ See Appendix B.

V
First Operatic Successes

The success of *Peter Grimes* was immediate and decisive. The London production was followed during the next three years by others in Stockholm, Basle, Antwerp, Zurich, Tanglewood, Milan, Hamburg, Mannheim, Berlin, Brno, Graz, Copenhagen, Budapest, New York, Stanford and Oldenburg, so that within a comparatively short time Britten's fame as an opera-composer was world-wide, and it became a matter of general interest to know what sort of an opera he was going to write next.

With the end of the war, however, the unstable operatic picture in Great Britain continued to shift and change. Perhaps the most important new factor was the avowed intention of a number of public-spirited persons to reopen the Royal Opera House, Covent Garden, which had been used as a dance-hall during the war years, and to run it as a national lyric theatre for opera and ballet. Messrs Boosey & Hawkes, the music publishers, took a lease of the building from the ground landlords and sub-let the theatre to a special Trust that was set up with Lord Keynes as its first Chairman. Financial backing from the State, which had never before shown any real interest in opera, was secured through the Arts Council; and immediate steps were taken to obtain resident opera and ballet companies. The Sadler's Wells Ballet, which had been created by Ninette de Valois and built up carefully during the last fifteen years from quite humble beginnings, accepted an invitation from the Covent Garden Trust to become its resident ballet company and gave a magnificent performance of Tchaikovsky's *Sleeping Beauty* at the gala reopening on 20 February 1946: but as no existing English opera company seemed suitable for transfer to Covent Garden, the Trustees decided to form their own company from scratch. Clearly it would take some time to assemble and train the singers; and, in actual fact, the new company's first performance was not given until January 1947.

Meanwhile, the general outlook was uncertain. Divided counsels in the management at Sadler's Wells led in March 1946 to a change of policy, 'the withdrawal of *Grimes* from the Wells' repertory at the composer's request, and the resignation of those who believed in the Wells as a progressive centre for British opera.'* In Britten's own words:† 'To some of the singers, writers and musicians involved in *Peter Grimes* this appeared to be the moment to start a group dedicated to the creation of new works, performed with the least possible expense and capable of attracting new audiences by being toured all over the country.' Accordingly, a new company was planned with the object of providing opportunities for the composition and performance of works that would forego the apparatus of large orchestras and choruses. As was explained in a preliminary manifesto:‡ 'The practical aim behind the formation of the Glyndebourne English Opera Company is towards providing a method by which singers of the first rank can devote five months of each year between June and October—slack months in the concert world—entirely to the rehearsal and performance of opera.' The scale of the new venture was to be kept as small as possible—at least to begin with—since it was only thus that 'the principles of high quality in singing, musicianship and preparation can be reconciled with the regular performance of new works'. To speed this venture, Britten agreed to write a new opera for eight singers and twelve musicians, to be produced by the Company at Glyndebourne for a limited run in the summer of 1946 and then to be taken on tour to the provinces and to London.

It happened that a friend of his, Ronald Duncan, had just written a verse play, *This Way to the Tomb*, in the form of a masque with anti-masque—the first part showing how in the fourteenth century Father Antony, Abbot of St Farrara on the island of Zante, withdrew to a mountain height with the firm resolve of fasting unto death, but was there assailed by various temptations, including the deadly sin of pride, and the second part depicting a television relay from the saint's tomb some five centuries later and the unacceptable miracle of the saint's return to life. For its production at the Mercury Theatre on 11 October 1945, Britten wrote incidental music—liturgical chants for a four-part choir using the Latin words of Psalm 69 and a Franciscan hymn, two songs with piano accompaniment for one of the novitiates, and various bits of jazz for piano (four-handed) and percussion in the television scene. These numbers were so well contrived that it was legitimate to claim that the play owed a considerable part of its success to Britten's music; and it was not unexpected, therefore, when this collaboration was carried a stage further by Duncan being invited to write the libretto for Britten's next opera, *The Rape of Lucretia*, the subject of which had already been suggested by Eric Crozier.

* From 'Peter Grimes' by Eric Crozier, originally written for *Music and Letters* in 1946, but rejected by the editor, Eric Blom, as being too controversial, and finally printed in *Opera*, June 1965.

† Special programme note by Benjamin Britten for the Salzburg Festival performance of *The Rape of Lucretia*, 1950.

‡ 'Benjamin Britten's Second Opera' by Eric Crozier. *Tempo*, March 1946.

Meanwhile, Britten had celebrated the completion of the score of *Peter Grimes* by plunging into the composition of various new works. At the beginning of August 1945, just after his return from a tour of Belsen and other German concentration camps which he had undertaken as Yehudi Menuhin's accompanist, he set nine of the *Holy Sonnets of John Donne* for high voice and piano and followed this up by finishing his second String Quartet on 14 October, both works being written as an act of homage to commemorate the 250th anniversary of the death of Henry Purcell which fell on 21 November of that year.

The Holy Sonnets of John Donne stand nearer to the *Seven Sonnets of Michelangelo* than to the Keats Sonnet in the *Serenade*; and over and above their Baroque display of rhetoric, they reveal a facility for musical conceits that not only closely matches the sombre metaphysical imagery of Donne's poetry with its agony of repentance in the shadow of death, but also recalls the fanciful and unorthodox side of Purcell's genius as well. Clearly, Britten's work as concert pianist and accompanist since his return from America had helped to familiarize him with the music of Purcell; and it might be said of him that, like Purcell, he never failed to 'find for words a music that exists in its own right as music'. This tribute is particularly true of the last Sonnet in the sequence, '*Death be not proud*' which, constructed as a *passacaglia* with a firm muscular ground bass, successfully embraces extremes, being both simple and fanciful, sensuous and austere, a masterpiece of feeling and form.

The second String Quartet was Britten's most ambitious attempt since the Piano and Violin Concertos to write a work in which form would be dictated, not by extraneous ideas, but by inner musical necessity. The result was a most impressive essay in sonata form expressed in terms of contemporary idiom.

Britten's interest in Purcell was by no means transitory. Shortly after the commemoration concert of 21 November 1945, he planned jointly with Peter Pears a performing edition of Purcell's works, for which he realized the figured bass with characteristic ingenuity and invention. The first volumes of this edition started to appear in 1946 and included the Golden Sonata and selections from *Orpheus Britannicus*, *Odes and Elegies* and Playford's *Harmonia Sacra*. He also chose a theme of Purcell's for the air on which he constructed a set of variations to accompany a Ministry of Education film on the instruments of the orchestra; and a new performing edition of *Dido and Aeneas* was planned and advertised in the 1946 Glyndebourne programme for production there the following year, though in fact the project did not materialize until 1951.

The sound track for the educational film entitled *Instruments of the Orchestra* was designed to show the orchestra as a whole, its four departments and the individual instruments; but it is written in such a way

Britten with his Rolls-Royce, outside the Old Mill, Snape, 1946

that it could be played as a concert piece as well, with or without spoken commentary. It was planned in the form of variations and a fugue on a dance tune from Purcell's incidental music to *Abdelazar, or The Moor's Revenge.* Every point in this lucid musical exposition was made with such directness and precision that the work became a kind of standard vade-mecum for the young listener.

Before settling down to the task of composing *The Rape of Lucretia*, he allowed himself the relaxation of writing incidental music to *The Dark Tower*, a radio parable play by Louis MacNeice inspired by Robert Browning's poem, '*Childe Roland to the Dark Tower Came*'. This was first broadcast in the BBC Home Service on 21 January 1946, with Britten's music played by a string orchestra of twenty-six players, together with percussion and one trumpet. The author's attitude to the composer's score was enthusiastic. 'Benjamin Britten', he wrote, 'provided this programme with music which is, I think, the best I have heard in a radio play. Without his music *The Dark Tower* lacks a dimension.'

The greater part of the winter and spring of 1946—apart from a concert tour with Peter Pears to Holland and Belgium—was taken up with the composition of *The Rape*; and during this period Britten collaborated closely, not only with his librettist, but also with Eric Crozier and John Piper, who had been chosen as producer and designer respectively. Rehearsals started at Glyndebourne in June; and the first performance was given on 12 July with Ernest Ansermet as conductor. A first-rate double cast had been assembled, the parts of Lucretia, Tarquinius, and the Male and Female Chorus being taken on alternate nights by Kathleen Ferrier and Nancy Evans, Otakar Kraus and Frank Rogier, Peter Pears and Aksel Schiotz, Joan Cross and Flora Nielsen. Reginald Goodall alternated as conductor with Ansermet.*

In this production, special praise should be given to the work of John Piper as designer. The double arcade setting used for the second scenes of Acts I and II was particularly memorable, though, as he himself has admitted,† its parallel arrangement was 'in essence pictorial or architectural rather than theatrical, and it threw a heavy burden on the producer if he was to make the scenes played in front of these arcades "work" in an interesting and lively way'. A real triumph was his drop cloth for Act II, the deep glowing and smouldering colours of which, depicting Our Lord in Majesty, recalled the best English stained glass of the thirteenth and fourteenth centuries.

Some of the critics who reviewed *The Rape* seemed to have difficulty in accepting the premises of the work. Looking for the mass effects of a second

* See Appendix B.

† *The Rape of Lucretia* (commemorative volume) ed. Eric Crozier. The Bodley Head, 1948.

Britten with W. H. Auden at Tanglewood, Lenox, Mass., August 1946

Peter Grimes, they found instead an opera built on austere chamber music lines, without a large chorus or orchestra. The Christian commentary of the single figures who act as Male and Female Chorus was objected to as a wilful anachronism, while the didactic tone of some of their historical information about the Romans and Etruscans—references that for the most part were modified or expunged in the revised version of 1947—was resented as an intrusion. Yet there was no doubt that the audience's attention was held throughout; and by the end of the summer the opera had been played about seventy-five times in Great Britain, the 100th performance being celebrated at Covent Garden on 17 October the following year.

When the tour to Manchester, Liverpool, Edinburgh, Glasgow, London (Sadler's Wells), Oxford and Holland was over, Britten and his supporters decided to relaunch the company in 1947 under the title of the English Opera Group. The arrangement with Glyndebourne had not worked altogether satisfactorily; but it was agreed that the new company, though now independent, would perform there as visitors in June 1947. The Group's aims and objects were restated by its promoters in the following terms: 'We believe the time has come when England, which has always

Britten, Audrey Mildmay (Mrs John Christie) and Eric Crozier at Glyndebourne, 1947

depended on a repertory of foreign works, can create its own operas. . . . This Group will give annual seasons of contemporary opera in English and suitable classical works including those of Purcell. It is part of the Group's purpose to encourage young composers to write for the operatic stage, also to encourage poets and playwrights to tackle the problem of writing libretti in collaboration with composers.' It was made clear that concerts as well as opera performances would come within its purview; and the new works commissioned for 1947 were an opera by Britten and a *Stabat Mater* by Lennox Berkeley.

Immediately after *The Rape of Lucretia*'s short initial run at Glyndebourne, Britten was invited to attend the first American production of *Peter Grimes* at Koussevitzky's Berkshire Music Center at Tanglewood, Lenox, Massachusetts (6, 7 and 8 August). On his return, he wrote an Occasional Overture in C (opus 38) for the opening orchestral concert of the new BBC Third Programme at the end of September. Later he decided to withdraw this composition, and it does not figure in his list of published works. About the same time he provided incidental music for Carl Czinner's New York production of Webster's *The Duchess of Malfi*, with Elizabeth Bergner in the title role.

In the winter of 1947, Britten undertook another Continental tour. He visited Zurich and there conducted performances of the *Serenade* and *The Young Person's Guide to the Orchestra* and, together with Peter Pears, gave recitals in Switzerland, Holland, Belgium and Scandinavia. On returning to England, he settled down to the composition of a new opera for the English Opera Group. In the past two years a number of possible themes had been suggested by Ronald Duncan, including *The Canterbury Tales*, *Abelard and Heloise*, and an action based on Jane Austen's *Mansfield Park* to be called *Letters to William*;* but in the event the choice of librettist fell on Eric Crozier. The problem confronting the composer and librettist was how to devise an opera made to the same measure as *The Rape of Lucretia*, but as different as possible in subject matter and style—in fact, a comedy instead of a tragedy, with a setting in the late nineteenth century instead of B.C. Guy de Maupassant's short story, *Le Rosier de Madame Husson*, gave them the basic idea; but the Gallic original was so freely adapted into East Anglian terms that the resulting lyrical comedy, *Albert Herring*, which was performed for the first time at Glyndebourne on 20 June, had much of the flavour of an original work.

Once again, scenery and costumes were entrusted to John Piper—with excellent results. Particularly admired were the scene in Mrs Herring's greengrocery in Loxford and the drop curtain showing the market-place with the rich fuscous gloom of its buildings enlivened only by the newly painted signboard of its inn glowing like a drop of blood. Frederick Ashton, widely known for his work as choreographer to the Sadler's Wells Ballet, produced. A first-rate cast was assembled, including Peter Pears in the title role and Joan Cross as Lady Billows, an elderly regal autocrat; and Britten himself conducted.†

Before the Glyndebourne season closed, *The Rape of Lucretia* was revived in a revised version; and both operas were included in the English Opera Group's tour abroad to the International Festival at Scheveningen, the Stadsschouwburg in Amsterdam and the Lucerne International Festival. During their visit to Switzerland, a concert was given at Zurich, at which Lennox Berkeley's *Stabat Mater* was performed for the first time; and back in England, they gave ten opera performances at Covent Garden and toured to Newcastle upon Tyne, Bournemouth and Oxford before dispersing for the winter.

Meanwhile, the Covent Garden Opera Company had prepared a new production of *Peter Grimes* under the direction of Tyrone Guthrie. This opened on 6 November, with Peter Pears and Joan Cross as guest artists singing their original parts; and, after a few performances, their roles were taken over by Richard Lewis and Doris Doree. New scenery and costumes

* See *How to Make Enemies* by Ronald Duncan. Rupert Hart-Davis, 1968.

† See Appendix B.

had been designed by Tanya Moiseiwitsch; but whereas Eric Crozier's production and Kenneth Green's designs at Sadler's Wells had been in a realistic vein (as specified in Montagu Slater's libretto), Tyrone Guthrie and Tanya Moiseiwitch had decided on a more abstract interpretation of the drama. The main Borough set, as used in the first scenes of Acts I and II and the whole of Act III, showed a spacious beach and implied an illimitable sea beyond, but left the Moot Hall, the church and *The Boar* entirely to the imagination. This meant that the dance at the beginning of Act III, which, with its four-piece band, is supposed to take place off-stage in the Moot Hall, was given on the beach in full view of the audience, a change which was not for the better. It must also be admitted that on the vast stage of Covent Garden the scene in *The Boar* failed to produce that feeling of claustrophilia which is so characteristic of English pubs. But, apart from these reservations, the production was a fine one, and it was specially admired in Brussels and Paris when the Covent Garden Company played there the following June.

VI
Festival Interlude

In 1947 Britten moved from Snape to Aldeburgh. There he took a house overlooking the sea that Crabbe had described so lovingly in *The Borough*:

> *Various and vast, sublime in all its forms,*
> *When lull'd by Zephyrs, or when rous'd by Storms,*
> *Its colours changing, when from Clouds and Sun*
> *Shades after shades upon the surface run.*

Shortly after the move he was driving by car from Holland to Switzerland with his friends Peter Pears and Eric Crozier. The English Opera Group had just played *The Rape of Lucretia* and *Albert Herring* at the Holland Festival and was due to appear a few days later at the Lucerne Festival. Eric Crozier has described* how the three of them felt 'proud that England was at last making some contribution to the traditions of international opera. And yet—there was something absurd about travelling so far to win success with British operas that Manchester, Edinburgh and London would not support. The cost of transporting forty people and their scenery was enormously high: despite packed houses in Holland, despite financial support from the British Council in Switzerland, it looked as if we should lose at least £3,000 on twelve Continental performances. It was exciting to represent British music at international festivals, but we could not hope to repeat the experiment another year. It was at this point that Peter Pears had an inspiration. "Why not make our own Festival?" he suggested. "A modest Festival with a few concerts given by friends? Why not have an Aldeburgh Festival?" '

During the following autumn and winter the idea was submitted to the local population, who greeted it with enthusiasm; and although Aldeburgh had only about two and a half thousand inhabitants, £1,400 was subscribed in advance guarantees. The programme was carefully planned; the artistic direction entrusted to the English Opera Group; the Arts Council of Great

* 'The Origin of the Aldeburgh Festival' by Eric Crozier. The *Aldeburgh Festival Programme Book*, 1948.

Britain offered a financial subsidy; and the first Aldeburgh Festival, with the Earl of Harewood as President, opened 5 June 1948, and lasted for nine days.

After the war, the idea of creating new festivals had been sparked off by the Edinburgh Festival (established in 1947); but that was by intent an international festival held in a capital city. What chance of success would a local East Anglian festival have, set in a small seaside town? Writing about the first Aldeburgh Festival shortly after it had been held, E. M. Forster said:* 'A festival should be festive. And it must possess something which is distinctive and which could not be so well presented elsewhere. . . . There exists in Aldeburgh the natural basis for a festival. It can offer a particular tradition, a special atmosphere which does not exist elsewhere in these islands: nothing overwhelming, but something that is its own, something of which it can be proud.' These are certainly prerequisites; but however unique the setting, the artistic direction must be first-rate if a festival is going to establish itself on the national—let alone the international—plane. And this, thanks to Benjamin Britten, the Aldeburgh Festival was able to achieve. At first the names of Benjamin Britten, Eric Crozier, and Peter Pears appeared as Founders, while the artistic direction was handled by the English Opera Group; but in 1955 the style was changed, Britten and Pears appearing as Artistic Directors, and the following year the two of them were joined by Imogen Holst. This triumvirate continued until 1968, when they were joined by Philip Ledger; Colin Graham was added to the group in 1969 and Steuart Bedford in 1974. After Britten's death in 1976, Mstislav Rostropovich was made an Artistic Director in 1978.

The 1948 Festival was a success, and the festival operation immediately established itself on an annual basis. It proved to be local in the best sense. Britten's compositions played an important but not preponderant part in the festival programmes. He and Peter Pears frequently appeared as executants; he and Imogen Holst conducted a number of the concerts. The members of the Aldeburgh Festival Singers were drawn from amateur singers in the neighbourhood. Lectures and exhibitions on East Anglian themes supplemented the opera performances, concerts and recitals. To begin with, performances were confined to Aldeburgh; but gradually, as it was seen how limited was the accommodation that Aldeburgh could provide, the Festival started to expand. The first extension was to Thorpeness, where madrigals were sung in the open air on the Meare in 1949, and the Workmen's Hall and the Country Club were used for cabaret, plays and concerts in subsequent years. Then some of the neighbouring country houses were laid under contribution; and a number of neighbouring East

* 'Looking back on the first Aldeburgh Festival', a talk by E. M. Forster, broadcast in June 1948 and reprinted in the *Aldeburgh Festival Programme Book*, 1949.

Anglian churches followed—Blythburgh in 1956, Framlingham in 1957, Orford in 1958 and (further afield) Ely Cathedral in 1964.

Britten saw to it that many contemporary composers were made warmly welcome at the Festival. Visitors from abroad included Francis Poulenc, Hans Werner Henze, Aaron Copland, Zoltán Kodály, and Witold Lutoslawski. A full list of British composers who have participated in the Festival since 1948 would run to over fifty names; but a short list—Malcolm Arnold, David Bedford, Arthur Benjamin, Richard Rodney Bennett, Lennox Berkeley, Harrison Birtwistle, Sir Arthur Bliss, Gordon Crosse, Peter Maxwell Davies, Peter Racine Fricker, Roberto Gerhard, Alexander Goehr, Oliver Knussen, Elizabeth Lutyens, Colin Matthews, Nicholas Maw, Priaulx Rainier, Alan Rawsthorne, Edmund Rubbra, Humphrey Searle, Matyas Seiber, Roger Smalley, John Tavener, Sir Michael Tippett, Sir William Walton, and Malcolm Williamson—is sufficient to show how wide and catholic the representation has been.

Many friends of Britten and Pears have been featured as executants; and some like Julian Bream and George Malcolm have returned to the Festival year after year. The great singer Kathleen Ferrier made only one appearance at Aldeburgh; but that was a most poignant one in the summer of 1952, just a year before her death. Britten himself has described her performance of his *Canticle II: Abraham and Isaac*.* 'Many people have said they will never forget the occasion: the beautiful church, her beauty and incredible courage, and the wonderful characterization of her performance, including every changing emotion of the boy Isaac—the boyish nonchalance of the walk up to the fatal hill, his bewilderment, his sudden terror, his touching resignation to his fate—the simplicity of the Envoi, but, above all, combining with the other voice, the remote and ethereal sounds as "God speaketh".'

In later years a remarkable feature has been the strength of the participation of artists from the USSR. Mstislav Rostropovich, the cellist, and his wife Galina Vishnevskaya, the soprano, first appeared at the 1961 Festival. In 1964 Sviatoslav Richter, the pianist, agreed at short notice to join Rostropovich in a special additional recital in the Parish Church (20 June). Close and friendly relations with these Russian executants led directly to the composition of Britten's *Cello Sonata in C*, the *Symphony for Cello and Orchestra* and the three *Suites for Cello Solo* for Rostropovich, and indirectly to the Pushkin song cycle, *The Poet's Echo*.

Most of the opera performances and music recitals were given in the Jubilee Hall, which has a minute stage and a capacity of only about 300. In default of a larger building to accommodate its main events, the Festival was

* From 'Three Premières' by Benjamin Britten in *Kathleen Ferrier: a memoir*. London, Hamish Hamilton, 1954.

Britten with members of Lancing College choir prior to the first performance of *Saint Nicolas* at Lancing, 1948

bound to remain small and intimate in scale; and this was indeed the case during its first nineteen years. It might have been thought that with high prices and limited accommodation, there would be a tendency for it to become exclusive and even a little snobbish. But no—from the beginning it was equally welcomed by local inhabitants and visitors. E. M. Forster had a revealing anecdote to tell* about the first performance of *Albert Herring* in the Jubilee Hall in 1948. 'During the first interval a man in a pub said: "I took a ticket for this show because it is local and I felt I had to. I'd have sold it to anyone for sixpence earlier on. I wouldn't part with it now for ten pounds." '

Although the price of tickets for opera and the top concerts never reached the figure of ten pounds, it is true to say that, even after making allowance for substantial subsidies from the Arts Council and from the large body of friendly subscribers that the Festival soon built up, prices remained comparatively high, and at first it was difficult to see how students and other young people could afford to go to the Festival in any numbers. In 1958 Princess Margaret of Hesse, who was herself a devoted festival-goer, decided that 'by some means or another it must be made financially possible for more young people to attend the Festival'. It was not long before she had enlisted the help of some friends and opened the fund which bears her name. A modest start was made in 1959 and about half a dozen students were given

* E. M. Forster, op. cit.

a limited number of tickets for different events. Each year the gates were opened wider and by 1962 the numbers had risen to thirty-four. The rules were that applicants must be under twenty-five years of age and that, although they need not necessarily be music students, they were expected to be playing some active part in the musical life of the community in which they lived or worked.'* This infusion of new blood was most welcome and did much to popularize the Festival among the younger generation.

A number of Britten's works have received their first performance at the Festival. The first Festival of all (1948) opened with his cantata *Saint Nicolas* to words by Eric Crozier. This had been written during the winter of 1947–8 specially for the centenary celebrations of Lancing College in July 1948. Its lay-out for tenor, mixed choirs, string orchestra, pianoforte and percussion and the fact that it included two familiar hymns for congregation and choirs made it particularly suitable for performance in the Aldeburgh Parish Church. Movements like The Birth of Nicolas with the innocent and joyful lilt of the sopranos' tune answered at the end of each verse by the boy Nicolas's treble '*God be glorified!*' and the strangely primitive story of Nicolas and the Pickled Boys fully justified E. M. Forster's comment:† 'It was one of those triumphs outside the rules of art which only the great artist can achieve.' The cantata was subsequently revived at the 1949, 1951, 1955 and 1961 Festivals.

Lachrymae, Reflections on a Song of Dowland, a set of ten variations for viola and piano, was first performed by William Primrose and the composer at the 1950 Festival.‡ The following year the *Six Metamorphoses after Ovid* for oboe solo were written for Joy Boughton and played by her at an open-air concert given on the Meare at Thorpeness. These short pieces take their place with Debussy's *Syrinx* and Stravinsky's Three Pieces for Clarinet Solo as being among the most outstanding compositions for an unaccompanied wind instrument that have been written in this century.

For the 1953 Festival a special work for string orchestra was commissioned. Six variations on the tune of *Sellinger's Round, or, The Beginning of the World* were written by Lennox Berkeley, Arthur Oldham, Humphrey Searle, Michael Tippett and William Walton as well as Britten himself. The identity of the actual composer of each movement was concealed at the festival performances and revealed only later. (Subsequently Michael Tippett took his variation and used it as the second movement of his *Divertimento on 'Sellinger's Round'* for chamber orchestra.)

Two of Britten's song cycles have been launched at the Festival—*Songs from the Chinese* for tenor and guitar (performed by Peter Pears and Julian Bream) in 1958 and *Songs and Proverbs of William Blake* for baritone and

* 'The Hesse Students' by Arthur Harrison. *Aldeburgh Festival Programme*, 1963.

† E. M. Forster, op. cit.

‡ Britten orchestrated the *Lachrymae* for viola and strings in 1975.

piano (performed by Dietrich Fischer-Dieskau and the composer) in 1965. *Nocturnal after John Dowland* was specially written for the guitarist Julian Bream and played by him at the 1964 Festival. The *Suite in C* for harp solo, which was specially written for the harpist Osian Ellis, was played by him at the 1969 Festival. Of the compositions written for Rostropovich, the *Sonata in C for Cello and Piano* and the first two *Suites for Cello Solo* received their first performances at the 1961, 1965 and 1968 Festivals respectively. The première of the *Symphony in D for Cello and Orchestra* was planned for a concert at Blythburgh Church on 30 June 1963, but had to be cancelled owing to Rostropovich's illness. Its first performance was eventually given in Moscow on 12 March 1964 with Britten conducting; and the first performance in England followed on 18 June 1964, when the work was heard at Blythburgh Church as originally planned. The third *Suite for Cello Solo* was first performed by Rostropovich at Snape Maltings on 21 December 1974.

A most unusual work was the *Gemini Variations* which received its first performance during the 1965 Festival. Describing its origin,* Britten wrote: 'When in Budapest in the spring of 1964 at a Music Club meeting for children, I was very taken by the musical gifts of two twelve-year-old twins. Each played the piano, one the flute and the other the violin: they sang, sight-read, and answered difficult musical questions. It turned out that they were the sons of one of Budapest's most distinguished flute players. At the end of the meeting they approached me and charmingly, if forcefully, asked me to write them a work. Though I claimed that I was too busy, my refusal was brushed aside: however, I insisted on one small bargaining point: I would do it only if they would write me a long letter telling me all about themselves, their work and their play—in *English*. I felt safe. After a week or two, however, the letter arrived, in vivid and idiosyncratic English, and I felt I must honour my promise. *Gemini Variations* is the result.' The theme used was no. 4 of Zoltán Kodály's *Epigrams* (1954). The boys were Zoltán and Gabriel Jeney.

Occasionally some of Britten's juvenile compositions have been given a hearing. Two movements were salvaged from a Christmas Suite called *Thy King's Birthday* written about 1930 or 1931—these were the fourth movement entitled *New Prince, New Pomp*, for soprano solo and chorus, performed at the 1955 Festival, and the second movement entitled *Sweet was the Song* for contralto solo and chorus of female voices at the 1966 Festival. For the 1969 Festival he dug out some early settings of lyrics by Walter de la Mare that he had written between the ages of fourteen and seventeen, and these were published under the title *Tit for Tat*.

If, as was the intention from the beginning, opera was to provide the

* In *Faber Music News*, Autumn 1966.

backbone of the Festival programmes, it was clear that it would have to be on an intimate scale. Fortunately the existence of the English Opera Group went a long way to overcome the inevitable difficulties inherent in presenting opera in the cramped conditions of the Jubilee Hall. The touring of the Group's productions of *The Rape of Lucretia* and *Albert Herring* in 1947 had been the factor that originally led to the idea of an Aldeburgh Festival: so it was appropriate that the opening opera at the 1948 Festival should be *Albert Herring.* Its East Anglian setting and local connotations proved particularly apt, and it was revived at several subsequent Festivals (in 1949, 1951, 1953, 1957 and 1963). The tenth anniversary performance (1957), when Joan Cross, Peter Pears and others returned to their original roles, was particularly impressive. *The Rape of Lucretia* was presented in 1949 and revived in 1954, 1959 and 1960. In 1949 came the first opera of Britten's to be created at the Festival—the extraordinarily popular entertainment for children of all ages called *Let's Make an Opera!*—and this was revived in 1950 and 1956, and also in 1965 with a revised Introduction. The opera in 1950 was Britten's realization of *The Beggar's Opera* with the keys of some of the movements transposed so that the part of Macheath could be sung by a baritone; in 1963 it was revived with Peter Pears singing the original tenor role. In 1951 (the year of the Festival of Britain) Britten's realization of Purcell's *Dido and Aeneas* was brought to Aldeburgh from London where it had been heard for the first time at the Lyric Theatre, Hammersmith. (It was revived at Aldeburgh in 1962.) *The Turn of the Screw* followed in 1955 (with a revival in 1961); and two years later *Noye's Fludde* was given its first performance in Orford Church and revived there in 1961. The boldest venture of all was in 1960, when the English Opera Group presented *A Midsummer Night's Dream* for the first time in the enlarged Jubilee Hall, a very complicated production to mount on the pocket-handkerchief stage. In 1964 came the première of the first of the parables for church performance, *Curlew River* (revived in 1965); in 1966 the second parable *The Burning Fiery Furnace* (revived in 1967); and in 1968 the third parable *The Prodigal Son* (revived in 1969)—all three of them (like *Noye's Fludde*) produced in Orford Church.

If the attractively edited programmes of the Aldeburgh Festival are examined, it will be seen that (apart from Britten himself) the main composers laid under contribution have been Purcell, Mozart, and Schubert. Not far behind in popularity are Dowland and Byrd, Bach and Haydn, Mahler and Berg, Holst and Bridge.

In addition to the general concert programmes, many of the Festivals have featured an outstanding series of programmes of Church Music specially devised by Imogen Holst and usually given in the Parish Church. These have been presented in conjunction with the BBC Transcription Service.

Lectures, poetry readings and recitals, the occasional play, and numerous exhibitions of paintings, drawings, and sculpture—all these have helped to build up a balanced festival programme.

From the beginning, the Festival had difficulties in finding the right sort of accommodation for its needs. It was difficult enough to fit in concerts, exhibitions, lectures, recitals and the occasional play; but opera was the most difficult of all, for the conditions in the Jubilee Hall were cramped and inadequate. It is true that in 1959/60 certain improvements were carried out which made it easier to produce *A Midsummer Night's Dream* in the summer of 1960. At the same time it was decided to purchase a property in the centre of the town and to adapt it as a festival club with a small gallery for exhibitions. To raise the extra money needed, various friends of the Festival—artists and collectors—were asked to help by contributing something (pictures, sculpture, books, or manuscripts) to an auction that was held by Christie's on 23 March 1961 and raised about £11,480. Among the items sold on this occasion were two important manuscripts of Britten's—the autograph full score (in pencil) of *The Young Person's Guide to the Orchestra* and the first sketches (also in pencil) of *Seven Sonnets of Michelangelo*—both of which were bought by James M. Osborn, Curator of the Osborn Collection in the Yale University Library.* The sketches and original manuscript full score of the *Cantata Academica* (*Carmen Basiliense*) had been bought prior to the sale by Dr and Mrs Paul Sacher of Basle.

The new Festival Club proved a great success; but the main problem of a new hall or opera-house still remained to be solved. In the 1957 Festival Programme Book an article by H. T. Cadbury-Brown called *Notes on an Opera House for Aldeburgh*, carried an illustration showing the site of a Festival Theatre as then proposed. This particular plan came to naught; but ten years later, an imaginative adaptation of part of the Maltings at Snape was carried out, one of the Malt Houses being turned into a concert hall seating about 820 with a restaurant and bar for the public as well as full dressing room facilities for the artists. At the same time the auditorium was made suitable for stereophonic recording by Decca, and a recording room was provided for Decca and the BBC.

The Maltings Concert Hall was opened by Her Majesty The Queen, who was accompanied by the Duke of Edinburgh, on 2 June 1967; and after hearing the first two pieces of music in the Inaugural Concert programme—Britten's setting of the National Anthem for chorus and orchestra, and his overture *The Building of the House* (composed specially for the occasion)—the audience realized that the new hall had extraordinarily fine acoustic

* It is worth remembering that at least two other important manuscript scores of Britten's are to be found in the United States. Both *Peter Grimes* and the String Quartet No. 1 are in the Library of Congress, Washington D.C.

properties. Other concerts followed, including the first performance by the Vienna Boys' Choir of Britten's vaudeville for boys and piano called *The Golden Vanity*; and the open platform was used for opera when *A Midsummer Night's Dream* was given in a new production.

The existence of this hall made it possible to plan future Festivals on a larger scale than hitherto: so it was a particularly traumatic experience when on 7 June 1969, shortly after the opening concert of the 1969 Festival, the building was destroyed by fire.

But temporary reverses like this could not affect the unique nature of the Festival. In the first place, there is the special attraction of this remarkable little seaside town. As Britten said in his speech on receiving the Freedom of the Borough of Aldeburgh on 22 October 1962: 'Everyone is charmed by its lovely position between sea and river, and the beach with the fishing boats and life-boat, the fine hotels, the golf course, wonderful river for sailing, the birds, the countryside, our magnificent churches, and of course the shops too.' And then it is the sort of place where friends meet, friendships are renewed, new friendships formed, and there is time to converse.

Referring to the Festival on the same occasion Britten said: 'It is a considerable achievement, in this small Borough in England, that we run year after year a first-class Festival of the Arts, and we make a huge success of it. And when I say "we" I mean "we". This Festival couldn't be the work of just one, two or three people, or a board, or a council—it must be the corporate effort of a whole town.' This is true up to a point: but ultimately everyone must recognize that, had it not been for its resident composer, the Aldeburgh Festival would not have come into being and could not have continued. As Rostropovich wrote after his first visit to Aldeburgh in 1961: 'Britten's energy and capacity for work during the Festival were phenomenal. He was the heart and brain of the Festival. He took part in it as pianist and conductor. He was at all the rehearsals and concerts, he looked into literally every trifle.'* He was indeed an exuberant and indefatigable host.

* From 'Dear Ben . . .' by Mstislav Rostropovich in *Tribute to Benjamin Britten on his Fiftieth Birthday*.

VII
Aldeburgh: Living in Crabbe Street

Britten's life was now following a fairly regular annual pattern. There was usually a new opera on the stocks; various other compositions to be squeezed in; a certain number of engagements as conductor and pianist; a recital tour with Peter Pears at home or abroad; and each summer would bring the busy but refreshing interlude of the Aldeburgh Festival.

About the time of his move to Crag House in Crabbe Street, Aldeburgh, he completed two vocal works: *Canticle I* and *A Charm of Lullabies*. The *Canticle*, a setting of a poem by Francis Quarles for tenor and piano, is a more extended composition for voice than any of the previous song-cycles. Peter Pears, writing just before *Canticle II* was composed, considered it to

Britten and Peter Pears buying vegetables from Jonah Baggott in the High Street, Aldeburgh, *c.* 1948

Britten's studio at Crag House, Aldeburgh

be 'Britten's finest piece of vocal music to date'.* He particularly praised the vocal line as being 'free, melismatic yet controlled, and independent throughout, whether as one or two or three parts in counterpoint or a melody with chordal accompaniment'. *A Charm of Lullabies* reverts to the earlier song-cycle pattern. Britten has chosen five contrasting lullabies—*A Cradle Song* (William Blake), *The Highland Balou* (Robert Burns), *Sephestia's Lullaby* (Robert Greene), *A Charm* (Thomas Randolph) and *The Nurse's Song* (John Philip)—and set them for mezzo-soprano and piano.

For the 1948 season of the English Opera Group, he decided to add to the company's repertory a new version, not of *Dido and Aeneas* as had been promised earlier, but of *The Beggar's Opera*. For this purpose, John Gay's text was slightly revised by Tyrone Guthrie, while Britten, ignoring all the numerous versions of the score that had appeared during the last two and a quarter centuries, went back to the sixty-nine airs originally chosen by Dr Pepusch and included all of them in his version except three. Since his return from America he had produced three volumes of folk song arrangements (two for the British Isles and one for France), which showed such sensitivity to the mood and mode of folk tunes and skill in their setting

* 'The Vocal Music' by Peter Pears in *Benjamin Britten: a commentary* (edited by Mitchell & Keller). Rockliff, 1952.

Eric Crozier, Benjamin Britten and Tyrone Guthrie at a rehearsal for *The Beggar's Opera*, 1948

that it was hardly surprising he should now find himself strongly attracted by the traditional tunes of *The Beggar's Opera*.

For the first performance at the Arts Theatre, Cambridge (24 May, 1948), Tyrone Guthrie was producer. Profiting by a hint in the original Prologue that the opera had previously been performed by the Company of Beggars in their 'great Room at St Giles's', he set the whole opera in this 'great room', which for some reason or other he imagined as a laundry. Unfortunately, the atmosphere of this laundry with its piles of clothes, whether dirty or clean, proved stifling, rather than inspiring, and the production never succeeded in fulfilling the producer's laudable aim of restoring the mordancy of the original satire. Britten wrote the part of Macheath for tenor voice; and the role was admirably sung by Peter Pears. When the opera was revived two years later, the part was transposed for baritone; but the result was not altogether satisfactory, some of the buoyancy and sparkle of the score being thereby lost.

After a week's run in Cambridge where it was conducted by Britten himself and Ivan Clayton, the opera was played by the English Opera Group at the Holland Festival, the Cheltenham Festival of Contemporary Music, the Festival du Littoral Belgique, Birmingham, and the Sadler's Wells Theatre and the People's Palace, London; and during the next two or three years it had separate productions in Austria, Switzerland and Germany.

Having produced a Young Person's Guide to the Orchestra, Britten seemed bound sooner or later to write a Young Person's Guide to Opera. The episodes in *Albert Herring* where the three children bounce their ball against the door of Mrs Herring's greengrocery shop and where Miss Wordsworth rehearses them in their festive song were among the most successful passages in that comic opera and seemed to show that such a work might well be written so as to provide parts to be played by children themselves. He believed there were many children in the country who were natural musicians and actors and was anxious to help provide an outlet for their artistic talent. In this he was ably aided and abetted by Eric Crozier. *Let's Make an Opera!* was planned in two parts: the first part showing a group of children who help two or three of their elders to plan, write, compose and rehearse an opera; and the second part being the opera itself, *The Little Sweep*. The music of this one-act opera is not continuous, but consists of eighteen musical numbers, and there is a certain amount of spoken dialogue. It was an ingenious stroke on the part of the authors of this entertainment for young people to implicate the audience in the performance of *The Little Sweep* as well as the children and the three or four professional adults that are called for in the cast. *Let's Make an Opera!* was an immediate success on its first production at the second Aldeburgh Festival (14 June, 1949). The conductor, who plays such an important part in knitting together the different musical strands of this entertainment, was Norman Del Mar; Basil Coleman produced; and the attractive setting was by John Lewis.*

To judge by statistics, *The Little Sweep* is easily Britten's most popular opera to date. As well as many professional productions in Europe, America, Asia and Australia, there have been innumerable amateur performances all over the world, particularly in schools. It is difficult to assess the long-term effect of all this; but Eric Crozier's words should be borne in mind: 'Many children write plays for their own performance. Few, I suspect, attempt opera. Perhaps, with the stimulus of an imaginative example before them, they may be prompted to explore the fascinating possibilities of expression and entertainment that it offers.'†

Britten continued to attract much attention abroad. By 1948 monographs on his work as a composer had appeared in France, Italy and Switzerland as well as Great Britain. In its first three years the English Opera Group had toured its productions of *The Rape of Lucretia*, *Albert Herring* and *The Beggar's Opera* to Holland, Belgium, Switzerland, Denmark and Norway. *Peter Grimes* reached the Scala, Milan, and the Opéra, Paris, in 1947, and the Metropolitan Opera House, New York, the following year. *The Rape of*

* See Appendix B.

† 'An Opera for Young People' by Eric Crozier. *Times Educational Supplement*, 19 March 1949.

Lucretia aroused considerable controversy when it was produced in America. In Chicago it was greeted by one of the local newspapers with the banner headline 'Bold, Bawdy and Beautiful'; but its run in New York at the end of 1947 came to an abrupt end after only twenty-three performances. On that occasion Olin Downes, music critic of the *New York Times*, performed a complete *volte face*. After attending the first night, he praised the work warmly; but a return visit led him to change his mind and he decided it was 'as arrant a piece of musico-dramatic twaddle as has been visited upon the public for years'.* Hostile criticism of Britten was also forthcoming from the USSR. The first All-Union Congress of Soviet Composers that met in Moscow from 19–25 April 1948, energetically denounced him, together with Menotti and Messiaen, as being 'impregnated with extreme subjectivism, mysticism and disgusting facetiousness', while it was said that Stravinsky 'actually showed by his idealization of the Middle Ages that he breathed the spirit of fascism'. But this attack of nerves over the 'reactionary formalist trends in the West' calmed down when Stalin disappeared from the scene; and by 1962 Stravinsky was being amicably received by Krushchev in the Kremlin in the course of a triumphal return to his native country nearly half a century after he had left it, and early in 1963 Britten was being warmly fêted in Moscow and Leningrad during a festival of British music.

During the autumn and winter of 1948–9 Britten was preoccupied with the *Spring Symphony*, the first performance of which was given at the Holland Festival, Amsterdam (9 July, 1949) by kind permission of Koussevitzky, who conducted the first American performance at the Berkshire Festival in Tanglewood (13 August, 1949). For two years he had been planning such a work, 'a symphony not only dealing with the Spring itself, but with the progress of Winter to Spring and the reawakening of the earth and life which that means'.† Apparently his original intention had been to use medieval Latin verse for this purpose; but 'a re-reading of much English lyric verse and a particularly lovely Spring day in East Suffolk, the Suffolk of Constable and Gainsborough', led him to change his mind and to substitute for his choice of Latin verse an anthology of English poems.

The *Spring Symphony* is written for three soloists (soprano, alto and tenor), mixed chorus, boys' choir, and large orchestra, including a cow-horn and a vibraphone. 'It is in the traditional four movement shape of a symphony, but with the movements divided into shorter sections bound together by a similar mood or point of view. Thus after an introduction, which is a prayer, in Winter, for Spring to come, the first movements deal with the arrival of Spring, the cuckoo, the birds, the flowers, the sun and "May months' beauty"; the second movements paint the darker side of

* See 'The Rape of Lucretia', *New York Times*, 30 December 1948, and 'Second Thoughts', *New York Times*, 9 January 1949.

† 'A Note on the Spring Symphony' by Benjamin Britten. *Music Survey*, Spring, 1950.

Britten and E. M. Forster on a walk, 1949

Spring—the fading violets, rain and night; the third is a series of dances, the love of young people; the fourth is a May-day Festival, a kind of bank holiday, which ends with the great thirteenth-century traditional song "Sumer is i-cumen in", sung or rather shouted by the boys.'*

The sentiments of this springtime anthology culled from Edmund Spenser, Thomas Nashe, George Peele, John Clare, John Milton, Robert Herrick, Henry Vaughan, Richard Barnefield, and Anon, are without specific indication of time or period, apart from the account of Elizabethan London in May extracted from Beaumont and Fletcher's *The Knight of the Burning Pestle* which forms the finale, and the four stanzas extracted from Auden's poem '*Out on the lawn I lie in bed*'† where the lulled listener is suddenly startled by the prophetic reference to Poland and war. Britten shows great skill in setting all this heterogeneous material in a unified musical idiom and in ordering it so as to give the work the specific gravity of a symphony instead of the running lightness of a suite.

After the *Spring Symphony* the collaboration with Ronald Duncan was resumed. Britten had already written incidental music, not only for Duncan's verse play *This Way to the Tomb*, but also a fanfare for his translation and adaptation of Jean Cocteau's play *The Eagle Has Two Heads*, which was produced by the Company of Four at the Lyric Theatre, Hammersmith, on 4 September, 1946. He now provided music for

* Ibid.

† From *Look, Stranger!*, 1936.

Duncan's new verse play, *Stratton*, which started a brief provincial tour at the Theatre Royal, Brighton, on 3 October, 1949, and asked Duncan to provide the words for *A Wedding Anthem* for the wedding of the Earl of Harewood and Miss Marion Stein. This work for soprano and tenor soli, choir and organ was performed at St Mark's Church, North Audley Street, London, on 29 September, 1949, by Joan Cross, Peter Pears and the Choir of St Mark's which had recently sung a number of Britten's choral works, including the early *Te Deum* (in C major) and *A Boy was Born.*

Shortly after the Harewood wedding, which was attended by the King and Queen and many members of the Royal Family, Britten and Pears left for a concert tour of North America. They crossed to the West Coast of the United States; and, while in Hollywood, Britten saw Carl Ebert rehearsing *Albert Herring* for production by the University of Southern California. Back in England by Christmas, he started to think about his next opera. He had already chosen Herman Melville's posthumous story, *Billy Budd, Foretopman*, as the subject, and E. M. Forster and Eric Crozier had agreed to write the libretto jointly. The work of composition was begun in February 1950 and finished in the autumn of 1951.

Britten accepted a commission from the Arts Council of Great Britain for the opera to be produced in connection with the Festival of Britain, 1951; but for some time the exact destination of the new opera was uncertain. At first it was intended that it should be produced by the Sadler's Wells Opera Company at the 1951 Edinburgh Festival, and this was announced in September 1950. Two months later, however, Sadler's Wells decided they would have to abandon the idea of producing it as it was likely to prove beyond their resources; and in December it was announced that *Billy Budd* would definitely be produced at the Royal Opera House, Covent Garden, in the autumn of 1951.

During the twenty months or so that *Billy Budd* was being composed, Britten allowed few extraneous matters to distract him. The only other compositions belonging to this period were the *Lachrymae*, for viola and piano (1950), and the *Six Metamorphoses after Ovid* for solo oboe (1951), both performed for the first time at the Aldeburgh Festival, and a set of *Five Flower Songs* for mixed chorus unaccompanied, dedicated to Leonard and Dorothy Elmhirst of Dartington Hall on the occasion of their 25th wedding anniversary (3 April, 1950). He also found time to prepare a new realization of *Dido and Aeneas* for the English Opera Group's Festival of Britain season.

About this period a number of ballets were adapted to existing scores of his. *Soirées Musicales* and *Matinées Musicales* (based on Rossini's music) were used once more for a ballet which was produced at the Théâtre de la Monnaie, Brussels, in 1948 under the title *Fantaisie Italienne.* The following June *The Young Person's Guide to the Orchestra* was used for a modern classical ballet *Oui ou Non?* (*Ballet de la Paix*) presented by the Association des Amis de la Danse at their annual gala performance at the Théâtre National Populaire du Palais de Chaillot, Paris. On 26 April, 1949, the Ballets de Paris de Roland Petit gave the first performance at the Prince's Theatre, London, of *Le Rêve de Léonor*, a surrealist ballet with choreography by Frederick Ashton to the *Variations on a Theme of Frank Bridge* arranged for full orchestra by Arthur Oldham. The same *Variations* were used in Lew Christensen's *Jinx*, the revised version of which was included in the New York City Ballet's repertory for its spring 1950 season and brought to Great Britain when the company visited Covent Garden in July 1950. The same company performed *Les Illuminations* as a ballet at City Center, New York, on 2 March 1950, with choreography by Frederick Ashton and décor by Cecil Beaton; and this too was performed at Covent Garden in the summer of the same year. The *Sinfonietta* was used for a little drama in ballet form called *Die Versunkene Stadt* with choreography by Mara Jovanovits which was given at the Stadttheater, St Gallen, Switzerland, on 26 April, 1950.

The production of Purcell's *Dido and Aeneas* by the English Opera Group represented the fulfilment of a long cherished ambition. Britten was closely associated with Imogen Holst in this work. Together they collated and compared all the extant manuscript material and copied the whole of the transcript made by some copyist in the latter part of the eighteenth century and preserved in the Library of St Michael's College, Tenbury.* They then examined Nahum Tate's printed libretto and were particularly struck by the fact that no setting by Purcell exists for the witches' chorus and dance at the end of Act II. In a note dated 4 April, 1951, printed in the Lyric Theatre, Hammersmith, programme, Britten wrote: 'Anyone who has taken part in, or indeed heard a concert or stage performance, must have been struck by the very peculiar and most unsatisfactory end of this Act II as it stands; Aeneas sings his very beautiful recitative in A minor and disappears without any curtain music or chorus (which occurs in all the other acts). The drama cries out for some strong dramatic music, and the whole key scheme of the opera (very carefully adhered to in each of the other scenes) demands a return to the key of the beginning of the act or its relative major (i.e. D, or F major). What is more, the contemporary printed libretto (a copy of which is preserved in the library of the Royal College of Music) has perfectly clear indications for a scene with the Sorceress and her Enchantresses, consisting of six lines of verse, and a dance to end the act. It is my considered opinion that music was certainly composed to this scene and has been lost. It is quite possible that it will be found, but each year makes it less likely. It is to me of prime importance dramatically as well as musically to include this missing scene, and so I have supplied other music of Purcell's to fit the six lines of the

* See 'Dido and Aeneas', and article by George Malcolm in *Benjamin Britten: a commentary* (edited by Mitchell & Keller). Rockliff, 1952.

libretto, and a dance to end in the appropriate key . . . The realization of the figured bass for harpsichord is, of course, my own responsibility; in Purcell's time it was the custom for the keyboard player to work it out afresh at each performance. Therefore, no definitive version of this part is possible or desirable . . .'

This realization of *Dido and Aeneas* was given in a dual bill with Monteverdi's *Combattimento di Tancredi e Clorinda* at the Lyric Theatre, Hammersmith, on 1 May, 1951. Nancy Evans was Dido, and Joan Cross produced. Britten conducted from the harpsichord. After the Hammersmith season, it was played at the Aldeburgh, Holland, Cheltenham and Liverpool Festivals.

That summer he was created a freeman of his birthplace, Lowestoft.

At the end of September, while engaged on the final stages of the orchestral score of *Billy Budd*, Britten, together with Peter Pears and a group of friends, set out on a short pleasure cruise that took them direct from Aldeburgh, across the North Sea and up the Rhine as far as Bonn. Later that autumn, Peter Pears returned to Germany and sang the title part in *Oedipus Rex* in a performance for the Nordwestdeutscher Rundfunk, Cologne, that was conducted by Stravinsky, whose new opera, *The Rake's Progress*, had just been given in Venice.

Shortly after Britten's return, rehearsals started for *Billy Budd*. From discussions between the producer (Basil Coleman) and designer (John Piper), the general conclusion emerged that the sea and the ship would have to be suggested and not portrayed in realistic terms, and that the sets would have to be made 'so abstract that the absence or presence of particular details would not be noticed, so long as the shapes themselves were all intensely *ship-like*, and so long as the practical demands of the libretto and the score were all satisfied'.* This, on the whole, they succeeded in doing—particularly in the scene on the berth-deck with its skeleton of wooden ribs, low headroom, swung hammocks and illusion of claustrophobia.

The first performance of *Billy Budd* took place at the Royal Opera House, Covent Garden, on 1 December, 1951. Britten conducted; and the cast included Theodor Uppman in the title part, Peter Pears as Captain Vere, and Frederick Dalberg as Claggart.† Despite the possibility that the special nature of the subject and its all-male cast might restrict public interest, the first six performances were played to capacity houses. The opera was then taken on tour to Cardiff, Manchester, Glasgow and Birmingham; and when it returned to Covent Garden after Easter it continued to attract quite good attendances. In May the Covent Garden Opera Company gave two performances of it at the Théâtre des Champs-Elysées, Paris, during the

* 'Billy Budd on the Stage' by Basil Coleman and John Piper. *Tempo*, Autumn 1951.

† See Appendix B.

Peter Pears, Kathleen Ferrier and Britten, 1952

Festival of Twentieth-Century Art. The attitude of the Parisian audience appears to have been rather tepid.

This was not so with the first German production at Wiesbaden in March 1952. Despite severe cuts that amounted almost to mutilations, the opera was an unqualified success with the public. The Earl of Harewood, who attended the sixth performance, wrote that the German audience's enthusiasm was something he could not 'remember ever having seen exceeded elsewhere'.*

True to his usual custom, Britten celebrated the completion of his new opera by composing a smaller-scale work. The text of *Canticle II: Abraham and Isaac* is taken from the Chester Miracle Play and is set for alto, tenor and piano. The first performance was given by Kathleen Ferrier and Peter Pears at Nottingham (21 January, 1952) with the composer at the piano. The work is a dramatic scene, in which the tenor is cast as Abraham, the alto as Isaac; and the two voices combine, whether in two parts or in unison, to form the voice of Jehovah. Just as the second String Quartet is an instrumental sequel

* 'Foreign Diary' by the Earl of Harewood. *Opera*, May 1952.

to *Peter Grimes*, this is a parergon to *Billy Budd*. Abraham's dilemma over Isaac is similar to the problem that confronts Captain Vere and Billy Budd; but in the opera there is no *deus ex machina*.

Shortly after George VI's death in February 1952, Britten had the idea of writing an opera on the theme of Elizabeth I and Essex. This subject had made a strong impression on him when young; and when HM Queen Elizabeth II gave him permission to compose an opera on the occasion of her Coronation, he received just the stimulus he needed. In the event, *Gloriana* was produced at a gala performance at the Royal Opera House, Covent Garden, on 8 June, 1953, in the presence of the Queen and members of the Royal Family. It was a unique occasion. As Ralph Vaughan Williams pointed out in a letter to *The Times*,* this was 'the first time in history the Sovereign has commanded an opera by a composer from these islands for a great occasion'.

As his librettist, Britten chose William Plomer. Lytton Strachey's tragic history, *Elizabeth and Essex*, was the starting point of their collaboration; but, in the course of the opera's composition, both Plomer and Britten became 'less concerned than Strachey with the amatory motives of the two principal characters and more concerned with the Queen's pre-eminence as a Queen, a woman and a personality'.† The opera was planned so as to give considerable scope for pageantry—particularly the scenes of the Masque at Norwich and the dancing at the Palace of Whitehall. Basil Coleman was the producer and John Piper the designer; and between them they devised a magnificent and beautiful production, fully worthy of the great occasion for which the opera was written. John Pritchard conducted.‡ Joan Cross was cast as Queen Elizabeth and gave one of the finest performances of her career. No opera-lover who was present will ever forget the extraordinary effect of Elizabeth I on the stage directly addressing the glittering audience grouped round Elizabeth II in the Royal Opera House with the following words: 'I have ever used to set the last Judgment Day before mine eyes, and when I have to answer the highest Judge, I mean to plead that never thought was cherished in my heart that tended not to my people's good. I count it the glory of my crown that I have reigned with your love, and there is no jewel that I prefer before that jewel.'

But it must be admitted that the special audience at that gala was for the most part unmusical and disinterested, and the atmosphere in the Royal Opera House, when compared with that of a normal opera or ballet performance, distinctly frigid. This gave certain elements an excuse to denigrate the opera and its composer, and to express disapproval of the

* 18 June 1953.
† 'Notes on the Libretto of Gloriana' by William Plomer. *Tempo*, Summer, 1953.
‡ See Appendix B.

circumstances that had led to its commissioning. As Martin Cooper wrote in the *Spectator* (19 June), 'the work has been very generally over-blamed, with an almost sadistic relish or glee that has little to do with musical merit or demerit', and he noted the feelings of resentment that had arisen and the envy of 'special patronage and special conditions of work and performance not accorded to other performers'.* Despite its mixed reception at the première, subsequent performances of *Gloriana* at Covent Garden drew nearly as full houses as for *Billy Budd*. Its first performance outside London was given by the Covent Garden Company at Bulawayo, Southern Rhodesia (8 August 1953), at the Rhodes Centennial Exhibition; and early in 1954 it was toured to Cardiff, Manchester, and Birmingham.

The schedule for the composition of *Gloriana* had been a particularly onerous one. The idea of the opera had probably first been mooted during a skiing holiday with the Harewoods in Austria in March 1952. By the end of April the suggestion had received Royal approval; and the official announcement, naming the date of the gala performance of the Coronation opera as (probably) 8 June of the following year was made on 28 May. By July part of the first act existed in rough draft; and by the following February the work was sufficiently far advanced for a private run through to be held at the Royal Opera House. The actual composition had to be fitted in a very busy diary of festival appearances in the summer of 1952—Aldeburgh, followed by Copenhagen, Aix-en-Provence, Menton and Salzburg—and it is doubtful whether Britten would have managed to finish the score on time, had it not been for the devoted help of Imogen Holst. Subsequently she described this collaboration in some detail:† 'It was while he was still having discussions with William Plomer about the libretto that I first began working for him in Aldeburgh. My job was to copy out his pencil sketches of the music for each scene as soon as he had finished writing it, and to make a piano arrangement that the singers could use at rehearsals. I already knew that he was as practical a composer as my father had been, but even so it was astonishing to see how strictly he could keep to his time-schedule of work. He was able to say in the middle of October, when he was just beginning Act I, that he would have finished the second act before the end of January . . . When he began work on the full score of the opera, he wrote at such a tremendous speed that I thought I should never keep pace with him. He managed to get through at least twenty vast pages a day, and it seemed as if he never had to stop and think.'

In September 1953, Britten completed the composition of a set of eight lyrics and ballads by Thomas Hardy for high voice and piano. These were

* See also 'Let's Crab an Opera' by William Plomer. The *London Magazine*, October 1963.

† *Britten* by Imogen Holst. Faber, 1966.

dedicated to John and Myfanwy Piper, and *Winter Words*, as the song sequence was called, was performed for the first time at Harewood House on 8 October by Peter Pears with the composer at the piano, as part of the Leeds Triennial Festival programme.

While composing *Gloriana*, Britten had already been thinking about his next opera, which had been commissioned for the Venice Biennale in 1954; but in the autumn of 1953 he fell ill with acute bursitis in his right shoulder and had for the time being to cancel all conducting and recital engagements. He refused, however, to allow his illness to interfere with his composition schedule and started to write down the music for *The Turn of the Screw* with his left hand. The libretto had been prepared by Myfanwy Piper. Ultimately the score was finished in time; and the production of the opera by the English Opera Group at the Teatro la Fenice on 14 September 1954 with the composer conducting was a great triumph. Some of the critics confessed themselves puzzled by the subject matter of Henry James's story; but all praised the ingenuity of the score, the designs by John Piper and the production by Basil Coleman.* The work was first heard in London during a fortnight's season given by the English Opera Group at Sadler's Wells Theatre at the beginning of October.

That autumn he completed a third canticle. His choice was a poem by Edith Sitwell, *Still falls the rain*, which he set for tenor, horn and piano. It was dedicated to the memory of Noel Mewton-Wood, the brilliant Australian pianist, who had recently committed suicide; and the first performance was announced for a memorial concert at the Wigmore Hall on 4 December 1954. This particular concert had to be postponed till 28 January 1955, however, owing to the indisposition of Peter Pears.

During 1955 the English Opera Group gave further performances of *The Turn of the Screw* at Munich, Schwetzingen, and Florence (as part of the Maggio Musicale), at the Aldeburgh Festival in June, and at the Scala Theatre, London, in September. There was also an autumn tour and a Christmas Season of *Let's Make an Opera!*

Towards the end of the year Britten and Pears left England on an extended tour that took them via Yugoslavia and Turkey to the Far East, where they visited Bali, Japan and India before returning to England the following spring.

At this period Britten was much preoccupied with thoughts of writing a full-length ballet. He greatly admired the work of John Cranko, the young choreographer who was attached to the Sadler's Wells Theatre Ballet; and in fact Cranko had been chosen to direct a new production of *Peter Grimes* at Covent Garden in November 1953 with sets by Roger Ramsdell. A preliminary announcement was made in January 1954 that Britten would

* See Appendix B.

write a ballet for Cranko to choreograph for the Sadler's Wells Theatre Ballet during its 1954/5 season; but in the event the composition of the score was delayed for nearly two years.

Meanwhile, a new crop of ballets appeared, based on existing Britten scores. At the time of the Coronation of HM The Queen, a ballet called *Fanfare* was mounted by the New York City Ballet with choreography by Jerome Robbins to Britten's *Young Person's Guide to the Orchestra*. The same score was used for a ballet entitled *Variations on a Theme of Purcell* given by the Sadler's Wells Ballet at Covent Garden (6 January 1955) with choreography by Frederick Ashton and scenery and costumes by Peter Snow. (The programme carried the following quotation from Ovid: 'If you have a voice, sing: if soft arms, dance—and with whatever gifts you have for pleasing—please!') The *Variations on a Theme of Frank Bridge* were used for three different ballets. John Cranko created a ballet called *Variations on a Theme* for the Ballet Rambert, which was danced to a version specially scored for small orchestra by James Bernard (21 June 1954). In February 1955 Alan Carter mounted a new version called *Haus der Schatten* with the Bayerischer Staatsopernballett in Munich. And on 10 February 1957 the American Ballet Theatre produced *Winter's Eve* in New York with choreography by Kenneth MacMillan and settings by Nicholas Georgiadis. At the end of 1955, a new ballet by Zachary Solov called *Soirée* was presented at the Metropolitan Opera, New York, with décor and costumes by Cecil Beaton. The action represented a masked ball, and the music was chosen from Britten's arrangement of Rossini's music in *Soirées Musicales*. In the summer of 1957 the José Limon Ballet gave a season at Sadler's Wells Theatre, in the course of which they used Britten's String Quartets 1 and 2 as accompaniment for a ballet entitled *Ruins and Visions* after the collection of poems by Stephen Spender.

During 1954 and 1955 Britten gave much preliminary thought to the ballet score he intended to write. Cranko had already prepared a draft scenario for a three-act ballet and, knowing that what he wanted was 'a vehicle for creative choreography rather than "classical" pastiche', had decided that a 'mythological fairy-tale would supply the framework needed', his idea being 'to make a series of images from traditional fairy stories, linked by a thread of plot which was as important or unimportant as the audience chose to make it. These images would provide the various divertissements . . .'* Accordingly, he prepared a rough outline for *The Prince of the Pagodas*. When Britten formally agreed to write the music, Cranko's early draft scenario was reviewed, the composer making it clear that in his music he would introduce 'various themes on which he would make variations short enough to provide the episodic dances, but which

* 'Making a Ballet' by John Cranko. The *Observer*, 13 and 20 January 1957.

would give the work as a whole a sense of continuity.'* A revised script was prepared, on which the composer based his score; and the choreographer found the music so compelling that he had to revisualize the entire choreography.

Britten's interest in oriental music and his voyage to the Far East had yielded a timely musical harvest. Cranko agreed with the designer, John Piper, that some of the more exotic episodes in *The Prince of the Pagodas* would be related 'to the strange edifices of Steinberg and Paul Klee',† and the scene with the pagodas (in the second part of Act II) offered the composer a cue for introducing special colour elements into the orchestra—vibraphone, celesta, piano, xylophone, bells, tomtoms, gongs, all joining in outbursts of gay, festive sound, reminiscent of the Javanese gamelan.

The scenario by virtue of its deliberate construction out of stock characters and situations and various props supposed to be common to the conventions of fairy tales did not completely avoid the trap of pastiche. Nevertheless, the shape of the plot showed that Cranko had devised a suitable armature for a full-length ballet so that the right dances came at the right moments. For instance, the second act opens with a beautiful travelling sequence, where the heroine, Belle Rose, travels through three of the elements (air, water, fire) ultimately to track the Prince to earth in the Kingdom of the Pagodas; and in the third act after the transformation scene there is an elaborate *divertissement* consisting of eleven varied dance numbers containing some of the most original and inventive music in the score.

The Prince of the Pagodas contains about thirty-six different dances—some of them character dances, some of them *divertissements*. To differentiate these dances in the course of a full-length ballet score requires great ingenuity on the part of the composer. As Erwin Stein said,‡ 'It is not only a question of inventing many good and diverse tunes, but also of co-ordinating and balancing them. And as rhythm is the life blood of dancing, it is especially the rhythmic shapes of the tunes that must be well defined and diversified.' Here Britten was extraordinarily successful. The absence of words to set seemed to cause him no inhibitions; and the score has a vitality and a variety of melody, metre, texture and form that puts it in the same category as Prokofiev's full-length ballets *Cinderella* and *Romeo and Juliet*.

The first performance of *The Prince of the Pagodas* was given by the Sadler's Wells Ballet at the Royal Opera House, Covent Garden. At first, the advertised date was 19 September 1956; but as Britten found he was behindhand with the instrumentation of the score, the première had to be postponed to 1 January 1957. The main roles of the Princess Belle Rose and

* Ibid. † Ibid.

‡ From 'The Prince of the Pagodas: The Music' by Erwin Stein. *Tempo*, Winter 1956/7.

the Prince of the Pagodas were danced by Svetlana Beriosova and David Blair. The composer conducted; and at the end of the performance he was presented with a giant laurel wreath. The ballet was dedicated by composer and choreographer to Imogen Holst and Ninette de Valois.

The Prince of the Pagodas was performed at the Metropolitan Opera, New York, when the Royal Ballet visited America at the end of the summer of 1957; but shortly after that it was dropped from the company's repertory. It was mounted at the Scala, Milan, in the early summer of 1957.

A small group of occasional pieces preceded the composition of *The Prince of the Pagodas*. In the winter of 1955, Britten went skiing with friends at Zermatt, and one of them, Mary Potter, hurt her leg and was laid up. To divert her, he wrote an *Alpine Suite* for three recorders, which the two of them together with Peter Pears used to play in the evenings. To the same year belongs a *Scherzo* for recorder quartet (dedicated to the Aldeburgh Music Club). For the quincentenary of St Peter Mancroft, Norwich, 1955, he supplied a *Hymn to St Peter* for choir and organ; and for the centenary of St Michael's College, Tenbury, 1956, an *Antiphon*, also for choir and organ.

In April 1957, he was elected an honorary member of the American Academy of Arts and Letters and of the National Institute of Arts and Letters. In presenting him with the insignia, the American Ambassador in London read the following citation: 'Your compositions for voice, chamber groups and orchestra have been received with delight in many lands beside your own. Aware of the musical values and the history of your country, often collaborating with poets of distinction, as their contemporaries did with Shakespeare, Jonson, Milton, and Dryden, you have recaptured the great English tradition of word, song, and instrument. Your operas, *Peter Grimes*, *Albert Herring* and *The Rape of Lucretia* among others, are in the world repertory. They do honour to your country and to you.'

In August and September 1957 the English Opera Group visited Canada and played *The Turn of the Screw* at Stratford, Ontario. In October it gave performances of the same opera in Berlin as part of the Berlin Festival. A number of these performances were conducted by Britten himself.

On his return to Aldeburgh in October he decided to start work on a new children's opera. There had been several occasions in the past when he had thought of writing a successor to *The Little Sweep*. In the summer of 1951 he had plans to compose *The Tale of Mr Tod*, after the story by Beatrix Potter, for production by the English Opera Group in 1952; but copyright difficulties intervened, and the project never got off the ground. About 1954 he discussed with William Plomer an opera for children based on a space travel theme. Recalling this abortive venture years later he said:* 'I did in

* From an interview with Britten on his return from Russia in 1964 printed in *The Times*.

fact start on [an opera on astronauts], for children, about ten years ago, with William Plomer—who'd written a superb first scene; we occasionally look back at it and I may finish it sometime. It had a character with the magnificent name of Madge Plato.' This time, however, he chose a biblical theme—the episode of the Flood from the Chester Miracle Plays. *Noye's Fludde* was written at great speed. It was started at Crag House, Crabbe Street, on 22 October and finished a few weeks later at the Red House, Aldeburgh, to which he had just moved.

VIII
Aldeburgh: At the Red House

The move from Crag House to the Red House in November 1957 was brought about partly because the former house could be so closely overlooked by people strolling along Crag Path that Britten inevitably suffered from a lack of privacy. The occupier of the Red House, situated in a secluded part of Aldeburgh near the Golf Club, was the artist, Mary Potter; and she now moved into the house in Crabbe Street that had been vacated by Britten and Pears. The Red House, with its attractive garden, was larger and more convenient from the composer's point of view; and his life continued to follow a fairly regular routine of composition interspersed with performances as conductor and pianist, and festival direction.

Britten playing tennis at the Red House, Aldeburgh. He is partnered by Mary Potter the painter

Britten's studio at the Red House, Aldeburgh

The first composition to be completed at the Red House was *Noye's Fludde* (on 15 December 1957), and this was produced with great success as part of the 1958 Aldeburgh Festival programme at the church in the neighbouring village of Orford. The producer was Colin Graham, and the designer Ceri Richards.* This Festival also featured the first performance of *Songs from the Chinese*, a setting of Chinese poems translated by Arthur Waley for high voice and guitar, which had been completed before the move to the Red House the previous autumn. These were performed by Peter Pears and Julian Bream.

Although Britten had never been particularly keen on writing as such, feeling his true medium was music, nevertheless he agreed to collaborate with Imogen Holst on a book entitled *The Story of Music*, which was published by Rathbone Books, London, in 1958. This was a popular manual, lavishly illustrated and with collages specially designed by Ceri Richards, dealing first with the essential components of music—sound and rhythm, songs and singers, instruments and players—and then with drama

* See Appendix B.

The Library at the Red House

in music, styles in music, and western music as compared with eastern music. The final section touches on the work of the composer; and this leads to a reference to twentieth-century experiments in distortion, particularly the twelve-note or twelve-tone system which is basic for the construction of 'serial' music. Here the two authors write: 'It is impossible for anyone to say whether this is to be the recognized music of the second half of the twentieth century. Some musicians think it is. Some think that there are still unlimited possibilities in the seven-note scale and the chords that grow out of it. Some think that it does not matter what style a composer chooses to write in, as long as he has something definite to say and says it clearly.'

Other occasional articles by Britten published about the same time include a tribute to the virtuoso horn-player, Dennis Brain, killed in a car crash in 1957 (*Tempo*, Winter 1958), and an essay 'On Realising the Continuo in Purcell's Songs' which was published in *Henry Purcell (1659–1695)*, a symposium edited by Imogen Holst in honour of the tercentenary of Purcell's birth (Oxford University Press, 1959). The Purcell celebrations included a performance of his *Ode for St Cecilia* conducted by Britten at the Royal Festival Hall (10 June 1959), on which occasion Dame

Edith Sitwell read a new poem entitled *Praise We Great Men*, which she had written in honour of the occasion and dedicated to Britten.

The previous summer Britten had broadcast a programme, 'Personal Choice', on the BBC Home Service (16 July 1958), in which he selected a number of his favourite poems, which were then read over the air. He excluded poems which he had already set to music; and the following were his choice (in many cases prophetic of settings to come):

Crabbed Age and Youth	William Shakespeare
When most I wink	William Shakespeare
Vertue	George Herbert
The Chimney Sweeper	William Blake
'The World is too much with us'	William Wordsworth
'Ah! Sun-flower!'	William Blake
From *The Wanderings of Cain*	S. T. Coleridge
'Break, break, break'	Alfred Lord Tennyson
'If it's ever Spring again'	Thomas Hardy
Strange Meeting	Wilfred Owen
The Youth with Red-gold Hair	Edith Sitwell
'Lay Your Sleeping Head, My Love'	W. H. Auden

He also included *Hälfte des Lebens* by Hölderlin, together with Michael Hamburger's translation into English.

He forthwith proceeded to make a new short anthology of poems connected with night and sleep and dreams, with the intention of setting them on similar lines to his *Serenade*. For this purpose he chose a few lines from Shelley's *Prometheus Unbound*, Tennyson's *The Kraken*, Coleridge's *The Wanderings of Cain*, Middleton's *Blurt, Master Constable*, an extract from Wordsworth's *The Prelude*, *The Kind Ghosts* by Wilfred Owen, *Sleep and Poetry* by Keats and Shakespeare's 43rd Sonnet ('When most I wink'). He set these for tenor solo and string orchestra; but whereas in the case of the *Serenade* he had chosen a single *obbligato* instrument (the horn) for the whole work, in the *Nocturne* he picked seven. The opening poem (by Shelley) is set for strings alone. A bassoon *obbligato* is added to the strings for the Tennyson; harp for the Coleridge; horn for the Middleton; timpani for the Wordsworth; English horn for the Owen; flute and clarinet for the Keats; and all seven solo instruments join together with the string orchestra for the Shakespeare finale. Each *obbligato* instrument gives a different tone colour to the movement it appears in. Particularly impressive are the bassoon's submarine wallowings and burblings in *The Kraken*, and the menace of the timpani in the passage from *The Prelude*:

But that night
When on my bed I lay, I was most mov'd

And felt most deeply in what world I was . . .
I thought of those September Massacres,
Divided from me by a little month,
And felt, and touch'd them, a substantial dread . . .
And in such way I wrought upon myself
Until I seem'd to hear a voice that cried
To the whole City, 'Sleep no more!'

This *Nocturne* is in the sort of lyrical elegiac vein that is both characteristic of Britten and reminiscent of Mahler; and it seemed most appropriate that the work should be dedicated to Mahler's widow, Mrs Alma Mahler Werfel. The first performance was given on 16 October 1958 as part of the Leeds Centenary Festival by Peter Pears with the BBC Symphony Orchestra conducted by Rudolf Schwarz.

Another poem from the BBC 'Personal Choice' programme provided the cue for his next song cycle. It was Prince Ludwig of Hesse and the Rhine who brought Britten's attention to Hölderlin and his poetry, and he now chose *Hälfte des Lebens* and five other poems, to make *Six Hölderlin Fragments*, which he set for tenor and piano. These were first performed at Schloss Wolfsgarten, near Frankfurt-am-Main, on Prince Ludwig's fiftieth birthday (20 November 1958). The poems are short, and the songs represent Britten's style at its pithiest. Even though he is dealing with a foreign language, his inflexions are impeccable; and he also allows the words and their meaning to provide an occasional cue for musical transliteration, e.g. the drooping melodic tendrils in *Hälfte des Lebens* and the wonderful scalic ladders that slowly intersect in *Die Linien des Lebens.*

In 1959 Britten received a very attractive commission. It came from the University of Basle and was an invitation to write a cantata in honour of the 500th anniversay of the University's foundation which would be celebrated in 1960. He accepted and agreed to set a Latin text compiled from the Charter of the University and from older orations in praise of Basle.

After the 1959 Aldeburgh Festival, certain adaptation work was carried out to the Jubilee Hall. The stage and orchestral pit were enlarged, the dressing-room accommodation improved, the seating capacity increased to 316, and proper ventilation installed. In order to celebrate these improvements, Britten decided to compose a new opera for performance at the 1960 Festival. As usual, the production was to be entrusted to the English Opera Group; but in view of the increased facilities at the Jubilee Hall, he felt he could now write for a somewhat larger orchestra than the usual English Opera Group ensemble of about a dozen solo instruments. In 1960 he himself described the inception of the opera as follows:* 'Last August it was

* 'A New Britten Opera' by Benjamin Britten. The *Observer*, 5 June 1960.

decided that for this year's Aldeburgh Festival I should write a full-length opera for the opening of the reconstructed Jubilee Hall. As this was a comparatively sudden decision there was no time to get a libretto written, so we took one that was ready to hand . . . I have always loved *A Midsummer Night's Dream.* As I get older, I find that I increasingly prefer the work either of the very young or of the very old. I always feel *A Midsummer Night's Dream* to be by a very young man, whatever Shakespeare's actual age when he wrote it. Operatically, it is especially exciting because there are three quite separate groups—the Lovers, the Rustics, and the Fairies—which nevertheless interact . . . In writing opera I have always found it very dangerous to start writing the music until the words are more or less fixed. One talks to a possible librettist, and decides together the shape of the subject and its treatment. In my case, when I worked with E. M. Forster or William Plomer, for instance, we blocked the opera out in the way an artist might block out a picture. With *A Midsummer Night's Dream*, the first task was to get it into manageable shape, which basically entailed simplifying and cutting an extremely complex story . . . I do not feel in the least guilty at having cut the play in half. The original Shakespeare will survive . . . I actually started work on the opera in October, and finished it on, I think, Good Friday—seven months for everything, including the score. This is not up to the speed of Mozart or Verdi, but these days, when the line of musical language is broken, it is much rarer. It is the fastest of any big opera I have written, though I wrote *Let's Make an Opera!* in a fortnight.'

Although the work of composition proceeded speedily, a number of checks and difficulties were encountered—illness for one—but he could not afford to allow his regular working schedule to be affected. 'A lot of the third act', he admits,* 'was written when I was not at all well with flu. I find that one's inclination, whether one wants to work or not, does not in the least affect the quality of the work done.'

Anyway, the work was finished on time. John Cranko was appointed producer; John Piper designed the sets; and Carl Toms was responsible for the costumes.† The first performance at Aldeburgh (11 June 1960) was an unqualified success. Later that month the opera was given by the English Opera Group as part of the Holland Festival programme. When it arrived at Covent Garden the following winter (2 February 1961) a larger complement of strings was used in the orchestra. Georg Solti conducted; and the production was entrusted to Sir John Gielgud. Within a year of its first production, the opera had also been staged in Hamburg, Zurich, Berlin, Pforzheim, Milan, Vancouver, Göteborg, Edinburgh, Schwetzingen, and Tokyo. This made it clear that *A Midsummer Night's Dream* was likely to

* Ibid. † See Appendix B.

prove the most popular in the international field of Britten's full-scale operas since *Peter Grimes*.

About this time a change occurred in the status of the English Opera Group. Originally it had been set up as a company limited by guarantee and had pursued an independent artistic policy, receiving an annual subsidy from the Arts Council of Great Britain. But now it was judged expedient for it to become closely associated with the Royal Opera House, Covent Garden, which henceforth undertook its direct management.

The first performance of *Cantata Academica* (*Carmen Basiliense*) took place in Basle on 1 July 1960 when it was performed by the Basle Chamber Choir and the Basle Chamber Orchestra under the direction of Paul Sacher. The work caught the imagination of the public with its infectious high spirits, good humour and academic ingenuities (e.g. Chorus *alla Rovescio*, *Tema Seriale con Fuga*, *etc*.).

During 1960 Britten completed a revision of *Billy Budd*, changing it from a four-act to a two-act opera and in the process shortening the end of the original Act 1. The new version was heard for the first time in a studio performance broadcast by the BBC (13 November 1960) and was staged at Covent Garden early in 1964.

In recent years it looked as if Britten had been composing more for the theatre and concert hall than for the church; but the time had now come to redress the balance. In 1959 he wrote the *Missa Brevis in D* as a parting present to George Malcolm, the retiring organist at Westminster Cathedral, who was well known as an excellent trainer of boys' voices and a doughty opponent of the artificial and unnatural sound known as 'Cathedral Tone'. He was a firm upholder of the belief that it was perfectly feasible 'to train a boy's voice—to refine it, and develop it, and turn it into a medium of real musical beauty—without destroying its natural timbre, and without removing from it the characteristics of the normal human Boy.'* In the *Missa Brevis*, the writing for boys' voices is particularly well fitted to the type of singing voice that Malcolm had trained so successfully in the Cathedral choir during his term as organist. The new work was first given during High Mass at Westminster Cathedral (22 July 1959).

A little later (1961) Britten wrote a *Jubilate Deo* for St George's Chapel, Windsor, at the request of HRH The Duke of Edinburgh, as a companion piece to the *Te Deum* of 1934.

But now the chance of a major church commission came his way, and he embraced it readily, though not without feeling slightly daunted at the magnitude of the task.

For some years the building of a new Cathedral in Coventry, designed by

* From 'Boys' Voices' by George Malcolm. *Tribute to Benjamin Britten on his Fiftieth Birthday*.

Sir Basil Spence and intended to complement the ruins of the bomb-damaged medieval Cathedral, had been under way; and many artists—including Graham Sutherland, Jacob Epstein, John Piper and John Hutton—had been engaged to beautify it. When the new Cathedral was seen to be approaching completion, it was agreed to celebrate its rededication with a special festival of the arts. A number of new works were required for the occasion, including a large-scale oratorio; and this commission was offered to Britten, who accepted it. He fully realized the importance of the occasion, for it would mark not only the phoenix-like resurgence of the new Cathedral at the side of the shattered shell of the old, but also the healing of many wounds. He wanted to make some public musical statement about the criminal futility of war, and this seemed a good opportunity to do so. Clearly a big work was called for—something for full orchestra and full chorus; something calculated for 'a big, reverberant acoustic'.* From the beginning the idea of the *Missa pro Defunctis* was in his mind—but this was to be a setting with a difference. When looking for something that would help him to contrast the spiritual pleadings and terrors and consolations of the *Missa pro Defunctis* with the realistic horror, suffering and desolation caused by twentieth-century war, he thought once again of his 1957 'Personal Choice' programme for the BBC and found what he required in Wilfred Owen's poem *Strange Meeting*. And in Owen's unpublished preface to his poems (*c.* 1918) lay the key to what was to be called *War Requiem*. '. . . I am not concerned with Poetry,' wrote Owen. '*My subject is War, and the pity of War. The Poetry is in the pity.* Yet these elegies are to this generation in no sense consolatory. They may be to the next. *All a poet can do to-day is to warn.* That is why the true Poets must be truthful.' (The italicized passages appear on the title page of the *War Requiem* as an epigraph.)

Britten now decided that on the big-scale level he would set part of the *Missa pro Defunctis* for chorus and full orchestra, while on a more intimate level (using soloists and chamber orchestra of twelve) he would set the text of nine of Owen's war poems, which would be inserted episodically into the six main movements of the Requiem. Two further musical decisions followed. The setting of the poem *Strange Meeting* seemed to postulate two male soloists, one symbolizing a British soldier (the poet) and the other a German soldier whom he had killed—here Britten chose a tenor and a baritone; and the setting of the rest of the song cycle was divided between them. This meant that, if only for purposes of contrast, it was preferable for the Requiem proper to have a female soloist (soprano); and a boys' choir was added in order to strengthen the high tessitura.

The Owen song cycle has the same sort of stature and importance as *Les*

* *On Receiving the First Aspen Award* by Benjamin Britten. Faber, 1964.

Illuminations or the *Nocturne*. Britten has set the following nine poems: 1. *Anthem for Doomed Youth*, 2. *Voices* (part only), 3. *The Next War*, 4. *Sonnet on Seeing a Piece of our Artillery Brought into Action* (six lines only), 5. *Futility*, 6. *The Parable of the Old Men and the Young*, 7. *The End*, 8. *At a Calvary near the Ancre*, and 9. *Strange Meeting* (thirty-three lines out of a total of forty-four). The songs are self-contained, with certain exceptions. *Futility* (which is treated as whispered recitative) is cross-cut with the *Lacrimosa dies illa* verse of the *Dies Irae* movement. A cue from the *Offertorium*—'*quam olim Abrahae promisisti, et semini ejus*'—leads into Owen's poem *The Parable of the Old Men and the Young* with its retelling of the Abraham and Isaac parable in twentieth-century terms:

When lo! an angel called him out of heaven,
Saying, Lay not thy hand upon the lad,
Neither do anything to him. Behold,
A ram, caught in a thicket by its horns;
Offer the Ram of Pride instead of him.
But the old man would not so, but slew his son,—
And half the seed of Europe, one by one.

And here the music deliberately recalls the parallel passage in Britten's *Canticle II*. The penultimate song *At a Calvary near the Ancre* is cross-cut with the *Agnus Dei* movement, and at the end the tenor soloist is drawn out of the Owen poems with a final ascending scalic phrase '*Dona nobis pacem*'. The final song, *Strange Meeting*, is treated as a duologue in recitative for tenor and baritone; and their last line '*Let us sleep now*' becomes a coda which is absorbed into the final chorus '*In paradisum deducant te Angeli*'.

There are many striking features in the *War Requiem*;* and it undoubtedly succeeds in what it sets out to do, in moving between two planes—the setting of the *Missa pro Defunctis* in Latin for soprano solo with full chorus and full orchestra, and the setting of the Owen poems for the two male soloists with chamber orchestra. But at times one wonders whether it is really possible to achieve a conciliation between these elements. '*Requiem aeternam dona eis, Domine*' sings the chorus, leading directly to the tenor soloist's agonized question '*What passing-bells for these who die as cattle?*' and his answer '*Only the monstrous anger of the guns.*' In the *Sanctus* movement, the choral cries of *Hosanna in excelsis!* are followed by Owen's poem *The End*, where the baritone soloist asks:

Shall life renew these bodies? Of a truth
All death will life annul, all tears assuage?

* An excellent study of the score of *War Requiem* by Peter Evans will be found in *Tempo*, Spring/Summer 1962.

Britten receiving the Freedom of the Borough of Aldeburgh in the Moot Hall, 22 October 1962

and Earth answers

My fiery heart shrinks, aching. It is death.
Mine ancient scars shall not be glorified,
Nor my titanic tears, the sea, be dried.

The first performance of *War Requiem* was given in St Michael's Cathedral, Coventry, on 30 May 1962. The soloists were Heather Harper, Peter Pears and Dietrich Fischer-Dieskau. The chorus and full orchestra were conducted by Meredith Davies and the chamber orchestra by the composer. The work made a profound impression both then and later when it was heard in London at Westminster Abbey (6 December 1962). By the end of 1963 it had been performed in more than a dozen cities abroad, including Berlin, Boston, Paris, Perugia and Prague. The Decca gramophone recording sold over 200,000 sets in only five months.

In May 1962, just before the first performance of *War Requiem*, Britten completed a setting of *Psalm 150* for two-part children's voices. This was intended for the centenary celebrations of his preparatory school, Old Buckenham Hall School (formerly South Lodge School) Lowestoft, and it was performed there in July, the first public performance being given the following year (1965) in the course of the Aldeburgh Festival.

To mark the fourteenth centenary of St Columba's missionary journey from Ireland to Iona, a *Hymn of St Columba* was written in May 1963 and given its first performance on 2 June 1963 at Gartan, County Donegal, the Saint's birthplace.

Meanwhile, Britten had gradually formed a number of friendships with Russian musicians that were to have an important effect on his work. In September 1960, he met the great Russian cellist, Mstislav Rostropovich, in London, and it was agreed that he should compose a special Cello Sonata for him. This was dispatched to Russia in the winter of 1961, and rehearsed in London at the beginning of March when Rostropovich was passing through on his way to South America. The first public performance was given by Rostropovich and the composer at the Aldeburgh Festival on 7 July 1961. During this Festival visit, Rostropovich was joined by his wife Galina Vishnevskaya, who gave a vocal recital in honour of the Festival. Britten was so impressed by her lovely voice that he hoped she would be able to sing the solo soprano part at the first performance of his *War Requiem*; but unfortunately her engagements did not permit her to do so. Another Russian musician, who became a constant visitor to the Aldeburgh Festival, was the great pianist, Sviatoslav Richter, whom Rostropovich introduced to Britten in London in 1961. The following year Dmitri Shostakovich heard *The Turn of the Screw* at the Edinburgh Festival in company with Rostropovich, and the music of the opera made a tremendous impact on him. So it was not surprising when an invitation came for Britten and Pears to visit the USSR during a festival of British music in March 1963.

The programme of this festival in Moscow and Leningrad included orchestral performances of the *Sinfonia da Requiem*, the *Serenade*, and the Sea Interludes and Passacaglia from *Peter Grimes*, and chamber music recitals which included the Sonata in C for Cello and Piano, *Winter Words* and the *Six Hölderlin Fragments*. This was the moment when the Second Plenary Meeting of the Board of the USSR Union of Composers was sitting in Moscow, and special attention was being given to the work of the younger generation of composers. The current attitude to contemporary British music seemed propitious, especially when contrasted with the hostile atmosphere of the All-Union Congress of Soviet Composers only fifteen years previously. Britten and Pears received a very warm reception from their Russian audiences.

During this visit, Britten gave an interview to a *Pravda* correspondent in which he said: 'I must own that until my arrival in USSR I was assailed with doubts whether the Soviet audiences would understand and accept our musical art which had been developing along different national lines than the Russian. I am happy at having had my doubts dispelled at the very first concert. The Soviet public proved not only unusually musical—that I knew all along—but showed an enviable breadth of artistic perception. It is a wonderful public.'

This interview was widely quoted in the international press and, coming when it did, it may have played a not unhelpful part in the improvement in Anglo-Soviet cultural relations.

Britten in Moscow in 1963, with Peter Pears and Galina Vishnevskaya (*left*) and Mstislav Rostropovich and Marion, Countess of Harewood—now Mrs Jeremy Thorpe (*right*)

On his return to Aldeburgh, Britten completed two important works: the *Symphony in D for Cello and Orchestra*, which was dedicated to Rostropovich, and the *Cantata Misericordium* for tenor and baritone solos, small chorus and string orchestra, piano, harp and timpani, written to celebrate the centenary of the foundation of the Red Cross and dedicated to the Countess of Cranbrook, the Chairman of the Aldeburgh Festival Council. The first performance of the *Symphony for Cello* was scheduled for the 1963 Aldeburgh Festival, but had to be cancelled owing to Rostropovich's illness. The first performance of the *Cantata Misericordium* took place in Geneva on 1 September 1963 as planned, with Peter Pears and Dietrich Fischer-Dieskau as soloists, the Motet Genève and the Orchestre de la Suisse-Romande, conducted by Ernest Ansermet. The first performance in Great Britain occurred on 12 September at the Royal Albert Hall in the course of a Promenade Concert devoted entirely to Britten's music.

This special 'Prom' programme marked the opening of an autumn season of productions and performances intended to honour his fiftieth birthday on 22 November. Another new work appeared in September entitled *Night Piece* (Notturno) for piano solo written as a test piece for competitors in the first Leeds International Pianoforte Competition. *Peter Grimes* was revived in a new production by Basil Coleman at Sadler's Wells (16 October).

On the actual birthday, a special tribute from about three dozen of his friends—including writers, artists, musicians—was published by Faber and Faber. Anthony Gishford was the editor; and in his Foreword he explained that the 'invitation to those of Mr Britten's friends and collaborators who we thought would like to join in such a gift specified only that they should contribute something that they themselves liked and that they thought would give the recipient pleasure'. This loose formula covered such contributions as a chapter from an unfinished novel by E. M. Forster, a study of Edward Fitzgerald by William Plomer, substantial extracts from the diary written by Prince Ludwig of Hesse and the Rhine when he accompanied Britten and Pears on their journey to the Far East in 1956, and three works which had been specially dedicated to Britten—Edith Sitwell's poem 'Praise We Great Men' (1959), Hans Werner Henze's *Kammermusik 1958*, and Michael Tippett's *Concerto for Orchestra*, which bears the superscription 'To Benjamin Britten with affection and admiration in the year of his fiftieth birthday'. These last two tributes were represented by page facsimiles from the manuscript scores.

Many tributes appeared also in the national daily and weekly press, in periodicals, and on radio and television.

On the evening of Britten's birthday, a concert performance of *Gloriana* at the Royal Festival Hall was presented as a tribute to the composer by the Polyphonia Orchestra with Bryan Fairfax as conductor. Sylvia Fisher sang the part of Queen Elizabeth I for the first time, and Peter Pears was heard in his original part of the Earl of Essex. The revival of this opera was warmly welcomed by the composer and the audience, but the pleasure generated by the occasion was sadly affected as the news of the assassination of President Kennedy earlier that day in Dallas started to seep through the auditorium.

In some ways Britten's fiftieth birthday proved a climacteric. For nearly thirty years the firm of Boosey & Hawkes had been the exclusive publishers of his music. Now he decided to make a change. His contract was not renewed, and he threw in his fortunes with a new music publishing venture started by Faber and Faber, whose ambitious plan was 'to build up a catalogue of the highest quality, comprising both old and new music'. The first work of Britten's they published was *Nocturnal* (after John Dowland) for guitar, op. 70. The second was *Curlew River*, a new type of opera styled 'a parable for church performance'. Unlike most of Britten's works this was not written at home in Aldeburgh, but abroad in Venice, where he went for a change of air in February 1964. The way in which he and his librettist, William Plomer, succeeded in adapting stylistic methods characteristic of the Japanese Noh plays to a new kind of operatic convention for church performance marked a new departure in his operatic practice, not the least revolutionary feature being the abolition of the conductor.

After Venice, he paid a brief visit to the USSR in order to conduct the first performance of the *Symphony in D for Cello and Orchestra* in Moscow on 12 March 1964 with Rostropovich as soloist. He went over to Leningrad for a few days; and while he was there a group of music students performed part of the *War Requiem* in his honour. A little later the first performance of *Peter Grimes* in the USSR was given in concert form in the large hall of the Leningrad Conservatoire by opera soloists, the Leningrad Radio chorus, and the Leningrad Philharmonic Orchestra under Dzhemal Dalgat; and this led to two performances at the Kirov Theatre, Leningrad, and one in Moscow at the end of the season.

In May 1964 Britten was named the first winner of the Aspen Award in the humanities. This had been established by Mr Robert O. Anderson of Roswell, New Mexico, chairman of the Institute of Humanistic Studies at Aspen, Colorado, to honour 'the individual anywhere in the world judged to have made the greatest contribution to the advancement of the humanities'. The award (of $30,000) was handed over on 31 July at a ceremony held in the amphitheatre at Aspen and attended by about 1,500 guests. In his speech of thanks, Britten referred again to a subject that was always near his heart—that of 'occasional' music—and emphasized the importance of the 'occasion'. He reminded his audience that 'Bach wrote his *St Matthew Passion* for performance on one day of the year only—the day which in the Christian church was the culmination of the year, to which the year's worship was leading' and went on to say 'it is one of the unhappiest results of the march of science and commerce that this unique work, at the turn of a switch, is at the mercy of any loud roomful of cocktail drinkers—to be listened to or switched off at will, without ceremony or occasion'.* He expressed his dismay that musical performances could be made 'audible in any corner of the globe, at any moment of the day or night, through a loudspeaker, without question of suitability or comprehensibility. Anyone, anywhere, at any time, can listen to the B minor Mass upon one condition only—that they possess a machine. No qualification is required of any sort—faith, virtue, education, experience, age.' These were brave words, and possibly words that some members of his audience would not be prepared to accept; but anyone acquainted with the scientific advances during the last half-century that have made it possible to popularize music on such a universal scale must realize that this has not necessarily brought with it an automatic rise in the standards of listening and appreciation—in fact, everywhere the dangers of aural debasement are only too real.

Britten placed the money from the Aspen Award in a special Trust Fund which had been set up for the purpose of helping and encouraging young musicians.

During the summer of 1964 the English Opera Group toured the successful Aldeburgh Festival production of *Curlew River* (first performance, Orford Church, 13 June 1964) to the Holland Festival, and subsequently to the City of London and King's Lynn Festivals. In the autumn it embarked on a tour of the USSR (Riga, Leningrad, and Moscow) with a repertory consisting of *The Rape of Lucretia*, *Albert Herring* and *The Turn of the Screw*. The Russian audiences were most responsive; and special interest in the scale and style of the English Opera Group productions and their suitability for touring was expressed by Madame Furtseva, the Soviet Minister of Culture.

In 1965 Britten and Pears made two important trips abroad. First, there was a visit to India early in the year. Then in the summer they were invited to visit the USSR and to stay for a period in the Composers' Home for Creative Work in Dilidjan, Armenia. Two days after a performance of the *Symphony for Cello* by Rostropovich at the Royal Festival Hall (1 August), they flew with Rostropovich and his wife Galina Vishnevskaya to Yerevan via Moscow. From there they motored to Dilidjan where all four of them stayed for just over three weeks.† On 28 August a Britten Festival opened in Yerevan and the composer attended the various concerts, whose programmes included performances of the *Peter Grimes* Interludes, *The Young Person's Guide to the Orchestra*, the 1st String Quartet, three movements of the *Sonata for Cello and Piano*, the first *Suite* for unaccompanied cello (first

* *On Receiving the First Aspen Award* by Benjamin Britten. Faber, 1964.

† *Armenian Holiday*, an attractively informal account of this holiday in diary form by Peter Pears, was privately published in 1966.

performance in the USSR), and various songs, including two extracts from a new Pushkin song cycle.

Britten had bought a copy of the Penguin edition of Pushkin when he was passing through London Airport on his way to the USSR and fallen in love with some of the lyrics. He thought that setting some of these poems might help his Russian, so he got Rostropovich and Vishnevskaya to read aloud the poems he had chosen from the literal English translation in the Penguin, and they set about teaching him to pronounce them properly. He then worked out a transliteration of six of them, and began setting them to music. By the time the holiday party left Armenia the new cycle (to be called *The Poet's Echo*) had been sketched out in rough. A fascinating account is given in Peter Pears's *Armenian Holiday** of a visit they paid to Pushkin's birthplace in the course of a special journey between Novgorod and Leningrad by car. '. . . It was not until 8 p.m. that we reached our destination, Pushkin's home, just twenty-four hours later than we were expected. Our hosts had waited for us all night. Slava† had not thought to telephone; but we were welcomed and greeted as if they had been in no way inconvenienced or put out . . . Before we retired our host took a torch and showed us Pushkin's house and museum, and outside the front door was the clock tower and its cracked clock which was there in Pushkin's time and still struck its old hours . . . After a meal of soup and excellent cold leg of lamb, and a sort of barley with meat balls (so good), marvellous coffee and plum syrup, our host begged to hear the Pushkin songs. We moved into the lamp-lit sitting-room with an upright piano in the corner, and started on the songs after an introduction by Slava. Galya sang her two, and I hummed the others. The last song of the set is the marvellous poem of insomnia, the ticking clock, persistent night-noises and the poet's cry for a meaning in them. Ben has started this with repeated staccato notes high-low high-low on the piano. Hardly had the little old piano begun its dry tick-tock tick-tock, than clear and silvery outside the window, a yard from our heads, came ding, ding, ding, not loud but clear, Pushkin's clock joining in his song. It seemed to strike far more than midnight, to go on all through the song, and afterwards we sat spell-bound. It was the most natural thing to have happened, and yet unique, astonishing, wonderful . . .'

As a coda to this Russian visit, *A Midsummer Night's Dream* received its first Russian production at the Bolshoi Theatre, Moscow, on 28 October 1965 with Gennadi Rozhdestvensky as conductor, Boris Pokrovsky as producer, and Nicolai Benois as designer.

Meanwhile there had been a plentiful outpouring of other new works. At the 1965 Aldeburgh Festival, the first *Suite* for unaccompanied cello, the *Gemini Variations* for piano duet, flute and violin, and *The Songs and*

* Ibid.

† Rostropovich.

Proverbs of William Blake, an extended song-cycle for baritone and piano, had all received their first performances. Rostropovich played the *Suite*; the Hungarian twins, Gabriel and Zoltán Jeney, performed the *Variations*; and the composer accompanied Dietrich Fischer-Dieskau in the Blake cycle.

Somewhat earlier Britten had accepted a commission from the United Nations for an anthem to mark their twentieth anniversary. The closing section was a setting of Virgil's fourth Eclogue—the vision of the Golden Age to come. *Voices for Today* (as it was called) was given a simultaneous première in New York, Paris and London on 24 October 1965. In his address delivered in the General Assembly Hall, U Thant, the Secretary-General of the United Nations, said: 'To Benjamin Britten, the ideal of peace is a matter of personal and abiding concern. At the head of an earlier composition (also about war and peace), he once wrote this stark preamble: "All the artist can do . . . is warn." Today he speaks for all of us, with an eloquence we lack, in a medium of which he is a master.'

For the 1966 Aldeburgh Festival Britten planned to compose a second parable for church performance as a companion piece to *Curlew River*. Once again William Plomer was invited to write the libretto; and the subject chosen was Nebuchadnezzar and the burning fiery furnace. But Britten's composition schedule was upset in the winter of 1966 by illness; and he had to undergo an operation for diverticulitis. Nevertheless, *The Burning Fiery Furnace* was ready on time and, like *Curlew River*, received its first performance in Orford Church (9 June 1966).

Earlier in the year, the film of *Curlew River*, made at Louvain in 1965 by the Belgian Television, was awarded first prize in the Monte Carlo 'Unda' Festival; and *The Burning Fiery Furnace* was telerecorded at Louvain later in the summer. The English Opera Group tour of *The Burning Fiery Furnace* also covered Holland, and the City of London and King's Lynn Festivals.

In the autumn *Gloriana* was successfully revived at Sadler's Wells. For this production (by Colin Graham), the composer made a few rather minor revisions to the score.

Recitals in Moscow and Leningrad at the end of December 1966 gave Pears and Britten a chance to remain a few days longer in Moscow so that they could celebrate the Russian New Year with Rostropovich, Vishnevskaya, Shostakovich and others. (A sparkling account of this trip is given in the extracts from Peter Pears's diary printed in the 1967 *Aldeburgh Festival Programme Book*.) An interesting incident occurred after the recital at the Philharmonic Hall in Leningrad, when a group of young dancers mainly from the Kirov Ballet, formed and organized by the horn player Bouyanowski, gave Britten a private performance of a ballet that had recently been devised to his *Metamorphoses* for oboe solo.

In England the year 1967 was notable for the completion of a number of new concert halls. In London two halls were opened on the South Bank: the Queen Elizabeth Hall on 1 March, and the Purcell Room two days later. Britten conducted the greater part of the inaugural concert at the Queen Elizabeth Hall in the presence of HM Queen Elizabeth II; and the programme included the first performance of his *Hankin Booby*,* a folk dance for wind and drums, that had been commissioned by the Greater London Council.

On 2 June came the opening of the new Maltings Concert Hall, Snape, by HM The Queen, who was accompanied by HRH The Duke of Edinburgh. This was the first event of the 1967 Aldeburgh Festival. The inaugural concert programme also contained a new work by Britten, an Overture (with chorus) called *The Building of the House*. This had been 'inspired by the excitement of the planning and building—and the haste!'† and it proved to be one of his most successful pieces of 'occasional music'. The new concert hall was generally acclaimed as one of the finest in the country; and when a new production of *A Midsummer Night's Dream*, which the English Opera Group had presented in Paris a few weeks previously, was mounted there on 7 June, it was seen to be suited for opera too. The availability of the new hall made a great difference to the general Festival planning. In fact the sales of tickets for the 1967 Festival rose to a figure well over double that of 1966. In 1968 the hall won a Civic Trust award.

A vaudeville for boys and piano based on the old West Country ballad of *The Golden Vanity* was another new work that received its première at the 1967 Festival when it was performed by the Vienna Boys' Choir (3 June) for whom it had been specially written. The work was staged imaginatively by its librettist, Colin Graham—in costume, but without scenery—and the action was mimed, in a simple way, a few basic properties being provided. The result was like a miniature opera.

In September the English Opera Group played *Curlew River* and *The Burning Fiery Furnace* at Expo '67, Montreal; and afterwards Britten and Pears embarked on a tour that took them, first to New York, and then through various countries of Latin America including Mexico, Peru, Chile, Argentina, Uraguay and Brazil. Each of their two recital programmes contained works by Britten: in the first there was *The Poet's Echo* and some of Britten's folk song arrangements; in the second the *Seven Sonnets of Michelangelo*, *Winter Words*, and the *Six Hölderlin Fragments*. Their reception everywhere was most enthusiastic.

A few years previously, after seeing Rembrandt's great painting *The Return of the Prodigal* in the Hermitage Museum, Leningrad, Britten had decided that this was to be the theme of his next church parable. William

* *Hankin Booby* was later incorporated into the *Suite on English Folk Tunes: 'A time there was . . .'* (1974).

† Programme Note by B.B. in the *Aldeburgh Festival Programme Book*, 1967.

Britten (in the orchestra pit) rehearsing Mozart's *Idomeneo* with the English Opera Group at Snape Maltings, June 1970

The Maltings Concert Hall, Snape

Plomer was once again chosen as librettist. A considerable part of the score was written during Britten's stay in Venice at the beginning of 1968. But on his return to Aldeburgh at the beginning of March he succumbed to an attack of fever which delayed the completion of the score for a few weeks. Fortunately he recovered in time for the new work (*The Prodigal Son*) to be rehearsed and produced at the 1968 Aldeburgh Festival, where it repeated the success of the two earlier church parables.

Early in January 1969 he completed *Children's Crusade*, a setting of Brecht's poem *Kinderkreuzzug* for boys' choir and orchestra; and on 19 May it was performed by the boys of Wandsworth School in the impressive setting of St Paul's Cathedral, London, to commemorate the fiftieth anniversary of the Save the Children Fund. But the events of the year were overshadowed by the disastrous fire that destroyed the Maltings Concert Hall, Snape, after the opening performance of the Aldeburgh Festival on 7 June.

Since its opening the hall had acquired an international reputation. In addition to Festival performances, it had been used for the following purposes: a Bach week-end, an Antique-Dealers' Fair, summer orchestral and band concerts, and a series of 'Jazz at the Maltings' for BBC Television. Recordings had been made there with Rostropovich, Vishnevskaya, Britten himself, Peter Pears, Philip Ledger, the English Chamber Orchestra, the Ambrosian Singers, and the Katchen-Suk-Starker Trio. The most ambitious operation, however, had been the television film of *Peter Grimes* made by the BBC during February 1969. And plans were under discussion for extending its use in other ways.

The fire put a temporary stop to all that. But it was clear that the same spirit of indefatigable determination that produced a revised programme for the 1969 Aldeburgh Festival in less than twenty-four hours and saw to it that the performances originally scheduled for the Maltings (including the stage production of Mozart's *Idomeneo*) were transferred elsewhere would be applied also to the rebuilding plans. In the event, after a year of intensive rebuilding activity the hall rose again like a phoenix from its ashes; and the fact that the opening concert on 5 June 1970 (entitled 'Music for a Royal Occasion') was attended by both HM The Queen and HRH The Duke of Edinburgh showed the continuity of royal interest. And later that summer, Britten and Pears were invited to give a recital at Sandringham House in honour of the seventieth birthday of HM Queen Elizabeth The Queen Mother.

Peter Pears, Britten and HM Queen Elizabeth, The Queen Mother (Patron of the Aldeburgh Festival) at the Red House, Aldeburgh, 13 June 1975

Britten and Peter Pears at Snape, 1974

About this time Britten began to show an increasing interest in television. Early in 1969 he agreed to conduct the BBC 2 colour production of *Peter Grimes*; and subsequently he accepted a commission to compose a new opera for television. As subject he chose *Owen Wingrave*, a short story by Henry James, which had much impressed him when he first read it twenty years or more ago, and as in the case of James's *The Turn of the Screw* he asked Myfanwy Piper to provide the libretto. Part of the music was written in Venice and Hessen during the winter of 1969/70; and the opera was 'shot' at the Maltings, Snape, in November 1970. The world première broadcast took place on 16 May 1971; and the first 'live' performance was given at Covent Garden (10 May 1973).

During his late fifties, he continued to tour extensively. He visited Australia in March 1970 with the English Opera Group, which presented all three of his church parables at the Adelaide Festival. In April the following year he returned to Moscow and Leningrad, this time with the London Symphony Orchestra, which he conducted in a programme that included his Piano Concerto and Symphony for Cello and Orchestra with his Russian friends, Richter and Rostropovich respectively, as soloists. The distinguished audience at the Moscow concert included Madame Ekaterina

Furtseva, Dmitri Shostakovich, and Madame Prokofiev. In later years, Sir Duncan Wilson, who acted as Britten's host in Moscow on this occasion, recalled how 'perhaps the most moving experience of all for an Englishman was to attend next day in his company part of a performance of *A Midsummer Night's Dream* at the Bolshoi Theatre, and to see, as he walked through the corridors at the interval, how the mainly young audience recognized and with obvious spontaneity applauded him'.*

By 1971 an important new opera was under way. Wishing to write something that would provide a specially varied and challenging role for Peter Pears, he chose Thomas Mann's story *Death in Venice* as his subject matter; and once again the work of adaptation was entrusted to Myfanwy Piper. By the beginning of 1973 the score was nearing completion, but Britten was beginning to feel seriously ill. His doctors examined him, and their diagnosis showed that one of the valves of his heart was defective and would have to be replaced. An operation took place in May; but unfortunately the replaced valve was not wholly successful, and the patient's condition was complicated by a slight stroke that occurred during the actual operation and paralysed his right side.

The last three and a half years of his life were those of an invalid, who was easily exhausted by the slightest exertion, and could summon up enough strength to devote only a very limited amount of his time to composition. Nevertheless, during this period he managed against all odds to complete over half a dozen important new works, including *The Death of St Narcissus*, a canticle for tenor and harp, *Phaedra*, a dramatic cantata for mezzo-soprano and small orchestra, and his Third String Quartet. He was engaged on a large-scale cantata, a setting of *Praise We Great Men*, a poem that had been written for him by Edith Sitwell some years previously, when death intervened.

He died at the Red House, Aldeburgh, on 4 December 1976 and was buried in the churchyard, within sight and sound of the sea he loved.

* *The Times*, 9 December 1976.

IX
Personal Postscript

Britten was supremely a professional musician. Composer, pianist, viola-player, conductor, research-scholar and musical editor—in the course of his career he was engaged in multifarious activities connected with music, and if he carried them out successfully and well, it was because he took the trouble to acquire the necessary skills. He always believed in the importance of technique. In his broadcast talk *The Composer and the Listener* (1946) he said: 'Obviously it is no use having a technique unless you have the ideas to use this technique; but there is, unfortunately, a tendency in many quarters today to believe that brilliance of technique is a danger rather than a help. This is sheer nonsense. There has never been a composer worth his salt who has not had supreme technique. I'll go further than that and say that in the work of your supreme artist you can't separate inspiration from technique. I'd like anyone to tell me where Mozart's inspiration ends and technique begins.'

For technical reasons, among others, he was always prepared to work to order. He did not believe in allowing his talents to rust. As an artist he wanted to serve the community and showed himself ready to accept commissions of every kind. He found virtue in serving all sorts of different persons and believed that even 'hackwork will not hurt an artist's integrity provided he does his best with every commission'.*

To have as many ideas as he had and to work as hard as he did argued not only extraordinary fertility and fluency but also great sensitivity. If an artist lacks feeling, he loses much of the impetus towards expression. Britten showed himself sensitive in many ways—particularly to cruelty and suffering. Many of his operas contain (or imply) scenes of almost sadistic cruelty, but they inevitably lead to episodes of warm compassion and pity. This intense sympathy with the victims of oppression lay at the heart of his pacifism. Hans Keller, in an interesting essay,† went so far as to suggest that

* Quoted in 'Benjamin Britten: Another Purcell' by Phoebe Douglas. *Town and Country*, December 1947.

† 'The Musical Character' by Hans Keller. *Benjamin Britten: a commentary*. Rockliff, 1952.

'what distinguishes Britten's musical personality is the violent repressive counterforce against his sadism; by dint of character, musical history and environment, he has become a musical *pacifist* too'.

He was also sensitive to critical misunderstanding, or lack of understanding, especially where it appeared to be the result of wilfulness or stupidity.* In his own case, it was not as if his music were particularly obscure or revolutionary. His style was eclectic; his idiom modal; his musical metrics often echoed the more or less familiar structure of English poetical metrics. The surface value of his music was quite easy to understand; but an appreciation merely of its superficial qualities would not reach the heart of the matter.

As an occasional composer he had a flair for the various elements that made an occasion unique, and his works were often supremely effective in the setting and circumstances for which they were designed. It was this feeling for what was likely 'to come off' in performance that stood him in such good stead in his music for the opera-house, theatre, cinema, radio and television.

Occasionally the effect on listeners was so strong that normal critical standards seemed to be swept away. E. M. Forster's comment on the first performance of *Saint Nicolas* at Aldeburgh has already been quoted—'It was one of those triumphs outside the rules of art which only the great artist can achieve.' The same work had a very similar effect on another critic. Donald Mitchell wrote:† 'I was so confused by its progressively overwhelming impact that all I could find to say was: "This is too beautiful".' Lord Clark, who spent the first fifteen years of his life on the other side of the river Alde from Aldeburgh, was similarly moved by *Noye's Fludde*.‡ 'To sit in Orford Church, where I had spent so many hours of my childhood dutifully awaiting some spark of divine fire, and then to receive it at last in the performance of *Noye's Fludde*, was an overwhelming experience.' Perhaps Auden in his poem 'The Composer'** found the best way of putting into words the inexplicable thrill that floods the mind and senses at such a moment:

Pour out your presence, O delight, cascading
The falls of the knee and the weirs of the spine,
Our climate of silence and doubt invading:
You alone, alone, O imaginary song,

* See 'Variations on a Critical Theme' by Benajmin Britten. *Opera*, March 1952.

† 'A Note on *Saint Nicolas*: Some points on Britten's Style' by Donald Mitchell. *Music Survey*, Spring 1950.

‡ 'The Other Side of the Alde' by Kenneth Clark from *Tribute to Benjamin Britten*, Faber 1963.

** *Another Time*, XXII.

Are unable to say an existence is wrong,
And pour out your forgiveness like a wine.

Britten always responded deeply to words and loved setting them. When he was a small boy of just ten years old, he chose the best of his juvenile songs and wrote them out neatly in a special manuscript book. Amongst his juvenilia there are 'settings of anonymous poems, poems by Tennyson, Longfellow, Shelley, Shakespeare, Kipling, a rather obscure poet writing under the pseudonym of "Chanticleer", pieces from the Bible, Thomas Hood, bits of plays, and poems in French too.'* Subsequently he turned to poems by Auden, Donne, Hardy, Blake for some of his song cycles. Although he had no great knowledge of any foreign language, he enjoyed reading foreign poems, sometimes with the help of cribs, and at various times set texts in French, German, Italian, Russian, and Latin.

He was sensitive to the relationship of words and music. He was not inhibited about words like some composers, but was capable of assessing the different values of the syllable, the word, and the idea behind the word, and knew how to give them a musical gravity of their own. Sometimes one had the feeling that his instrumental music aspired to the condition of vocal or choral music; and sometimes in the vocal and choral music one had the conviction that the word had been made music and the music had taken on a new dimension. If critics object that the issue is being confused by the presence of an extra-musical element, the answer must be that precisely this combination of disparate elements lies at the heart of the problem of opera, and Britten approached excitingly near to one of the possible solutions.

There were many aspects of his character that could be pursued if one felt inclined. His sense of humour (or perhaps one should say his sense of proportion); his brisk fancy and ambivalent imagination; his fondness for children; his deep religious conviction.

As a man he recalled with pleasure his youth in East Anglia—fêtes and obstacle races, bicycle rides, tennis tournaments, bathing parties, making friends and making music—and projected himself without difficulty into the minds and hearts of young people of a later age. That was why he wrote such good music about children and for them to listen to and play. He was always interested in their problems and prepared to go out of his way to give them advice and show sympathy. At the same time he did not lower his sights, but expected work of the highest quality from them.

His religious beliefs were central to his life and his work. As a devout and practising Christian, he was keen, wherever possible, to work within the framework of the Church of England, and many of his compositions were planned accordingly.

* From *Personal Choice*, a broadcast talk by Benjamin Britten, BBC Home Service, 16 July 1958.

His talent for music manifested itself at an astonishingly early age, and his precocity as a composer startled audiences when he was in his twenties. He reached complete musical maturity in his early thirties; and by his thirty-fifth year (1948) the full extent of his remarkable gifts had been revealed—the fluency, the protean variety, the feeling for effect, the love of setting words to music, and the deceptive simplicity of the melodic and harmonic means employed.

Although his success occasionally excited opposition and jealousy, his career did not go unhonoured.

The first university to honour him was Queen's University, Belfast (1951). The initiative shown by Northern Ireland was soon followed up by England, and honorary degrees (all D.Mus.) were conferred on him by the Universities of Cambridge, Nottingham, Hull, Oxford, Manchester, London, Leicester, East Anglia, Wales and Warwick. In 1957 he was made an honorary member of the American Academy and the National Institute of Arts and Letters; and in 1961 he was awarded the Hanseatic Goethe Prize. The following year he was created Commander of the Royal Order of the Pole Star (Sweden); the Aspen Award followed in 1964, and the Wihuri-Sibelius Prize the following year. On 25 November 1964 he was presented with the Gold Medal of the Royal Philharmonic Society. He was made an Honorary Fellow of Magdalene College, Cambridge and an Honorary Member of Worcester College, Oxford, and he received the Freedom of the Worshipful Company of Musicians in 1966. The Mahler Medal (awarded by the Bruckner and Mahler Society) and the Leone Sonning Prize (Denmark) followed in 1967 and 1968 respectively. In 1973 he became the first recipient of the Ernst Siemens–Musikpreis; and the following year he received the Ravel Foundation Prize, which was awarded to composers who revealed in their work 'qualities recalling the scrupulous attention to detail, the search for beauty of expression, sonority and invention which characterize the music of Ravel'. The very last honour he received was the Mozart Medal for 1976, awarded by the Mozartgemeinde, Vienna.

Suffolk was his home county. He was born there, and lived there for the greater part of his life. Some of his operas were set there—*Peter Grimes*, *Albert Herring*, *The Little Sweep* and *Curlew River*. Of all the numerous honours he received, he probably valued most highly the compliments paid him when he received the freedom, first in 1951 of the Borough of Lowestoft, the town where he was born, and then in 1962 of the Borough of Aldeburgh, the town where he chose to reside. In his speech of thanks on the former occasion, he took the opportunity of confirming his allegiance to that part of England. He said: 'Suffolk, the birthplace and inspiration of Constable and Gainsborough, the loveliest of English painters; the home of Crabbe, the most English of poets; Suffolk with its rolling, intimate countryside; its heavenly Gothic churches, big and small; its marshes, with those wild seabirds; its grand ports and its little fishing villages. I am firmly rooted in this glorious county. And I proved this to myself when I once tried to live somewhere else.'

His services to English music were outstanding; and it was largely due to him that today it is better known and stands higher in the esteem of countries abroad than was ever the case before. The tributes were well merited, therefore, when he was made a Companion of Honour in the Coronation Honours of 1952, awarded the Order of Merit in 1965, and created Baron Britten of Aldeburgh in the Birthday Honours of 1976.

Part Two

THE OPERAS

The opening chorus of the Prologue to *Paul Bunyan* in Britten's original composition sketch

I
Paul Bunyan

At the time of its first performance *Paul Bunyan* was described by its authors as a choral operetta with many small parts rather than a few star roles.

For his subject Auden took the legend of Paul Bunyan. This giant lumberman, who was reputed to stand forty-two axe handles high and to sport a twist of chewing tobacco between his horns, was among the pioneers working in the American wilderness who helped prepare the way for the advance of civilization westwards. Auden considered America to be unique in being the only country to create myths after the industrial revolution, and this particular legend to be not only American but universal in its implications. He looked on Paul Bunyan as 'a projection of the collective state of mind of a people whose tasks were primarily the physical mastery of nature'* and intended that the operetta should present 'in a compressed fairy-story form the development of the continent from a virgin forest before the birth of Paul Bunyan to settlement and cultivation when Paul Bunyan says goodbye because he is no longer needed, i.e. the human task is now a different one, of how to live well in a country that the pioneers have made it possible to live in.'†

In a newspaper article,‡ he set out his attitude to Bunyan and his friends in some detail: 'Appearing so late in history, Paul Bunyan has no magical powers; what he does is what any man could do if he were as big and as inventive; in fact, what Bunyan accomplishes as an individual is precisely what the lumbermen managed to accomplish as a team with the help of machinery. Moreover, he is like them as a character; his dreams have all the native swaggering optimism of the nineteenth century. . . .' Babe the Blue Ox, who gave Bunyan advice, Auden found something of a puzzle—'I conceive of her quite arbitrarily as a symbol of his anima'—and he omitted her as a character. He went on to say: 'Associated with Bunyan are a number of satellite human figures, of which the most interesting are Hel Helson, his

* Quotation from the *Paul Bunyan* programme. † Ibid.

‡ From 'Opera on an American Legend' by W. H. Auden. *New York Times*, 4 May 1941.

Swedish foreman, and Johnny Inkslinger, his book-keeper. These eternal human types; Helson, the man of brawn but no brains, invaluable as long as he has somebody to give him orders whom he trusts, but dangerous when his consciousness of lacking intelligence turns into suspicion and hatred of those who possess it; and Inkslinger, the man of speculative and critical intelligence, whose temptation is to despise those who do the manual work that makes the thought possible. Both of them learn a lesson in their relations with Paul Bunyan; Helson through a physical fight in which he is the loser, Inkslinger through his stomach.'

In writing an operetta about Bunyan, Auden found three main difficulties confronted him. In view of his previous record as poet and playwright, he was hardly likely to approach his subject from a literal or realistic angle; and it is not surprising that he tried to surmount these difficulties in ways consistent with the didactic style of epic drama as advocated by Brecht. 'In the first place [Bunyan's] size and general mythical characteristics prevent his physical appearance on the stage—he is presented as a voice and, in order to differentiate him from the human characters, as a speaking voice. In consequence some one else had to be found to play the chief dramatic role and Inkslinger seemed the most suitable, as satisfying Henry James's plea for a fine lucid intelligence as a compositional centre. Inkslinger, in fact, is the only person capable of understanding who Paul Bunyan really is, and, in a sense, the operetta is an account of his process of discovery. In the second place, the theatrical presentation of the majority of Bunyan's exploits would require the resources of Bayreuth, but not to refer to them at all would leave his character all too vaguely in the air. To get round this difficulty, the librettists interposed simple narrative ballads between the scenes, as it were, as solo Greek chorus. Lastly, an opera with no female voices would be hard to produce and harder to listen to, yet in its earlier stages at least the conversion of forests into lumber is an exclusively male occupation. Accordingly the collaborators introduced *a camp dog* and *two camp cats* sung by a coloratura soprano and two mezzo-sopranos respectively.'*

In his article from which the above quotations are taken, Auden went on to say: 'The principal interest of the Bunyan legend today is as a reflection of the cultural problems that occur during the first stage of every civilization, the stage of colonization of the land and the conquest of nature. The operetta, therefore, begins with a prologue in which America is still a virgin forest and Paul Bunyan has not yet been born, and ends with a Christmas party at which he bids farewell to his men because now he is no longer needed. External physical nature has been mastered, and for this very reason can no longer dictate to man what they should do. Now their task is one of their human relations with each other and, for this, a collective mythical

* Ibid.

Paul Bunyan: The lumberjacks, Moppet and Poppet (the camp cats) and Fido (the camp dog) in Act I from the English Music Theatre revival in 1976

figure is no use, because the requirements of each relation are unique. Faith is essentially invisible.'

Finally, he pointed out that the implications of the Bunyan legend were not only American, but also universal.

Paul Bunyan was presented on 5 May 1941,* for a week's run by the Columbia Theater Associates of Columbia University, with the co-operation of the Columbia University Department of Music and a chorus from the New York Schola Cantorum. It was financed by a grant from the Alice M. Ditson Fund. The producer was Milton Smith, and the conductor Hugh Ross.

CHARACTERS

In the Prologue

Old Trees	Young Trees	Three Wild Geese

* There had been a preview the previous evening for members of the League of Composers.

In the Interludes Narrator

In the Play The Voice of Paul Bunyan
Cross Crosshaulson John Shears Sam Sharkey
Ben Benny Jen Jenson Pete Peterson
Andy Anderson Other Lumberjacks
Western Union Boy Hel Helson Johnny Inkslinger
Fido* Moppet* Poppet*
The Defeated
Slim Tiny
The Film Stars and Models
Frontier Women

Scene: A Grove in a Western Forest

	Prologue	—	Night
Act I	Scene i	—	A Spring Morning
	Scene ii	—	Summer
Act II	Scene i	—	Autumn
	Scene ii	—	Christmas

On the whole the work was received by the New York critics with dismay. *Time*, suspicious of this 'anemic operetta put up by two British expatriates', complained that it was 'as bewildering and irritating a treatment of the outsize lumberman as any two Englishmen could have devised'. *The New Yorker* said that though on paper or in conference there may have been certain items that 'looked like the makings of something pretty exciting . . . in the theatre *Paul Bunyan* didn't jell'. A more revealing description of the music came from Robert Bagar in *World Telegraph*. 'Mr. Britten, who is an up and coming composer, has written some worth-while tunes in this score. It ranges, in passing, from part-writing to single jingle. Its rhythms are often interesting and the harmonies fit rather well. There are arias, recitatives, small ensembles and big choral sequences. Most of the last named are good. The music makes occasional reference to *Cavalleria Rusticana* and one item, a stuttering bit, goes back to *The Bartered Bride*.'

Under the heading 'Musico-Theatrical Flop', Virgil Thomson, writing in the *New York Herald Tribune*, attacked the form of the work, which he considered fell into the category of 'the Auden semi-poetic play', going on to assert that on the stage the Auden style had 'always been a flop. It is flaccid and spineless and without energy.' Turning to Britten, he showed similar lack of enthusiasm over the music: 'Benjamin Britten's music, here as elsewhere, has considerable animation. His style is eclectic though not without savour. Its particular blend of melodic "appeal" with irresponsible

* These are the camp dog and two camp cats mentioned above.

counterpoint and semi-acidulous instrumentation is easily recognisable as that considered by the BBC to be at once modernistic and safe. Its real model is, I think, the music of Shostakovich, also eclectic, but higher in physical energy content than that of Mr. Britten. Mr. Britten's work in *Paul Bunyan* is sort of witty at its best. Otherwise it is undistinguished. . . .'

But the most perceptive review came from Olin Downes writing in the *New York Times*. Like Virgil Thomson, he found Britten's style 'eclectic' and thought his sources ranged widely 'from Prokofiev to Mascagni, from Rimsky-Korsakov to Gilbert and Sullivan'. Although he had a few reservations to make, he admitted that Britten 'knows how to set a text, how to orchestrate in an economical and telling fashion, how to underscore dialogue with orchestral commentary'. He added: 'What is done by Mr. Britten shows more clearly than ever that opera written for a small stage, with relatively modest forces for the presentation, in the English language, and in ways pleasantly free from the stiff tradition of either grand or light opera of the past, is not only a possibility but a development nearly upon us.'

At first neither score nor libretto was published. In fact, it was hinted that during *Paul Bunyan*'s brief run in New York, the work had been subjected to so many changes, cuts, and revisions that no definitive version could be said to exist. But after Auden's death in 1973 this attitude began to change. A number of people expressed interest in the work and asked for the material to be made accessible; a recording of one of its original performances was deposited in the Brander Matthews Dramatic Museum at Columbia University; and the value of this operetta could be assessed more justly in the light of the subsequent achievements of both composer and librettist in the operatic field. In 1975 Britten agreed to release it for performance. The score was edited and revised for stage performance and was produced by the English Music Theatre Company on 4 June at the 1976 Aldeburgh Festival. It was immediately recognized as an enjoyable, carefree entertainment that was fun to listen to and fun to perform.

Whether there could have been a future to this particular collaboration if the two partners had decided to pursue it is difficult to say. Although Auden appeared to be successful with some of his subsequent librettos, such as *The Rake's Progress* for Stravinsky and *The Bassarids* for Henze, one has the feeling that in the long run Britten and Auden would not have worked happily together. Auden, the elder character, was fairly dogmatic in his attitude to opera and usually took the view that he knew most of the answers to most of the questions. It is unlikely that a person of Britten's shy and sensitive nature could have flourished in this rather overbearing atmosphere.* Anyway, surmise is useless, because after *Paul Bunyan* the partnership was not resumed.

* For a fascinating insight into the problems in this relationship see *Britten and Auden in the Thirties* by Donald Mitchell. Faber, 1981.

II
Peter Grimes

I

When Britten approached Montagu Slater in 1942 and asked him to write a libretto for the opera that had been commissioned by the Koussevitzky Music Foundation, the theme was already fixed—Aldeburgh was to be the scene and the subject Peter Grimes, the story of whose life is told by Crabbe in *The Borough*.

Aldeburgh was Crabbe's birthplace. He was born there on 1 January 1755. His son described it as a poor and wretched place lying between 'a low hill or cliff, on which only the old church and a few better houses were then situated, and the beach of the German Ocean. It consisted of two parallel and unpaved streets, running between mean and scrambling houses, the abodes of seafaring men, pilots and fishers. The range of houses nearest to the sea had suffered so much from repeated invasions of the waves, that only a few scattered tenements appeared erect among the desolation.' As for the beach, then as now it consisted of 'large rolled stones, then loose shingle, and, at the fall of the tide, a stripe of fine hard sand. Vessels of all sorts, from the large heavy troll-boat to the yawl and prame, drawn up along the shore—fishermen preparing their tackle, or sorting their spoil—and, nearer the gloomy old town-hall (the only indication of municipal dignity) a few groups of mariners, chiefly pilots, taking their quick, short walk backwards and forwards, every eye watchful of a signal from the offing—such was the squalid scene that first opened on the author of *The Village*.'* And such was the place and community that in 1810 Crabbe described so vividly in his poem *The Borough* by means of a series of twenty-four letters written in heroic couplets.

In the first of these letters he gives a general description of the Borough. He mentions the River Alde, which (as his son explains) 'approaches the sea close to Aldeburgh, within a few hundred yards, and then turning abruptly continues to run about ten miles parallel to the beach, until it at length finds

* *The Life of George Crabbe, by his Son*, 1834.

its embouchure at Orford'; the craft on the river—'hoys, pinks and sloops; brigs, brigantines and snows'—and also the quayside with its clamour of sailors and carters and lumber of 'package and parcel, hogshead, chest, and case.' After night-fall some of the inhabitants of the Borough pass their times at parties, whist-drives, concerts, plays or taverns, while—

Others advent'rous walk abroad and meet
Returning Parties pacing through the Street . . .
When Tavern-Lights flit on from Room to Room,
And guide the tippling Sailor staggering home:
There as we pass the jingling Bells betray,
How Business rises with the closing Day:
Now walking silent, by the River's side,
The Ear perceives the rimpling of the Tide;
Or measur'd cadence of the Lads who tow
Some enter'd Hoy, to fix her in her row;
Or hollow sound, which from the Parish-Bell,
To some departed Spirit bids farewell!

Crabbe then proceeds to deal with the various professions and trades in the Borough. Letter XI enumerates the inns—particularly *The Boar.*

There dwells a kind old Aunt, and there you see
Some kind young Nieces in her company;
Poor village Nieces, whom the tender Dame
Invites to Town, and gives their Beauty fame.

No fewer than ten of the later letters are devoted to the inhabitants of the almshouse and to the poor; and among the latter figure Abel Keene, a clerk in office (Letter XXI), Ellen Orford, the widowed school mistress (Letter XX), and Peter Grimes, a fisherman (Letter XXII). From the first, Slater borrowed no more than his surname, which he attached to Ned, the quack (who is described in Letter VII); the second he elevated to the principal female part; and the third became the protagonist of the opera.

Edward Fitzgerald, who was a friend of Crabbe's son, has left it on record that the Peter Grimes of the poem was based on an actual fisherman named Tom Brown, who lived in Aldeburgh in the middle of the eighteenth century. According to Crabbe, there were few redeeming features about Peter Grimes. As soon as he was out of his teens, he became impatient of parental control and started to knock his father about. Then he went to live on his own and 'fished by water and filched by land'; but he was dissatisfied so long as there was no unfortunate victim living with him on whom he could wreak his strength at any hour of the day or night. Presently he heard of workhouse-clearing men in London who were prepared to bind orphan parish-boys to needy tradesmen. He obtained such an apprentice for himself and was at last able to give full rein to his sadistic instincts and his lust for power. The first apprentice, Sam, lived for three years and then was found lifeless in his bed. The second fell one night from the main-mast of the fishing boat and was killed. The third died in the course of a stormy voyage from Aldeburgh to London. After his death, the conscience of the Borough was thoroughly roused; and the Mayor himself forbade Grimes to take any more apprentices to work for him. Thenceforward he was ostracized. Gradually his mind began to fail and, as he sailed up and down the river, he was haunted by the spirits of his father and two of the dead boys. In raving delirium shortly before his death he described one such scene:

In one fierce Summer-day, when my poor Brain
Was burning-hot and cruel was my Pain,
Then came this Father-foe, and there he stood
With his two Boys again upon the Flood;
There was more Mischief in their Eyes, more Glee
In their pale Faces when they glar'd at me:
Still did they force me on the Oar to rest,
And when they saw me fainting and opprest,
He, with his Hand, the old Man, scoop'd the Flood,
And there came Flame about him mix'd with Blood;
He bade me stoop and look upon the place,
Then flung the hot-red Liquor in my Face;
Burning it blaz'd, and then I roar'd for Pain,
I thought the Daemons would have turn'd my Brain.

In the Preface to *The Borough*, Crabbe embarks on a brief analysis of the character of Peter Grimes. 'The mind here exhibited', he says, 'is one untouched by pity, unstung by remorse, and uncorrected by shame; yet is this hardihood of temper and spirit broken by want, disease, solitude and disappointment; and he becomes the victim of a distempered and horror-stricken fancy. . . . The corrosion of hopeless want, the wasting of unabating disease, and the gloom of unvaried solitude, will have their effect on every nature; and the harder that nature is, and the longer time required to work upon it, so much the more strong and indelible is the impression.'

If Peter Grimes was to become the hero of a twentieth-century opera and win the sympathy of a modern audience, some of these eighteenth-century values would have to be altered and adjusted. Slater accordingly embarked on a reinterpretation of the character, as a result of which Crabbe's grim fisherman became something of a Borough Byron, too proud and self-willed to come to terms with society, and yet sufficiently imaginative to be fully conscious of his loss. A clue to this new reading is perhaps to be found in an episode of Grimes's childhood, which becomes even more poignant when it is remembered that Crabbe too as a boy had been bitterly hostile to his own father. Grimes recalled

How, when the Father in his Bible read,
He in contempt and anger left the Shed:
'It is the Word of Life', the Parent cried;
—'This is the Life itself', the Boy replied.

To fit his more modern interpretation, Slater decided to post-date the action of the drama from the latter part of the eighteenth-century, when the stories related in *The Borough* actually took place, to 1830 when the tide of Byronism was in full flood. In view of the usual time-lag between metropolitan and provincial fashions, little or no injury was thereby done to the accuracy of the general description of the Borough and its inhabitants as based on Crabbe; but the new date accentuated the rift between Grimes and the rest of the community—between, on the one hand, the comparatively modern type of the psychopathic introvert, divided against himself and against the world, and, on the other, reactionary extrovert society.

For the purpose of his plot, Slater omitted Peter's father and reduced the number of his apprentices from three to two, the first of whom has just died at sea when the opera opens. Ellen Orford, the widowed school-mistress, is promoted to the position of Peter's friend and confidante—in fact, there is a moment when Peter deludes himself into thinking his problems would be solved if he could marry her. At the end of the inquest into the apprentice's death, Ellen asks Peter to come away with her; but he feels he cannot accept until he has rehabilitated himself in the eyes of Borough—and to him rehabilitation means money, wealth. He explains this to Captain Balstrode, a retired sea-captain, during the storm in Act I:

These Borough gossips
Listen to money,
Only to money.
I'll fish the sea dry,
Sell the good catches.
That wealthy merchant
Grimes will set up
Household and shop.
You will all see it!
I'll marry Ellen!

Balstrode replies:

Man—go and ask her,
Without your booty,
She'll have you now.

But when Peter demurs at the idea of being accepted out of pity, Balstrode realizes that it is too late to remedy the defects in his character and that sooner or later the fatal pattern of the former tragedy is bound to be repeated. And so it turns out. The new apprentice arrives; but although he is ill-treated by Peter, it is accident rather than deliberate cruelty that ultimately brings about his death. By then, however, the Borough conscience has been thoroughly aroused—the man-hunt is up—and Balstrode realizes that the best thing for Peter will be to disappear. But how? At an earlier point in the action, Peter, asked why he didn't leave the Borough to 'try the wider sea with merchantman or privateer', replied:

I am native, rooted here . . .
By familiar fields,
Marsh and sand,
Ordinary streets,
Prevailing wind.

As exile is out of the question, the only alternative appears to be suicide; and on Balstrode's advice, he sails his fishing boat out to sea and scuttles it.

Through his imagination Peter is aware of wider universal issues at stake at the same time as he wrestles with the immediate problems caused by the flaws in his nature. This is made clear from his soliloquy in the crowded pub during the storm in Act I:

Now the Great Bear and Pleiades
where earth moves
Are drawing up the clouds
of human grief
Breathing solemnity in the deep night.
But if the horoscope's
bewildering . . .
Who can turn the skies back and begin again?

And this intensity of vision helps to raise to the tragic plane what might otherwise have been merely a sordid drama of realism.

Here is a synopsis of the libretto:

Prologue. The interior of the Moot Hall. At the end of the inquest into the death of Peter Grimes's apprentice, Mr Swallow, the coroner, brings in a verdict of death in accidental circumstances; but Peter complains that this verdict does not really clear him of the charge, for the case will still go on in people's minds. Act I, scene i. A street by the sea a few days later, showing the exterior of the Moot Hall and *The Boar*. Peter is already experiencing difficulty in working his fishing boat single-handed; but Ned Keene, the apothecary, tells him he has found another apprentice boy, whom Ellen Orford, despite the general disapproval of the Borough, agrees to fetch by

Peter Grimes: Peter Pears as Grimes and Joan Cross as Ellen Orford in their duet from the Prologue

the carrier's cart. Shortly after her departure, a storm breaks, which is all the more to be feared because it comes with a spring tide. The boats are made fast, the nets brought in and the windows of the houses shuttered. After a dialogue between Peter and Captain Balstrode, the scene changes to *The Boar* (Act I, scene ii) on the evening of the same day. Although it is past closing time, the pub is full, and people are still coming in out of the storm for shelter and refreshment. News is brought that the coast road has been flooded and a landslide has swept away part of the cliff up by Peter Grimes's hut. A quarrel or two break out among the topers; a round is sung; and when at last Ellen Orford arrives back with the boy, Peter—to everyone's consternation—insists on taking him away at once to his desolate hut through the storm.

Act II, scene i. The scene is the same as in Act I, scene i; the time a Sunday morning a few weeks later. Ellen and Peter's new apprentice sit in the sun on the beach, while morning service goes on in the Parish Church. By chance she discovers the boy's clothes are torn and his body bruised; and when Peter, who has just caught sight of a shoal, arrives to take him out fishing, her reproaches lead to an open quarrel between the two, which is overseen and overheard by some of the neighbours. By the time the church service is over, the news has spread round the Borough that '*Grimes is at his exercise!*' and a party of men sets out to investigate. Meanwhile, Peter and the apprentice have reached Peter's hut, which is made out of an old upturned boat (Act II, scene ii). Here he gathers together his fishing gear; but the boy's blubbering delays him and when, after a clumsy attempt to soothe the lad, he hears the sound of the neighbours coming up the hill, he suddenly decides to make a quick get-away. He flings his nets and tackle out of the cliff-side door; but the boy, as he starts to climb down the cliff, slips and is dashed to death. Peter scrambles down after him. On arrival, the search party—to its surprise—finds the hut empty, neatly kept and reasonably clean, but there is no sign of its recent occupants.

Act III, scene i. The scene is the same as in the first scenes of Acts I and II; the time, two or three nights later. A subscription dance is taking place in the Moot Hall, and there is considerable traffic between the Hall and *The Boar*. Though neither Peter nor his apprentice has been seen during the last few days, it is assumed that both are away fishing, until Mrs Sedley, one of the leading gossips in the Borough with a keen nose for scenting out crime as well as scandal, overhears Ellen telling Balstrode that the jersey she embroidered for the boy some time ago has been found washed up on the beach. Seeing that Peter's boat is now back, Mrs Sedley imparts her suspicions to Swallow, who in his capacity as Mayor summons the constable of the Borough and bids him take a posse of men to apprehend Grimes. A few hours later (Act III, scene ii) when the dance in the Moot Hall is over, a fog has crept up from the sea, and only the occasional cries of the man-hunt and the moan of a fog-horn break the stillness of the night as Peter creeps back to his hut. There Ellen and Balstrode find him, hungry, wet, exhausted, almost insane. It is Balstrode who proposes the way out—that he take his boat out to sea, scuttle it and sink with it—and this Peter does, as dawn breaks. Gradually the Borough reawakes to life. Lights appear at windows. Shutters are drawn back. The coastguard station reports a boat sinking far out at sea, but the news is dismissed as an idle rumour; and as the light of the morning waxes, the people of the Borough start to go about their daily tasks. It is the beginning of another day.

This outline is sufficient to show how far Slater's libretto is removed from Crabbe and *The Borough*, and how fundamentally different a character Slater's Grimes is from Crabbe's. Slater himself explained that 'the story as worked out in the opera uses Crabbe's poem only as a starting-point. Crabbe produced character sketches of some of the main persons of the drama. I have taken these character sketches as clues and woven them into a story against the background of the Borough: but it is my story and the composer's (the idea was originally not mine but Britten's), and I have to take the responsibility for its shape as well as its words.'*

In writing his libretto, Slater avoided the heroic couplet as used by Crabbe and blank verse, because he felt that the five-stress line was 'out of key with contemporary modes of thought and speech'.† Instead, he adopted a 'four-stress line with rough rhymes for the body of the drama', while the Prologue was written in prose and various metres used for the set numbers.

There are at least five different published versions of the text. The first is in Montagu Slater's *Peter Grimes and other poems* published by The Bodley Head in 1946.‡ This may be called the literary text—as Slater explains in his Preface, it is 'to all intents and purposes the one to which the music was composed', but omits 'some of the repetitions and inversions required by the music'. The second is a text that has not been published in full, but extensive passages are quoted from it in an essay of Slater's included in the Sadler's Wells Opera Book devoted to *Peter Grimes* (The Bodley Head, 1945). The third is the libretto of the opera published by Boosey & Hawkes in 1945 (and reissued with minor revisions in 1961); but this does not contain all the amendments and corrections that appeared in the fourth and near-final text as printed in the vocal score published by Boosey & Hawkes also in 1945. The final version of the libretto *as performed* was not published by Boosey & Hawkes until 1979.

The main divergencies between the literary text and the others are to be found in Peter's monologues in the second scenes of Acts II and III; and these changes were clearly made to meet the composer's musical exigencies. It may be of interest, however, to take a different passage and to compare the various versions of Ellen's monologue at the beginning of Act II, scene i as they appear in the four different texts:

Text 1 *The sun in*
His own morning
And upward climb
Makes the world warm.
Night rolled
Away with cold.
The summer morning
Is for growing.

* *Peter Grimes* (*Sadler's Wells Opera Books No.* 3 edited by Eric Crozier). The Bodley Head, 1945.

† *Peter Grimes and other poems* by Montagu Slater. The Bodley Head, 1946.

‡ Ibid.

Text 2
The sun in
His fair morning
And upward climb
Makes the world warm . . .

[*Cetera desunt*]

Text 3
Glitter of sun
On curling billows,
The earth is warm
Old ocean gently flows.
Man alone
Has a debt to pay
In this tranquility
*Mindful of yesterday.**

Text 4
Glitter of waves
and glitter of sunlight
Bid us rejoice
And lift our hearts on high.
Man alone
has a soul to save,
And goes to church
to worship on a Sunday.

Whatever the poetic merits of these different versions, there is no doubt that the final one was the best suited to its context. It clinches the impression made by the orchestral interlude at the beginning of the act and puts the forthcoming church service into perspective.

II

When Britten started to set this libretto, he was confronted by various problems.

In the first place, the division of each of the three acts of the opera into two scenes, the action of which was continuous or nearly continuous or partly overlapping, made it possible for him to decide to compose each act as an unbroken piece of music; but as there were scene changes between scenes i and ii of Acts I and II, interludes would be needed there, and a further interlude of some sort was indicated between scenes i and ii of Act III to mark the passing of time. There was also the formal problem of the Prologue to consider. Prosaic though it might be, it gave such back history as was needed, provided an exposition of the theme and introduced the main

* But in the 1961 revision of this libretto, text 4 has been substituted for text 3.

Peter Grimes: Peter Pears as Grimes in the pub scene (Act I, scene ii) from the BBC television production recorded at Snape Maltings in 1969

characters of the opera by name—all this so expeditiously and succinctly that it could hardly be expected to stand alone. Clearly, it ought to be joined to Act I; and this would entail another interlude to cover the necessary scene change. To complete the scheme, he added introductions to Acts II and III, making a total of six orchestral 'interludes' in all.

And then he had also to take into account the fact that each act of Slater's libretto contained cues for actual sound or song effects as opposed to the music to be composed in accordance with operatic convention. For instance, the scene in *The Boar* works up to a moment when a song is suggested and someone spontaneously starts up a round, '*Old Joe has gone fishing*', in which the rest of the company joins. The following Act opens with Ellen talking to the boy apprentice on the beach, while from the neighbouring church are overheard strains of the Sunday morning service. Later that morning, some of the men of the Borough form a procession and, led by Hobson the carter playing a tenor drum, go off to Peter's hut, chanting a sinister marching song. In the last Act, the dance band at the Moot Hall, consisting of fiddle, double-bass, two clarinets and percussion, is heard playing fragments of a barn dance, waltz *alla Ländler*, hornpipe and galop. And later that night, when the man-hunt is up, the search for Grimes is punctuated by the slow booming of a fog-horn.

In the scene in *The Boar*, not only was it important for the round to stand out properly in its context; but there was the added complication of storm without and warmth and drink-happy company within. Here he profited by his experience in writing for radio drama. The technique of the mixing panel had shown him how varied were the possibilities of using music at different levels—background, foreground or intermediate—and how with two or more distinct streams of sound, one could be brought up into the foreground while the other was faded out, or (if necessary) the two streams could be mixed together. He accordingly decided to depict the storm in its full fury in Interlude ii and shut it out as soon as the curtain went up. Most of the scene in *The Boar* is accordingly set to an animated form of free recitative, punctuated by brief fragments of the storm that burst through the doorway as various characters enter from outside; and this provides an excellent setting for the round. Thanks to the cross-fading device, the music of the storm, having been heard in full in Interlude ii, continues by implication unbrokenly throughout this scene.

Cross-fading is also used for the church service, the song chanted by the procession that visits Peter's hut, and the Moot Hall dance.

As for the fog-horn, Britten realized that here was an unique opportunity for dramatic effect. As the first half of the second scene of Act III is virtually a soliloquy by Grimes, he let the orchestra be silent after the *fortissimo* shouts of the chorus at the end of the previous scene and let Grimes's monologue be accompanied only by the fog-horn and occasional cries from the distant man-hunt. Then when he has sailed out to sea to drown himself and life returns to the Borough with the dawn of another day, the repetition of the orchestral music from the opening of Act I is particularly impressive.

The first Interlude, joining the Prologue to Act I, is based on three motifs:

Ex. 1

(*a*) The high unison strings that faintly outline the key of A minor cling hard and long to each holding note, and the tension is emphasized by the grace notes; (*b*) in the middle register, *arpeggii* of diatonic thirds from the harp reinforced by clarinets and violas, describe fragmentary arcs of sound; and this musical superstructure is underpinned by (*c*) a sequence of slowly shifting bass chords from the brass—A major against the shrill A minor of the upper strings. It is not over-fanciful to find these three motifs evocative of (*a*) the wind that 'is holding back the tide', as it blows through the rigging of the boats on the beach and over the chimney-pots of the Borough, (*b*) the lapping of the water, and (*c*) the scrunch of the shingle beneath the tide. The clash between major and minor gives an extraordinarily salty tang to the scene.

Interlude ii is a storm of almost symphonic stature, which might take the following lines of Crabbe as motto:

> *But nearer Land you may the Billows trace,*
> *As if contending in their watery chace . . .*
> *Curl'd as they come, they strike with furious force,*
> *And then re-flowing, take their grating course,*
> *Raking the rounded Flints, which ages past*
> *Roll'd by their rage, and shall to ages last.*

It follows directly on the unresolved cadence of Peter's monologue at the end of Act I, scene i, and its four main episodes are: (*a*) a theme (*presto con fuoco*), which is treated fugally at its first appearance, and whose periodic recurrence in different forms gives this Interlude something of the character of a rondo; (*b*) an altered form of the brass groundswell theme from the first Interlude, with a particularly grinding passage of close imitation at the interval of a minor ninth; (*c*) a grotesque bitonal passage in triplets (*molto animato*), where the gale indulges in particularly malicious pranks in the keys of D natural and E flat simultaneously; and (*d*) a reprise and development of the music of Peter's unresolved monologue from the end of the previous scene.

This Interlude is broken off short by the rise of the curtain on the scene in the interior of *The Boar*; but, as explained above, its continuance is implicit in the fragmentary bits of storm that burst into the pub each time someone opens the door. These make it clear that the episodes of the storm Interlude are following each other in the same order as above; but when a strangely altered phrase from (*d*) ushers in Peter's arrival, it serves as direct introduction to his soliloquy, '*Now the Great Bear and Pleiades*', which is thereby given a wider significance.

The Third Interlude is an impressionist description of the sea on a warm Sunday morning—the greatest possible contrast to the storm of the previous Act (A major after E flat minor). An *ostinato* by the horns playing contiguous but overlapping thirds gives a kind of blurred background to a merry toccata-like theme for woodwind. This with the syncopated

Ex. 2

reiteration of its notes recalls the animated glitter of sunlight on water. After a brief episode consisting of a sustained tune from cellos and violas rising and then falling back through an octave, the toccata material is repeated and leads directly to the rise of the curtain and Ellen's opening *arioso*, '*Glitter of waves and glitter of sunlight*', which is set to the tune from the preceding episode, but now appearing a fourth higher and in the key of D.

As in Shostakovich's *Lady Macbeth of Mtsensk*, the central Interlude is a passacaglia. The turning-point of the opera has been reached in the middle of Act II, scene i, when, after striking Ellen at the end of their quarrel, Peter is overcome by the full realization of their failure and cries out '*God have mercy upon me!*' The musical phrase to which these words are sung becomes

Ex. 3

a key motif for the rest of the opera. After providing the main theme of the following chorus, '*Grimes is at his exercise!*' it serves (in augmented form) as

Ex. 4

the ground-bass of the passacaglia and later will be found inverted.

This large-scale passacaglia Interlude, in which it may be claimed that Peter's apprentice who has been mute throughout the opera at last becomes musically articulate, consists of a poignant air for solo viola:

Ex. 5

followed by nine variations, developed freely over this unchanging ground-bass (key of F). The last variation, a fugal *stretto*, leads directly into the next scene, which opens with a series of disjointed ejaculations from Peter, punctuated by scrappy orchestral references to eight of the foregoing variations. In this way, Britten makes it clear that just as Interlude ii depicted the fury of the storm as it impinged on the senses, so Interlude iv reflects the agony that is undermining Peter's mind. The true close of the passacaglia is deferred until the end of Act II, just after the apprentice's death. Then, through a whispering *bisbigliando* figure for celesta, the solo

Ex. 6

viola repeats the original air inverted, at the end of which the ground-bass returns for a single final statement (key of C).

The two remaining Interludes are not so fully developed from the musical point of view. Like those introducing Acts I and II, Interlude V is a descriptive piece. By skilful placing, a sequence of almost static, carefully punctuated swell chords (mainly in their first and second inversions), strung together on a thread of quietly moving inner parts, is made to suggest the tranquil beauty of the sea and Borough under the moon. A secondary theme played by flutes and harp, which gives the impression of an occasional glint of reflected moonlight from wave or slaty roof or weather-vane, should be contrasted with the gayer and more glittering daylight toccata theme of Interlude iii.

The last Interlude is a cadenza freely improvised by various instruments over, under and through a ghostlike chord of the dominant. This chord arises like a faint overtone between the mighty shouts of '*Peter Grimes!*' at the end of the previous scene, is sustained by the muted horns *pianissimo* throughout the movement, and at the beginning of the last scene melts into the distant voices (off) still shouting '*Grimes!*' The effect of this *ostinato* is to emphasize the all-pervasive featureless fog, while the free improvisation of the orchestra, based on snatches of many previous themes, shows something of the raging turbulence and agony of Peter's mind.

The main purpose of these Interludes was to serve as impressionist and expressionist introductions to the realistic scenes of the opera, in much the same way as Virginia Woolf used the device of prose poems about the sea to introduce each different section and period of her novel *The Waves*, and also to secure continuity within the acts.

As for vocal presentation, Britten decided (in his own words) to embrace 'the classical practice of separate numbers that crystallize and hold the emotion of a dramatic situation at chosen moments'.* He did not, however, make each number complete and self-contained, but by following a method of construction similar to that used (for instance) by Verdi in *Falstaff* succeeded in reconciling the classical practice of separate numbers with an uninterrupted musical action. *Peter Grimes* shows with what remarkable skill he managed the transitions between the various degrees of intensity needed for recitatives, airs, *ariosi* and concerted numbers, and how he usually allowed the emotion engendered by each number to lead on to its sequel before the musical construction could reach a full close. The music flows accordingly without check or hiatus from the beginning to the end of each act, and this continuity of development is achieved at the expense of any sense of interim relaxation.

The nearest approach to the fully developed air is to be found in Ellen's solos in Act I and III; '*Let her among you without fault cast the first stone*' and '*Embroidery in childhood was a luxury of idleness*'. Her song in Act II, '*We planned that their lives should have a new start*', would fall into this category too, were it not for the fact that it excites the comments and interruptions of so many bystanders that after a few bars it becomes an eleven-part concerted ensemble and then the full chorus joins in.

As for Peter, his solos are in the nature of monologues or soliloquies; and their construction is looser and more rhapsodic accordingly. It has already been shown how his solo at the end of Act I, scene i is at first interrupted and then resumed by the storm Interlude, and how it is (as it were) completed by his soliloquy, '*Now the Great Bear and Pleiades*', in the middle of the subsequent scene. It may also be argued that his air in the hut, '*And she will soon forget her schoolhouse ways*', is a further instalment of the same large utterance, for it shows its strong family likeness to the earlier passages by its use of diatonic idiom and its consistent loyalty to the tonality of sharp keys (e.g. A and E).

There is one other fully developed musical number that deserves special mention, and that is the impassive quartet of women's voices that occurs at the end of Act II, scene i and forms such an excellent contrast to the all-male vocal writing of the following scene. When the procession of men has marched off to Peter's hut, Ellen, Auntie (the proprietress of *The Boar*) and her two nieces remain behind and dejectedly reflect on women's lot. A *ritornello* of bedraggled, trailing diatonic seconds played by the flutes separates each phrase of this trio, and the vocal parts, which are generally a major second lower than the notes of the accompaniment, betray a sluttish weariness—which conforms well with the character of Auntie and her nieces.

Most of the minor characters have an opportunity of singing memorable

* *Peter Grimes* (*Sadler's Wells Opera Books No.* 3).

snatches of song, generally in stanza form and sometimes with a refrain, and these can perhaps best be described as half-numbers. Such are Hobson's song (Act I, scene i), '*I have to go from pub to pub*', in which the second verse is sung by Ellen; Auntie's song (I, ii) with its refrain '*A joke's a joke and fun is fun*'; Balstrode's song in the same scene, '*Pub conversation should depend*' with its refrain '*We live and let live and look we keep our hands to ourselves!*'; and in Act III, scene i, Swallow's tipsy '*Assign your prettiness to me*' and the Rector's goodnight '*I'll water my roses*' with its male-voice sextet accompaniment. In addition, there is the capstan shanty in Act I, scene i, '*I'll give a hand*', which is started up by Balstrode, who is subsequently joined by Keene as helper and Auntie and Bob Boles, the Methodist, as lookers-on.

Stimulated but also kept on tenterhooks by these half-measures, the listener longs for the satisfaction of a fully completed musical number and in this state of tension welcomes any chance of relief however slight. Such a moment comes during Ellen's quarrel with Peter in Act II, scene i. The music leading up to this has been superimposed on the church service (off) with its in-going voluntary, morning hymn, responses, Gloria and Benedicite. As the Credo is reached, Peter and Ellen start to quarrel; and at this point the rift between the two musical streams widens, the Credo being intoned by the Rector and congregation to an F held by the organ, while Ellen cross-examines Peter (in the key of D flat) about the boy's bruises:

Ex. 7

After a particularly obstinate clash has developed between the subdominant of Ellen's key and the organ's F, her two-bar *dolce* phrase, '*Were we*

Ex. 8

mistaken?' in which her G flat appears to have modulated to F, has the surprise and relief of a final reconciliation. This relief is only momentary, however, for the passage leads directly to Peter's cry of despair, '*God have mercy upon me!*' (Ex. 3) and all the tumult released by that pregnant musical phrase.

As for the recitative in the opera, Britten's purpose can best be expressed in his own words:* 'Good recitative should transform the natural intonations and rhythms of everyday speech into memorable musical phrases (as with Purcell), but in more stylized music the composer should not deliberately avoid unnatural stresses if the prosody of the poem and the emotional situation demand them, nor be afraid of a high-handed treatment of words, which may need prolongation far beyond their common speech length, or a speed of delivery that would be impossible in conversation.' In *Peter Grimes*, there are numerous examples of both natural and unnatural intonation and rhythm. For instance, as the orchestra is playing the final bars of Ellen's air '*Let her among you without fault*', Ellen drops her voice to a *parlando* level and, turning to the carter, says: '*Mister Hobson, where's your cart? I'm ready.*' The unforced naturalness of this passage should be

Ex. 9

contrasted with another piece of recitative. At the beginning of Act II, after her short *arioso*, '*Glitter of waves*', she also drops her voice to a *parlando* level and asks Peter's apprentice '*Shall we not go to church this Sunday?*' Her words are set to the glittering toccata-like theme just heard in Interlude iii (Ex. 2) whose wide intervals and syncopated measure are utterly at variance with natural conversational idiom.

Ex. 10

The chorus plays an important part in the opera. The opening chorus of Act I, scene i, sung partly in unison and partly in parallel thirds, is sufficiently stolid with its diatonic hymnlike tune to bring out the drab as well as the picturesque aspect of life in a little fishing port; and its recapitulation at the end of Act III, where the whole musical structure is cut through in cross-section at its climax so that the opera ends with the same

* *Peter Grimes* (*Sadler's Wells Opera Books No.* 3).

abruptness as the East Anglian coast with its eroded cliffs facing the sea, constitutes an essential element of construction. Later in the opening scene of Act I, at the approach of the storm, the chorus is given a simple but moving appeal, '*O tide that waits for no man, spare our coasts!*' But its most impressive moment—and in some ways the climax of the whole opera—comes at the end of the first scene of Act III with its unaccompanied fortissimo shouts of '*Peter Grimes! Peter Grimes! Grimes!*' If this passage is to obtain its full effect, the chorus must be sufficiently strong for its cries to resound through the theatre and 'lift the roof'. Otherwise, the device of complete musical silence broken only by Balstrode's spoken words at the climax of the following scene (Grimes's suicide) loses some of its power by contrast.

Some critics, after comparing *Peter Grimes* with *Boris Godunov*, have suggested that *Grimes* is an opera whose protagonist is the chorus. But the analogy is misleading. The statement may well be true of Mussorgsky's opera, for the Russians tend to exalt the collective or communal ideal at the expense of the individual, but not of Britten's. Although the majority of the inhabitants of the Borough are prejudiced bigots, they nevertheless remain closely defined individuals who are absorbed into the general community only when their finer feelings are submerged by the herd instinct—as on the occasion of the man-hunt. The changes of focus whereby Balstrode, Boles, the Rector, Swallow, Keene, Hobson, Mrs Sedley, Auntie and her two nieces appear sometimes as individuals (with short solos to sing), sometimes as neighbours (with parts in an ensemble), and sometimes as members of the general chorus, are deliberately designed by Slater and Britten as a means of obtaining a degree of characterization in depth.

Whereas in his musical dramas Wagner was thinking first and foremost of his orchestral texture and his peculiar form of symphonic development led to an apparently unbroken flow of melody into which the vocal parts fitted like additional instruments, Britten's prime concern in *Peter Grimes* is to display the voices of protagonists, minor characters and chorus to the best possible advantage. This means, not that the vocal writing is necessarily easy and uncomplicated, but that, with the exception of the six Interludes, the orchestra is definitely used in a subordinate position as a means of accompaniment. How important this is can be seen from the scene in *The Boar* where, thanks to the preceding Interlude, the orchestra is able to allude to the furious storm outside without drowning the singers or, indeed, making it necessary for them (for the most part) to lift their voices above the level of normal recitative. Despite the use of a full symphony orchestra and of certain symphonic effects in the Interludes, *Peter Grimes* owes its characteristic movement and idiom to Britten's imaginative treatment of the voices.

Peter Grimes himself as portrayed in Slater's libretto is what might be called a maladjusted aggressive psychopath. There is a chasm, which he fails to bridge, between himself and the external world; and Britten has shown much ingenuity in finding appropriate devices to express this maladjustment in musical terms. Peter's disturbed state of mind leads, not only to the fragmentary style of utterance on which his monologue in Act I scene ii and his soliloquy in Act II scene ii are built up, but also to a disjunct motion in his vocal line and a tendency to use intervals wider than the octave. The minor ninth seems to be particularly symptomatic of his difficulty in adjusting himself to the outside world, and an upward leap of this interval occurs several times in his narration of the events that led up to the death of his first apprentice. But when he sees in Ellen a possible solution

Ex. 11

of his troubles, this interval does not resolve on the octave, but widens to the *major* ninth:

Ex. 12

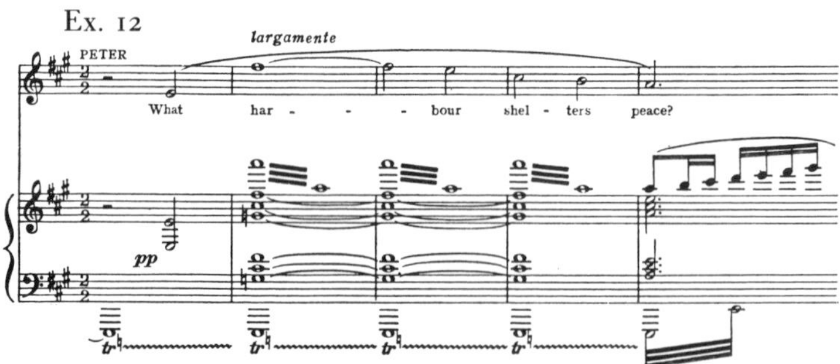

In so far as Peter is different from the rest of the Borough, augmentation and inversion are particularly associated with his music—augmentation when during the inquest in the Prologue he takes the oath and, later (I, ii), when he joins the round in *The Boar* (Ex. 13); inversion in the hut scene (II, ii) when to an inverted version of Ex. 3 he turns on his apprentice and accuses him of being the cause of all his troubles (Ex. 14). Another example of inversion deserves special mention. In the Prologue, the chorus is accompanied by the woodwind with a simple staccato chattering figure

(Ex. 15 (*a*)), which clearly becomes associated in Peter's mind with the persecution of Borough gossip. It reappears, inverted, in his soliloquy at the end of Act I, scene i (Ex. 15 (*b*)).

Ex. 13

Ex. 14

Ex. 15

Occasionally Britten feels justified in using bitonality to emphasize Peter's maladjustment, and then he sometimes tries to reconcile the simultaneous use of hostile keys by enharmonic means. An excellent example occurs at the end of the Prologue, when Peter and Ellen, left alone in the Moot Hall after the inquest, sing an unaccompanied duet. At first, Peter's key is F minor and Ellen's E major; but as the voices intertwine, Peter, thanks to the enharmonic mediation of A flat and G sharp, is won over

Ex. 16

to Ellen's key, and the duet ends with both singing in unison. Exactly the same bitonal clash (F minor and E major) is to be found in the violent tremolo passage for full orchestra that punctuates the chorus's shouts at the end of the first scene of Act III.

Ex. 17

A similar example of bitonality reconciled by enharmony occurs in the first scene of Act II. There a simple sequence of notes—E flat, F natural, E flat, D natural—is harmonized by organ chords in the key of C minor and

Ex. 18

becomes the sung Gloria in the church service (off). The enharmonic equivalent of this theme—D sharp, E sharp, D sharp, C double sharp—then appears in the theatre orchestra, harmonized in the key of B major, and becomes the accompaniment to Ellen's *arioso*, '*Child, you're not too young to know where roots of sorrow are*':

Ex. 19

These enharmonic and bitonal devices which are used to express Grimes's maladjustment, together with the various passages where by cross-fading two musical streams impinge implicitly, if not explicitly, upon the ear, at first cause a kind of auditory dichotomy on the part of the listener. But as this new idiom became more familiar and acceptable, it was realized that in *Peter Grimes* Britten had certainly widened the boundaries of opera by introducing new and stimulating ideas culled from cinema and radio technique and had shown himself a remarkably subtle delineator in musical terms of complex psychological states of mind.

The originality of the work remains unimpaired, even after one has made allowances for such unconscious or subconscious echoes as the resemblance between the A Lydian of Peter's '*And she will soon forget her schoolhouse ways*' and the D Lydian of Ping's '*Ho una casa nell' Homan*' in *Turandot*, and the unresolved cadence at the end of Act I scene i repeated faster and faster until it almost becomes a trill just like the curtain to the first act of *Wozzeck*. Britten himself considered it the most realistic of all his operas.* This East Anglian story comes from an East Anglian heart, and in its operatic form it is never likely to lose the exciting force of its original impact.

* See 'Producing the Operas' by Basil Coleman. The *London Magazine*, October 1963.

III
The Rape of Lucretia

I

When *The Rape of Lucretia* was first performed at Glyndebourne, the programme note explained that Ronald Duncan's libretto had been written 'after the play *Le Viol de Lucrèce* by André Obey and based on the works of Livy, Shakespeare, Nathaniel Lee, Thomas Heywood and F. Ponsard'.

The main Latin sources for this story of Roman virtue outraged by Etruscan lust and treachery are Livy and Ovid; but at the end of the Renaissance, Shakespeare made this story so much his own, partly by direct narration in his early poem *The Rape of Lucrece* and partly by references in some of his later plays (notably *Macbeth* and *Cymbeline*), that echoes of his voice are likely to be heard in any subsequent attempt to dramatize it. This is particularly true of *Le Viol de Lucrèce*, which André Obey wrote in 1931 for Jacques Copeau's Compagnie des Quinze. In fact, the play quotes from Shakespeare's poem such passages as the description of Lucrèce asleep in her bed, her arraignment of Opportunity after the rape, and the invocation of Philomel ('*Poor bird* . . .') as she contemplates suicide. To comment on the action, Obey decided to have a Chorus of both sexes, but reduced it from plural to singular numbers, the Male and Female Chorus being endowed with special insight into the characters of Tarquin and Lucrèce respectively. In this way, he was able to expand the Shakespearean device of the soliloquy and throw a revelatory beam on the subconscious workings of the two protagonists' minds. At the same time, both Choruses were free to comment on the action; and this they did from a more or less contemporary angle, occasionally quoting fragments of Shakespeare or Livy when it suited their purpose.

Obey arranged his tragedy in four acts, according to the following scheme. Act I, scene i. During the siege of Ardea, two sentinels overhear the Etruscan and Roman generals carousing in a tent and describing how, in the course of a surprise visit to Rome the previous night to make trial of their wives, only the virtue and chastity of Collatinus' wife Lucrèce had been triumphantly vindicated. Inflamed by this account, Tarquin steals from the

The Rape of Lucretia: Kathleen Ferrier as Lucretia in the original 1946 production by the English Opera Group

tent and sets off for Rome on his steed. Scene ii. The same evening, Lucrèce is discovered, spinning, with her maids at home. Tarquin arrives unexpectedly and is offered hospitality for the night. Act II. Lucrèce's bedchamber: the same night. Tarquin enters her room, wakes and ravishes her. Act III. The same scene: the following morning. Lucrèce awakens and sends for Collatinus. Act IV, scene i. A commentary, mainly by the Male and Female Chorus, on the revolutionary state of feeling in Rome. Scene ii. The same scene as Act I, scene ii. After telling the story of her rape, Lucrèce stabs herself. Brutus, on behalf of the other Romans there present, swears revenge on the Etruscans.

The presence of the Male and Female Chorus on the stage and their commentary on the action made it necessary for the actors to develop a style that could merge almost imperceptibly from acting into mime as occasion demanded and produced a kind of extra dimension that seemed to transcend the normal limitations of realistic stagecraft. As produced by Michel St Denis for Copeau's company in the early years of the 1930s, *Le Viol de Lucrèce* lives in the memories of those who saw it as one of the masterpieces of twentieth-century theatre.

For his libretto, Duncan kept fairly closely to Obey's play. He slightly reduced the number of *dramatis personae* by doing away with a few of the servants and a pair of sentinels, but adopted without change the device of the Male and Female Chorus. He compressed the action into two acts, instead of four. Act I: *Prologue.* Male and Female Chorus: general exposition. Scene i. The generals' tent in the camp outside Rome. (This loosely follows Obey's Act I, scene i.) *Interlude.* Male Chorus: description of Tarquinius' ride to Rome. Scene ii. A room in Lucretia's house in Rome the same evening. (This closely follows Obey's Act I, scene ii.) Act II: *Prologue.* Male and Female Chorus: further exposition. Scene i. Lucretia's bedroom. (This follows Obey's Act II.) *Interlude.* Male and Female Chorus: chorale. Scene ii. A room in Lucretia's house the next morning. (This partly amalgamates Obey's Act III and Act IV, scene ii.) *Epilogue.* Male and Female Chorus: final commentary.

It will be seen that, according to Duncan's scheme, the rape comes three-quarters instead of half-way through the action, with the result that, whereas in *Le Viol* there was a long gradual diminution of tension during the last half of the play—especially in Act III where Lucrèce soliloquizes alone for a considerable part of the scene—in *The Rape* dramatic interest is built up comparatively slowly during the first act and the action gathers impetus during the second act.

In an essay describing his method of writing the libretto,* Duncan maintains that 'the legend of Lucretia has much in common with Etruscan mythology'. He adds: 'Just as fertility or life is devoured by death, so is spirit defiled by fate. Lucretia is, to my mind, the symbol of the former, Tarquinius the embodiment of the latter.' In a further attempt to magnify the symbolic significance of this simple tale and to universalize its values, he has placed the Male and Female Chorus outside the temporal framework of the action and allowed them to submit it to Christian interpretation.

Whilst we as two observers stand between
This present audience and that scene;
We'll view these human passions and these years
Through eyes which once have wept with Christ's own tears.

And from this lofty religious viewpoint, they offer (in the Epilogue) the consolation of general absolution.

FEMALE CHORUS: *Is this all? Is this it all?*
MALE CHORUS: *It is not all.*
. . . yet now
He bears our sin and does not fall
And He, carrying all,
turns round

* *The Rape of Lucretia* (commemorative volume), ed. Eric Crozier.

Stoned with our doubt and then forgives
us all.

This is a gloss that is always likely to provoke critical comment. The severely dogmatic tone of Duncan's Chorus is far removed from the pagan spirit of Shakespeare and Obey; but in the Epilogue it certainly provides the composer with a cue for a musical coda of great solemnity.

Fortified by his experience in writing *Peter Grimes*, Britten laid great store by the close collaboration of poet and composer and in his preface to the published libretto maintained that this seemed to be 'one of the secrets of writing a good opera. In the general discussion on the shape of the work—the plot, the division into recitatives, arias, ensembles and so on—the musician will have many ideas that may stimulate and influence the poet. Similarly when the libretto is written and the composer is working on the music, possible alterations may be suggested by the flow of the music, and the libretto altered accordingly. In rehearsals, as the work becomes realized aurally and visually, other changes are often seen to be necessary.' Duncan's libretto reveals nearly as many variations in its various texts as Slater's libretto for *Peter Grimes*. The initial text is to be found in the libretto published by Boosey & Hawkes in 1946, a corrected version of which was printed the same year in the vocal score. The following year, a revised edition of both score and text was issued by Boosey & Hawkes, together with a German translation by Elizabeth Mayer. This is substantially the same text as was reprinted in the commemorative volume of 1948* and the library edition of 1953.†

The effect of some of these changes has been to make the information imparted by the Male and Female Chorus rather less didactic in tone. For instance, in the first version of the Prologue to Act II, the Female Chorus, reading from a book, explained that:

The prosperity of the Etruscans was due
To the richness of their native soil,
the virility of their men,
and the fertility of their women—
See Virgil, Book Eleven, verse five three three,
'Sic fortis Etruria crevit' etcetera.
All authorities agree
that the Etruscan conquest of Rome
dates from six hundred B.C.—
that is, approximately.

In the revised edition, the last six lines are omitted entirely. Other changes are probably due to the need for simplification. Duncan learned that in his

* Published by The Bodley Head. † Published by Faber and Faber.

role as librettist he must avoid writing complicated sentences. As he says: 'The poet must drive his metaphor to the point of clarity and contain in one image the condensation of a mood. He must never forget that the audience is listening to both words and music, and that their concentration, thus divided, cannot be imposed on.' An example of such simplification is to be found at the beginning of Act I, scene i, where the Male Chorus's original comment on the generals' drinking bout:

The grape's as wanton as the golden boy
Whom the Naiads drew to the whispers of the well
But these generals drink to drown his wanton echo.

was later changed to

The night is weeping with its tears of stars
But these men laugh—for what is sad is folly.
And so they drink to drown their melancholy.

Here, a rather intricate, if not confused, simile has given way to a clearer and simpler contrast between the natural sorrow of the unclouded night and the forced laughter of the generals flushed with wine.

But the main alterations affect two of the characters: Junius and Lucia. In the revised version, Junius' devouring jealousy of Collatinus is established more firmly in Act I, scene i, and this helps to render more credible his sudden irruption with Collatinus just before Lucretia's suicide in the last scene. Meanwhile, Lucia who appeared in the earlier version as a young, frivolous and slightly over-sexed maid-servant, regains a measure of her not yet lost innocence and is given a charming *arioso*, '*I often wonder whether Lucretia's love is the flower of her beauty*'—her only one in the opera—which helps to establish her character musically.

II

As has already been shown, both natural predilection and economic necessity influenced Britten in deciding to choose an instrumental contingent of chamber orchestra dimensions for the *The Rape of Lucretia*. A quarter of a century previously, when Stravinsky, partly for reasons of wartime economy, had felt a similar urge in planning *The Soldier's Tale*, he had chosen representative outer-range instruments from each of the main orchestral groups and had found that seven was his irreducible minimum. *The Soldier's Tale* was accordingly written for violin and double-bass, clarinet and bassoon, cornet and trombone, and percussion. Britten's solution was different: a string quintet, a woodwind quartet (with the flute doubling piccolo and bass-flute, the oboe doubling cor anglais, and the clarinet doubling bass-clarinet) and a miscellaneous trio consisting of horn, harp and percussion—a dozen players in all—with the *recitativo secco* accompanied by the conductor on a piano. (A similar ensemble was chosen by Menotti about the same time for his operas, *The Telephone* and *The Medium.*)

Although this meant that *The Rape* would be a chamber opera in the sense that every executant (vocalist or instrumentalist) would be a solo performer, it did not necessarily presuppose intimate chamber conditions of performance. The doublings in the instrumentation of works for symphony orchestra increase the volume of sound to only a limited extent—as Stravinsky says in the sixth lecture in his *Poetics of Music*, they thicken without strengthening, and above a certain point the impression of intensity is diminished rather than increased and sensation is blunted. Their main purpose is to blend and bind instrumental tone colour; and this may be compared with the custom of covering oil paintings with a heavy layer of varnish. Just as modern taste is in favour of removing these varnishes to reveal the original colours of a painting in all their unsubdued vigour, so one would like to think that modern audiences, suffering a revulsion from the inflated performances of super-orchestras, are prepared to demand a scaling-down of forces and to accept the convention whereby instrumental tone colours are presented directly in their primary state without any attempt to blend them before they reach the ear.

In the light of the experience gained in touring *The Rape* in England and abroad, it appeared (according to Eric Crozier) that 'the quality and vitality of the voices with instruments were much better in large theatres than in small. There were no complaints of thinness or raggedness in texture.'* On the other hand, there were moments when the voices, instead of being sustained by the blended accompaniment that comes from a full body of strings, had to fight for audibility on equal terms with each solo instrument and were in danger of being drowned or rendered insignificant by the unsubdued tone colour of a handful of instruments. As Edward Sackville-West wrote in the Preamble to *The Rescue*, 'it is, paradoxically, impossible to produce an overall orchestral pianissimo without using a considerable body of instruments, whereas a double *forte* requires only the minimum'.

In short, chamber opera demands the highest virtuoso standards from each individual executant—the slightest lapse is liable to prejudice the total effect. It makes similar demands of its audience too. The equipoise between voices and instruments is too precarious for the listener ever to be lulled into a sense of complete relaxation and security; and many listeners—particularly those reared on a rich diet of lush orchestral fare—are apt to resent the necessity of making this special effort. This is one of the problems that Britten and his collaborators had to face when producing *The Rape of*

* In *The Rape of Lucretia* (commemorative volume), ed. Eric Crozier.

Lucretia, *Albert Herring*, *The Beggar's Opera*, *The Turn of the Screw*, *Curlew River* and the other church parable operas, and one that they surmounted with extraordinary success.

III

Whether the conflict in *The Rape of Lucretia* is spirit defiled by fate or, more prosaically, Lucretia ravished by Tarquinius, Britten needed two simply contrasted musical ideas to express it. He found them by taking the melodic contents of the interval of the diminished fourth and arranging the notes in two different ways. The first (*a*), a descending scale-passage, is identified with Tarquinius; the second (*b*), a sequence of two thirds in contrary motion, is the kernel of the Lucretia motif. By extension, the idea of a scale-

Ex. 20a Ex. 20b

passage (whether descending or ascending) becomes identified with the male element. This is aptly summarized in the Prologue, where the Male and Female Chorus sing a solemn hymn, which combines both elements.

Ex. 21

With this key, it is possible to unlock many of the secrets of the score.

Lucretia's motif, moving both forwards and backwards, serves as the generals' flamboyant toast in Act I, scene i. In diminution, it is frequently

Ex. 22

used as an accompanying figure—for example, in Junius' outburst '*Lucretia! I'm sick of that name!*', also in the following comment by the Male Chorus,

> *Oh, it is plain*
> *That nothing pleases*
> *Your friends so much*
> *As your dishonour*

and in the Male Chorus's subsequent apostrophe, when he perceives what is going on in the privacy of Junius' heart and how like an empty vessel it is suddenly flooded with jealousy. Here in the swirling accompaniment, the

Ex. 23

minor third interval becomes widened progressively to major third, fourth and even fifth. During the same scene, Tarquinius' motif is not much in evidence, though it is clearly referred to in the Male Chorus's opening air which depicts the sultry atmosphere of the evening outside Rome, and three notes of it, repeated by the harp in diminution, become identified with the noise of the crickets (Ex. 24). In the Interlude, however, the male element dominates the furious ride of Tarquinius and his steed (Ex. 25). It is only when horse and rider, after being momentarily checked in their course by the sudden obstacle of the Tiber, plunge into the river and swim across that

Ex. 24

Ex. 25

the Lucretia motif returns, the music of Ex. 23, now accompanied by the cool metallic hiss of a cymbal tremolo, being repeated to the following words with their prophetic symbolism:

Now stallion and rider
Wake the sleep of water
Disturbing its cool dream
With hot flank and shoulder.

In the second scene, with Lucretia sewing, Bianca and Lucia spinning, and the Chorus interpolating her commentary, interlinked feminine thirds run riot in the harp accompaniment to the vocal quartet. The rising

Ex. 26

intonation of Lucretia's apostrophe to her absent husband may be thought of as an altered version of the Tarquinius motif, which naturally plays an important part a little later when Tarquinius arrives unexpectedly. A particularly subtle touch is to be found in the passage where this motif, preluded by its inversion, is accompanied by a figure made up of both the Tarquinius and Lucretia motifs in diminution. The final series of

Ex. 27

goodnights, when Lucretia leads Tarquinius to his bedchamber, contains the Tarquinius motif augmented and harmonized with thirds over a ground-bass of compound thirds rising by thirds:

Ex. 28

At the beginning of the second Act, the interval of the third—and also its inversion, the sixth—are predominant in Tarquinius' air, '*Within this frail crucible of light*', sung while Lucretia is still asleep; but when she awakens and in her agitation asks what he wants from her, the music gives an explicit answer, the brassed horn frenziedly attempting to fill the open interval of the

Ex. 29

cor anglais's minor third. The new figure formed thereby (*c*) becomes closely identified with Tarquinius' lust during the remainder of the scene, until near its climax Lucretia interrupts him with a broad and dignified rebuke based on the original Tarquinius motif in augmentation (Ex. 30). In the unaccompanied quartet with which the scene ends ('*See how the rampant*

centaur mounts the sky') will be found a recapitulation of the jealousy theme (Ex. 23) sung by Lucretia, together with fragments of the Lucretia, Tarquinius and lust motifs.

For the opening of the last scene, where Bianca and Lucia greet the sunny morning and then start to arrange the flowers the gardener has brought,

both accompaniment and voices describe festoons of rising and falling thirds. When Lucretia enters and is told by Bianca that they have left the orchids for her to arrange, she bursts out hysterically, and the music at once refers to the lust theme. Just before her suicide there are two passages where use of the Lucretia motif deserves special notice. The first comes when she asks Bianca if she remembers teaching her as a child to weave garlands of wild flowers. '*Do you remember!*' In a brief aria, Bianca replies:

Ex. 33

and nothing could sound gayer than this carefree scherzo, with its sparkling accompaniment based on the Lucretia motif in diminution and in a major mode. Later when Collatinus arrives and Lucretia dressed in mourning makes her confession, the Lucretia motif returns to the minor mode, but is tenderly harmonized with a major chord. Meanwhile, her silent entry has

Ex. 34

been made all the more pitiful by the way in which both the regularly moving ground-bass and the hesitant sobbing phrases of the cor anglais are

Ex. 35

formed out of scale passages. As she stabs herself, her last words fall in thirds through the compass of two octaves:

Now I'll be forever chaste
With only death to ravish me.
See, how my wanton blood
Washes my shame away!

A funeral march in passacaglia form follows, with a ground-bass (Ex. 36) that brings to mind the Chorus's solemn hymn (Ex. 21) that has been heard in both Prologues. Over this ostinato, a magnificent sextet is built up, in

Ex. 36

which each vocal part is developed with full regard for the characters of the various persons concerned. At the end, special prominence is given to the repeated demi-semiquaver figure; and this figure persists throughout the Epilogue so that when the opera ends with a recapitulation of Ex. 21, the accompaniment is powdered with major and minor thirds—the minor predominating—spread over the entire orchestral compass, like stars that come out in the firmament after sunset.

Although these musical germs or cells have been spoken of as motifs, and their permutations and transformations traced in some detail, it must not be thought that in *The Rape* Britten has adopted a comprehensive *leitmotif* system of construction. Many beauties lie outside the passages quoted above—to take a single example, the marvellous lullaby at the beginning of the second Act, one of his most original and memorable passages. But just as in the *Symphony of Psalms*, Stravinsky used the device of two interlinked ascending thirds (rather similar to the Lucretia motif) to unify the thematic material in each of its three movements, so Britten has used his motifs to emphasize the persistence of the fundamental conflict in the action and to achieve a remarkably homogeneous texture in his score.

IV
Albert Herring

Albert Herring was intended to be both a companion piece and a contrast to *The Rape of Lucretia*: a companion piece since it is written for the same vocal and instrumental contingent; a contrast in the sense that its subject is comic as opposed to the tragedy of *The Rape*.

Eric Crozier adapted Guy de Maupassant's short story, *Le Rosier de Madame Husson*, with considerable skill. He transferred the action from Normandy to East Anglia; and although in the process something of the malicious sparkle of the Gallic original may have been lost, what remains is in most essentials faithful to the letter, if not the spirit, of the original.

The main outline of the plot is soon told. Lady Billows, virtuous herself and the self-appointed guardian of virtue in others, is anxious to select a May Queen in Loxford; but, in default of suitable female candidates, she decides on a May King, and her choice falls on young Albert Herring, who works in a greengrocer's shop and has a reputation for unassailable innocence and chastity. During the May Day celebrations, he is fêted and plied with lemonade that has been surreptitiously laced with rum. So fortified, he breaks out and escapes that evening from the stifling atmosphere of his home. When his absence is discovered the following morning, search parties are sent out. At first, it is feared he may have been killed; but just as his death is being lamented, he arrives back, dirty, dishevelled and defiant after a bibulous night out.

This is the point where opera and short story begin to diverge. According to Crozier, Albert Herring's night out consisted only of a pub-crawl, in the course of which he was thrown out of *The Dog and Duck* and *The Horse and Groom*. Although Herring himself refers to it as 'a night that was a nightmare example of drunkenness, and dirt, and worse', it seems mildly innocuous when contrasted with the virtuous Isidore's escapade in *Le Rosier de Madame Husson*. 'Isidore was drunk, dead drunk, besotted after a week of dissipation, and not merely drunk, but so filthy that a dustman would have refused to touch him. . . . He smelt of the sewer and the gutter and every haunt of vice.' This would have set too serious a note for the simple honest fun of Crozier's libretto. Nevertheless, the character of Herring remains slightly embarrassing; and when the curtain falls, one does not feel convinced that the experience gained in the course of this or any other drinking bout would have been sufficient to free him from the shackles of his painful inhibitions. Isidore eventually died of *delirium tremens*; Albert Herring, one suspects, lived down the momentary scandal of his May Day intoxication and became a respected citizen of Loxford.

Crozier aimed at clarity and simplicity in his libretto and wrote 'to be sung, not to be read from a printed page'. In his series of lectures on *The Poetic Image*, C. Day Lewis, speaking from the poet's point of view, explained the distinction as follows: 'The writing of words for music demands an entirely different technique from the writing of lyric poetry as we now understand the term. Words for music are like water-weed: they live only in the streams and eddies of melody. When we take them out of their element, they lose their colour, their grace, their vital fluency: on paper they look delicate perhaps, but flat and unenterprising.' It is to Crozier's credit that he understood this, and consequently his libretto is most successful when it is most self-effacing.

Writing in 1938 of Britten's early works, Henry Boys gave it as his opinion that if Britten chose, 'he could undoubtedly become the most original and probably the most successful maker of light music in England since Sullivan'.* In *Albert Herring* this prophecy is fulfilled. The music is light and loose, mercurial and full of fun. It recaptures something of the boyish high spirits of his earlier works. '*Avanti!*' cries the composer to his woodwind in the Interlude between the two scenes of Act I, just as eleven years before he had written the same direction in the first movement ('*Rats away!*') of *Our Hunting Fathers*. Sid, the butcher's assistant, laces Albert Herring's glass of lemonade with rum; and a sinister coil of chromatics arises from the orchestra to remind one of the love potion motif in *Tristan und Isolde*. Police Superintendent Budd complains in the last act, when the hunt for Albert Herring is on:

Give me a robbery with force
Or a criminal case of rape,
But God preserve me from these disappearing cases!

And as he mentions rape, the orchestra refers slyly (but *fortissimo*) to the Lucretia motif (cf. Ex. 20b).

One of the score's most distinctive characteristics is to be seen in the handling of the recitative. Not only are there examples of every shade of *recitativo secco* and *recitativo stromentato*, but many of these show an extraordinary freedom in rhythm, the voices (*ad libitum*) often going a

* 'The Younger English Composers: V. Benjamin Britten' by Henry Boys. *Monthly Musical Record*, October 1938.

Albert Herring: Lady Billows (Joan Cross), The Vicar (William Parsons), and Miss Wordsworth (Margaret Ritchie) in the committee meeting from Act I in the original 1947 English Opera Group production

completely different way from the accompaniment—as in the *recitativo quasi ballata* of Act I, scene i—while others combine in contrapuntal patterns to form recitative ensembles of great complexity. There are three such ensembles in Act II, scene i, where each character is directed to sing his or her line at the natural speed of the diction without paying any regard to the other voices or the accompaniment; and the last one, which occurs as the coronation feast begins and just before the curtain falls, contains six independent recitative solos, two recitative duets (between Nancy and Sid, and the Mayor and the Police Superintendent), and a canon for the three village children.

In a three-act comic opera like *Albert Herring*, where the music is continuous, the composer has an enormous canvas to fill. As Erwin Stein says, in comic opera 'there are fewer opportunities for slow movements and lyrical expansion than in musical drama'.* Although by the use of recitative the composer is able to get over much of the ground at a spanking pace, it becomes all the more necessary for him to strengthen the tension and

* 'Form in Opera: *Albert Herring* Examined' by Erwin Stein. *Tempo*, Autumn 1947.

specific gravity of his music at the nodal points. This is done mainly by increasing the contrapuntal interest of the musical texture. For instance, there are fugal choruses, '*We've made our own investigations*' and '*May King! May King!*' in Act I, scene i; in the following scene, the 'pleasures of love' duet, where Nancy and Sid singing in unison are accompanied by a perky woodwind canon at the octave; the fugal Interlude between scenes i and ii of Act II; and, in particular, the magnificent nine-part threnody in the last Act. This is built up on a ground chorus in the minor mode. Above this

Ex. 37

the individual verses of lament are freely developed. The Vicar's contribution is marked *espressivo*, Nancy's *piangendo*, the Mayor's *marcato ed eroico*, Lady Billows's *brillante*, her housekeeper's *con forza*, the Superintendent's *pesante*, the schoolmistress's *lamentoso*, Sid's *con gravità* and Mrs Herring's *appassionato*. Towards the end, all these nine characteristic laments, after alteration to fit the major mode, are repeated together over a roll from the timpani and fused into a wonderfully intricate knot of polyphony.

It is the opera's special glory that frequently a character or episode is treated with a mixture of satire and sentiment that produces as unforgettable a vignette as a drawing by Rowlandson or a poem by Betjeman. There is the bland and hesitant Vicar trying to reassure Lady Billows on the subject of virtue:

Ex. 38

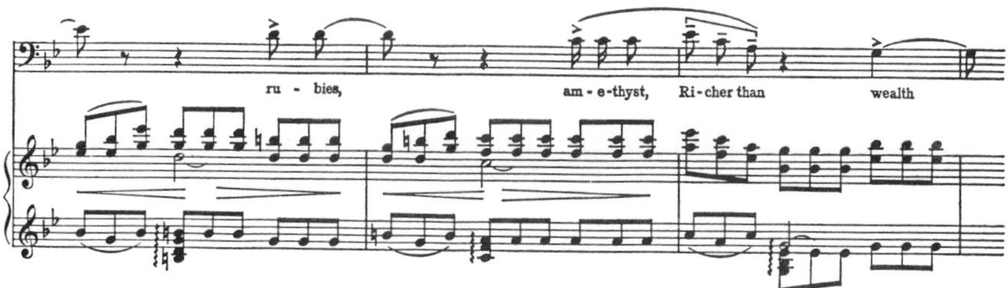

the twittering Miss Wordsworth nervously rehearsing the school children in the festive song:

Ex. 39

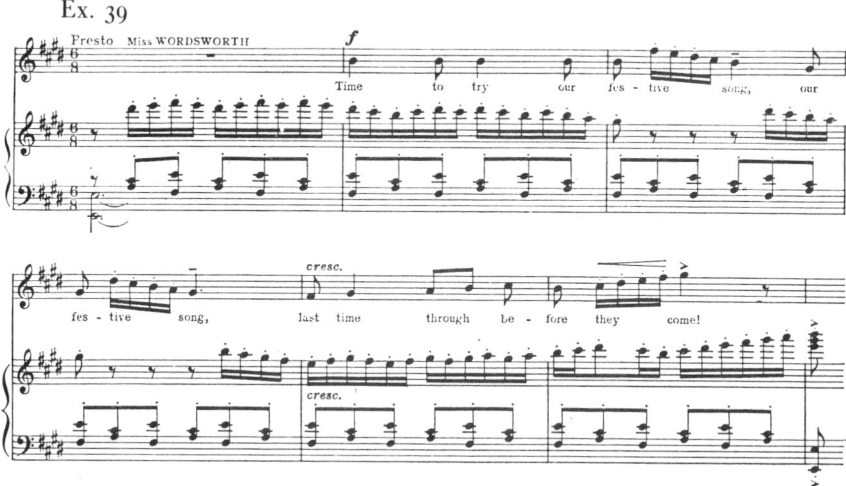

Mrs Herring clutching the faded framed photo of her son as a little boy:

Ex. 40

and Albert when, returning in the evening from the feast, he enters the greengrocer's shop in the dark and looks round for matches to light the gas to the accompaniment of the exquisite nocturne for bass flute and bass clarinet first heard in the previous interlude:

Ex. 41

It might be thought that in foreign countries *Albert Herring* would be handicapped by the slang element in its libretto; but this does not seem to be the case. In translation the opera has proved a great success in Germany and other countries; and in the original nowhere has it been more enthusiastically acclaimed than in Aldeburgh, which is only a few miles as the crow flies from Loxford itself.

V
The Beggar's Opera

Planned by John Gay as a Newgate comedy, *The Beggar's Opera* was an immediate hit when produced at the Theatre in Lincoln's Inn Fields on 29 January 1728. Its record run of sixty-two performances, of which the first thirty-two were consecutive, remained unbroken until the production of *The Duenna* at Covent Garden in 1775. It made the fortunes of a number of persons connected with it. Lavinia Fenton, the original Polly, became the toast of the town and ultimately married the Duke of Bolton. It is calculated that from his four benefit nights (third, sixth, ninth and fifteenth performances), John Gay, the author, received between £700 and £800. Details of the emoluments of Dr Pepusch, who adapted the music, are not known; but Rich, the manager, seems to have netted a profit of over £6,000 on the first season, and £1,000 or more the following (1728–9) season.* This must have contributed substantially to the capital needed a few years later when he promoted the building of the new Covent Garden Theatre.

The fame of *The Beggar's Opera* spread quickly through the provinces and there were performances in Dublin, Glasgow and Haddington in 1728. It was the second piece to be produced at Covent Garden (16 December 1732). The following year a company took it to the West Indies, where Polly had already gone in Gay's published but for many years unacted sequel, and subsequently it was played in North America. It set a fashion for ballad opera which swept London and persisted for about ten years—at least 120 ballad operas were produced during the period 1728–38—and later the type developed into *pasticcio* opera which flourished during the latter part of the eighteenth century. In both ballad and *pasticcio* operas the predominating role was the playwright's, while the composer had the function of a musical director, who arranged and scored the music selected. But whereas the majority of the tunes used in the ballad operas were popular and anonymous—for instance, fifty-one out of the sixty-nine in *The Beggar's Opera*—the numbers in the *pasticcio* operas had nearly all been composed by

* These figures are based on the calculations in Sir St Vincent Troubridge's article 'Making Gay Rich, and Rich Gay'. *Theatre Notebook*, October 1951.

contemporary musicians, many of them probably by the arranger himself.

It is not known for certain whether Dr Pepusch was solely responsible for the music in *The Beggar's Opera* or whether Gay himself played some part in the choice of tunes. The music as published with the libretto consisted of Dr Pepusch's Overture printed in four-part score and the tunes of the sixty-nine airs given without any indication of harmony. When the songs were separately engraved as Dr Pepusch's composition, an unfigured bass was added. Other musical editors soon started to make additions and alterations to Dr Pepusch's score. Dr T. A. Arne was one of the first; and his dance of prisoners in chains (Act III, scene xii), for which Dr Pepusch had specified no music, was later incorporated into the Frederic Austin version. Many others followed.

In default of an authoritative version of the original score, each revival has had to solve afresh the problem of musical presentation. After the first world war, when Nigel Playfair produced *The Beggar's Opera* at the Lyric Theatre, Hammersmith, the text was carefully revised by Arnold Bennett and all offensive matter removed. Frederic Austin, basing his score fairly closely on a previous version by J. L. Hatton, set about two-thirds of the original tunes in a style that was an elegant *pastiche* of the eighteenth century, scoring the numbers for string quintet, flute, oboe and harpsichord with occasional use of the viola d'amore and viola da gamba. He inserted a number of dances and instrumental interludes, mainly of his own composition; and Lovat Fraser designed a gay colourful setting. The production was pretty and had panache. It proved to be exactly suited to the taste of the post-war public and ran for 1,463 performances, being frequently revived later in the 1920s and during the early 1930s.

By 1940, when Glyndebourne produced *The Beggar's Opera* on tour and later brought it to the Haymarket Theatre, London, the Austin version was becoming outmoded. John Gielgud, who on this occasion was the producer, moved away from the emasculated prettiness of the Playfair-Fraser entertainment towards a more realistic treatment of the miseries of London; but he chose the early Victorian period depicted in the style of Cruikshank, and in this inappropriate setting the Austin score was a complete misfit. About the same time Edward J. Dent made a new version of the score at the request of Sadler's Wells; and this was based as far as possible on the original edition. In the event, the Dent version was performed for the first time, not by the Sadler's Wells Opera Company, but by the Clarion Singers, Birmingham, and there have been several subsequent amateur productions.

When Britten decided to make a new adaptation of *The Beggar's Opera* for the English Opera Group in 1948, he turned to Tyrone Guthrie as his collaborator. Guthrie wished to restore the opera's original pungency. He saw it literally as a *beggar's* if not a *beggars'* opera—in his own words, 'the expression of people made reckless, even desperate by poverty, but in whose

The Beggar's Opera: Polly Peachum (Nancy Evans), Macheath (Peter Pears) and Lucy Lockit (Rose Hill) in the original 1948 production by the English Opera Group

despair there is none the less a vitality and gaiety that the art of elegant and fashionable people often misses'—and he edited the text and planned his production accordingly. The same intention had underlain *Die Dreigroschenoper* which Brecht wrote in 1928 for production at the Theater am Schiffbauerdamm, Berlin: but whereas Brecht retained the essential framework of the characters and the plot (although he transferred the period from the early eighteenth century to the last years of Queen Victoria's reign during the Boer War), Kurt Weill removed all the original airs from his score, except the *Morgenchoral des Peachum*, which was based on Peachum's opening song '*Through all the Employments of Life*', and even this was dropped after the dress rehearsal.

As far as Britten was concerned, there was no temptation to cut the original airs. Quite the contrary. He himself said: 'These tunes to which John Gay wrote his apt and witty lyrics are among our finest national songs. These seventeenth- and eighteenth-century airs, known usually as "traditional tunes", seem to me to be the most characteristically *English* of any of our folk-songs. They are often strangely like Handel and Purcell: may, perhaps, have influenced them, or have been influenced by them. They have strong, leaping intervals, sometimes in peculiar modes, and are often strange and severe in mood. While recognizing that the definitive arrangement of them can never be achieved, since each generation sees them from a different aspect, I feel that most previous arrangements have avoided their toughness and strangeness, and have concentrated only on their lyrical prettiness. For my arrangements of the tunes I have gone to a contemporary edition of the original arrangements by Dr Pepusch. Apart from one or two extensions and repetitions, I have left the tunes exactly as they stood (except for one or two spots where the original seemed confused and inaccurate).'

In actual fact he used sixty-six out of the sixty-nine airs of the original 1728 version, as against the forty-five set by Austin. Twice he combined two of these airs: the first time to create a duet between Lucy (Air XXXI*—'*Is then his Fate decreed, Sir?*') and Lockit (Air XXXII—'*You'll think e'er many Days ensue*'); the second to create a trio between Macheath (Air XXXV—'*How happy could I be with either*') and Polly and Lucy (Air XXXVI—'*I'm bubbled—I'm bubbled*'). Britten's solution of the scene in the condemned hold where Macheath tosses off glasses of wine and bumpers of brandy in the hope of working up sufficient courage to face being hanged upon Tyburn tree is a *tour de force*. The original 1728 version specified a sequence of ten different airs, several of them fragmentary. Austin quite frankly shirked the problem by omitting six of the ten airs. Dent tackled it by giving the original tunes to the orchestra complete as far as possible and allowing Macheath to come in with his fragmentary ejaculations as and when they occurred. Britten's solution was to set the final air '*Green Sleeves*' in such a way that its bass could be used as a ground linking the previous airs. Seven times this ground bass is broken at different points to allow the interpolation of fragmentary airs; twice the fragments fit it exactly; and the tenth time it sinks into its proper place as the bass to the concluding '*Green Sleeves*'.

Although, as the Beggar boasts in the Prologue, there is nothing in the opera so unnatural as recitative, occasional passages of melodrama occur where music underlines spoken dialogue and eases some of the transitions from song to speech and speech to song. There is a particularly ambitious passage of this kind in the form of a series of nine cadenzas introducing eight ladies of the town and a harper in the scene of the tavern near Newgate.

A somewhat similar musical introduction of characters was carried out in Britten's Overture, which replaced Dr Pepusch's. Guthrie's intention was that after the Beggar had spoken his introduction the curtain would rise and the orchestra would play the Overture while the actors were seen getting ready for the performance and setting the scene of Peachum's lock. Britten accordingly composed an episodic overture introducing tunes connected with the main characters, starting with Lucy Lockit (fugue) and ending with Mr Peachum's air '*Through all the employments of life*', which is also the

* The numbering of the airs is that of the original 1728 edition.

opening number of Act I. The effect is attractive so long as the producer can ensure that the end of the Overture and beginning of the Opera are clearly differentiated so that the actors can get the ictus they need for the start of the action proper.

Another change made by Guthrie was the lengthening of Act I to include the first scene (A Tavern near Newgate) of Gay's Act II. The effect of this was to bring the curtain down on Macheath's arrest and to confine the next act to the Newgate scenes covering Macheath's imprisonment and escape.

Careful attention was paid by Britten to the keys of the different numbers. Thirty-six airs were presented in their original keys. The transpositions of the remaining thirty were carried out mainly with an eye to emphasizing two important tendencies—of numbers concerned with Macheath and Polly, and their love for each other, to gravitate round B flat major and its related keys, and of numbers concerned with Newgate to gravitate round E minor and A major and their related keys. The opera's central tonality is F. The Overture opens in F major; Act I starts with Peachum's first air in F minor; Macheath's scene in the condemned hold is in F minor; and the following trio '*Would I might be hanged*' is in F major. This marks the end of the opera proper, the dance in G minor which comes after the reprise being of the nature of an afterthought, a kind of jig to wind up the proceedings.

Throughout the opera Britten takes special pains to set off the modal characteristics of the airs and not to force them into the straight-jacket of academic major/minor harmonization. An interesting example of his treatment is to be found in the duet between Polly and Lucy '*A curse attends a women's love*'. The original tune was '*O Bessy Bell*' and the first half of it is given in Gay's original version of *The Beggar's Opera* as follows:

Ex. 42

Austin, being apparently nervous of the 'strong, leaping intervals' in the vocal part, altered the tune and set it as follows:

Ex. 43

Britten's version is not only faithful to the original, but captures the real non-modulatory spirit of the flattened seventh and sets it in proper relief by the oboe phrase with its false relations:

Ex. 44

Quotations illustrating the numerous ingenuities of Britten's settings of these tunes could easily be multiplied—the augmentations and diminutions, the metric subtleties, the daring harmonic progressions that occasionally seem to modulate against the vocal line, the startling stab of bitonality in the chorus '*Let us take the road*', the use of canon and imitation, the free development of counter themes, the cunning instrumentation, and so on. But even more important than any of these is the fact that Britten still knows when mere cleverness is out-of-place and when it behoves him to be absolutely unaffected and simple. For instance, his setting of the duet between Mrs Peachum and Polly '*O Polly, you might have toy'd and kist*' is most lovely and haunting. It will be found that here too Britten's vocal line differs from the Austin version, the reason being that Britten has literally followed the original tune '*O Jenny, O Jenny, where hast thou been*' as given in the original editions.

The orchestra for this version of *The Beggar's Opera* consists of flute (doubling piccolo), oboe (doubling cor anglais), clarinet, bassoon, horn, percussion, harp, string quartet and double-bass. From it Britten obtains a maximum variety of instrumental effects. Examples that stick in the mind are the tremolo flute motif in Polly's air '*The Turtle thus with plaintive crying*'; the lace-like edging provided by the harp to the sturdy cotillon '*Youth's the season made for joys*'; the sensitive flutterings of the flute in Polly's air '*Thus when the swallow seeking prey*'; the savage unison strings with their dotted quaver motif in Lockit's air '*Thus Gamesters united in friendship are found*'; the rumbling of the low timpani bass accompanying the air sung by that deep drinker Mrs Trapes '*In the days of my youth*'; the sinister liquid gurgling of the clarinet *arpeggii* as Lucy urges Polly to '*take a chirping glass*'; and the vibration of the tremolo bell chords, the tolling of which punctuates the trio '*Would I might be hanged!*'

Britten's version of *The Beggar's Opera* is not the definitive version—no version will ever be that*—but it is to date not only the most brilliant musical version, but also the one in which the operatic nature of the work has been successfully emphasized. For the first time in its long history, *The Beggar's Opera* needs singers rather than actors to interpret it; and the result is that, whereas none of the earlier versions made much headway abroad, except in the United States and British Commonwealth, *The Beggar's Opera* in Britten's version has been played in many of the opera houses in Europe, and the work is at long last becoming universally recognized as one of the masterpieces of comic opera.

* In 1953 another version of the score was made by Sir Arthur Bliss for the film directed by Peter Brook with Sir Laurence Olivier as Captain Macheath.

VI
The Little Sweep

The Little Sweep is the opera that forms part of the entertainment for young people called *Let's Make an Opera!* Whereas in *Peter Grimes* the apprentice boy was a mute character, here Sam, the sweep-master's eight-year-old apprentice, becomes the hero of the opera, and a fully vocal hero too.

The story of how a number of children living at Iken Hall, Suffolk, in 1810 meet Sam, a new sweep-boy, while he is sweeping one of the chimneys, and succeed in rescuing him from his bullying master, Black Bob, was based by Eric Crozier, not on Lotte Reiniger's silhouette film *The Little Chimney Sweep* (1935), nor Charles Kingsley's *The Water Babies* (though Britten himself was brought up on Kingsley's book as a boy), nor Elia's mannered essay, *The Praise of Chimney-Sweepers* (1822), but on William Blake's Songs of Innocence, *The Chimney Sweeper*:

When my mother died I was very young,
And my father sold me while yet my tongue
Could scarcely cry "'weep! 'weep! 'weep!"
so your chimneys I sweep, and in soot I sleep.

Despite its surface gaiety, the atmosphere of this little opera is surcharged with intense pity and indignation for the plight of the hapless sweep-boy sold into servitude because of his parents' poverty. If to readers of Lamb and Kingsley the note of cruelty implicit in this tale seems rather exaggerated, they will find more than sufficient justification for Crozier's attitude if they consult *A People's Conscience** where the case of the climbing boys is presented on the basis of evidence contained in the reports of various Select Committees of the House of Commons. No wonder that as Blake wandered through the London streets he heard

How the chimney-sweeper's cry
Every black'ning church appals.

The practice of using young boys to sweep the more difficult and dangerous

* By Strathearn Gordon and T. G. B. Cocks. Constable, 1952.

flues was not really abolished until the latter part of the nineteenth century; and as late as June 1949, the month and year in which *Let's Make an Opera!* was first performed, the last of the chimney boys—Mr Joseph Lawrence of Windlesham, Surrey—celebrated his one hundred and fourth birthday.

It is to the credit of Britten and Crozier that, while not shirking the fundamental problem of this opera, they presented it in such a cheerful and sympathetic guise as completely to beguile the audience; and this audience, it must not be forgotten, included children and young people as well as adults.

Sam, the little sweep, is eight years old. A party of half a dozen children, three of them living at Iken Hall and three of them on a visit there, rescue him from the flue where he has stuck and eventually deliver him from his master. As against these seven child actors—all the boys with unbroken voices—there are six adult parts, two of which can be doubled. The cast of eleven is accordingly a mixture of amateurs and professionals; and Britten and Crozier had the audacious but brilliant idea to increase the amateur element by implicating the whole of the audience in the performance. This they did by giving the audience four songs to sing in the course of the opera: *The Sweep's Song* by way of overture, *Sammy's Bath* and *The Night Song* as interludes between scenes i and ii, and scenes ii and iii, and the *Coaching Song* that forms the finale.

Such an unorthodox plan could be carried out successfully only if the audience had an opportunity to rehearse their songs; and this gave Britten and Crozier the cue they needed for the earlier part of the entertainment. Clearly the opera must be shown in rehearsal; and this in fact was how *Let's Make an Opera!* was first presented at Aldeburgh. Later, however, Crozier revised this first part, expanding it into two acts so as to show quite clearly the conception, writing and composition of the opera as well as its stage production.* Although these two acts are in the form of a play, they contain a certain amount of incidental music. For instance, the first scene ends with a musical toast in the form of a round on the words '*Let's Make an Opera!*' and later on the local builder who is roped in to play the roles of the Sweepmaster's assistant and the gardener takes part in an audition at which he sings '*Early One Morning*'. Earlier, there is a glimpse of the composer at work on the scene where Sam, just after his rescue from the chimney, begs the children '*Please don't send me up again!*' During the second act, the

* Subsequently (1965) he revised it again, condensing the two acts into one. But in the most recent edition of the published libretto for *The Little Sweep* Eric Crozier writes in the Foreword: 'This preliminary play served its purpose at the time, but it does not wear so well as the opera. Ideally, it should be rewritten to suit the local circumstances and characters of any group performing *The Little Sweep*. We have therefore decided not to reprint it any longer, but copies will continue to be available from the Hire Library at Boosey & Hawkes Ltd. for you to adopt or adapt at your pleasure. But if the opera is to be performed, without the play, it should still be preceded by a short rehearsal of the audience songs.'

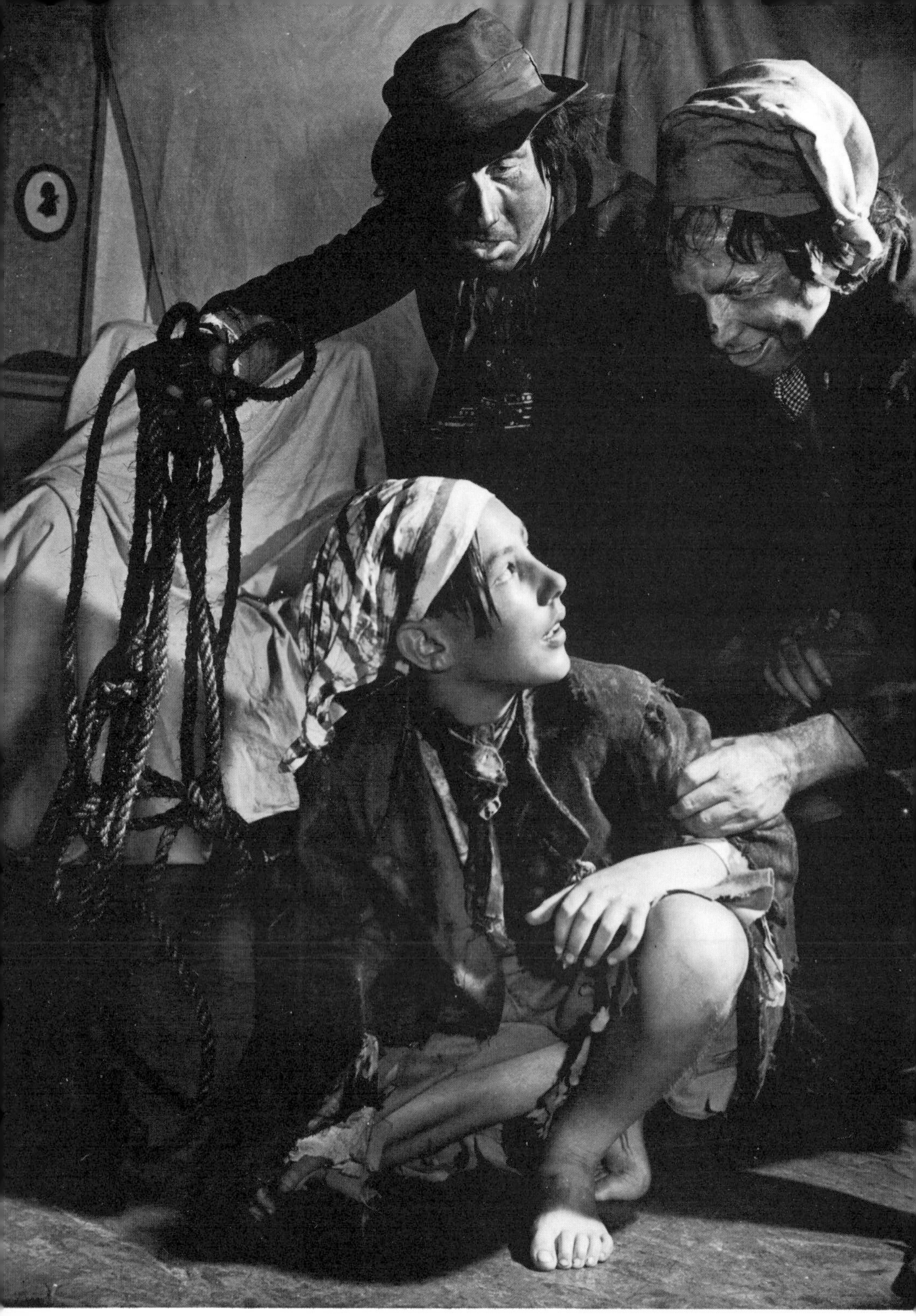

The Little Sweep: Black Bob (Norman Lumsden), Clem (Max Worthley) and Sam the sweep boy (John Moules) from the original 1949 production by the English Opera Group

audience is given a chance not only to learn its four songs, but also to see three of the children's ensembles being rehearsed: so by the time the opera proper is reached, the work of preparation has been so thorough that much of the music is greeted with the thrill of recognition.

The orchestra is smaller even than that used for *The Rape of Lucretia*, *Albert Herring* and *The Beggar's Opera*, and consists of a string quartet, piano (four hands) and percussion (single player).

The music is not continuous. There is spoken dialogue between the numbers, and practically no recitative.

The score is distinguished by the straightforward appeal of the vocal line; but the setting and presentation of the melodies often show a considerable degree of sophistication. The basic tunes of all four audience songs are so simple that some of them (particularly the Night Song) bid fair to attain an independent popularity; but in their setting they are distinguished by metrical and harmonic touches of considerable subtlety. For instance, each verse of the first audience song is prefaced by the cry '*Sweep!*' and the opening phrase of the catchy tune is:

Ex. 45

But Britten sets it in 5/4 time, which gives a fascinating contrast between the groups of nine hurrying triplet quavers and the more measured tread of the crotchets, and he makes ingenious use of the fact that a large concourse of people of all ages singing in unison often produces a slightly indeterminate pitch:

Ex. 46

The cry 'Sweep!' is harmonized differently on every appearance, with the result that although the tune never varies, the song in the course of its five verses modulates from D minor through B flat major, G minor, E flat major to D minor (ending on a chord of the major). Ex. 47 shows the transition between verses three and four:

Ex. 47

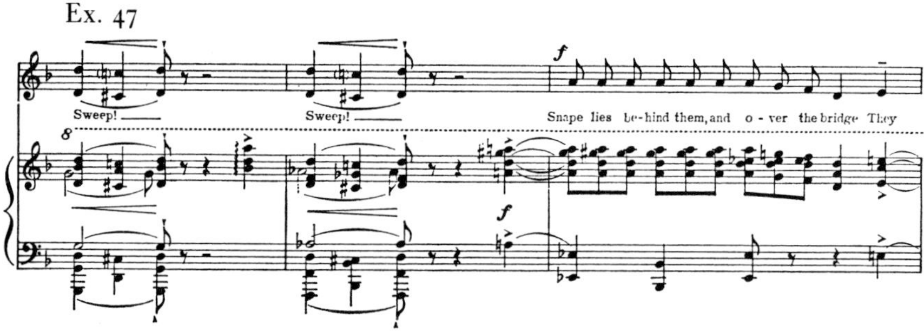

Another example of the special effects to be obtained from shifting harmonies while the tune remains constant is to be found in the Ensemble '*O why do you weep through the working day?*' At the end of each verse a three-part phrase sung by the children leads to Sam's repeated, unforgettably poignant cry '*How shall I laugh and play?*' The first and last verses are given in Ex. 48; and it will be seen how natural and moving is the clash between the F natural and the F sharp in the final cadence:

Ex. 48

Although Britten takes considerable pains to protect the children's voices from anything too complicated in the way of melody, he does not hesitate to allow them to take part in a contrapuntal movement like the finale to scene ii, which is really a passacaglia on a ground bass formed by the rising scale of D major:

Ex. 49

Since Purcell produced *Dido and Aeneas* for Josias Priest's girls' school at Chelsea, no more beautiful opera for child performers has been written. Its immediate popularity as an entertainment, not only in this country but all over the world, has been phenomenal; but what is more difficult as yet to assess is the extent of its influence in introducing children to opera. In some countries a new generation is growing up that, thanks partly to its example, is prepared to accept opera and its conventions as a natural and familiar art form.

The Little Sweep is an opera of innocence—of innocence betrayed and rescued—and it is fully worthy of the singer of innocence who inspired it.

VII
Billy Budd

I

At the first Aldeburgh Festival in 1948, E. M. Forster gave a lecture on George Crabbe and Peter Grimes. The crowded audience, which included Benjamin Britten, sat on the hard benches of the Baptist Chapel that warm summer afternoon and heard the lecturer talk about the far-reaching alterations Montagu Slater had made when constructing his opera libretto on the basis of Crabbe's poem. Having enumerated some of these changes, he went on to say: 'It amuses me to think what an opera on Peter Grimes would have been like if I had written it. I should certainly have starred the murdered apprentices. I should have introduced their ghosts in the last scene, rising out of the estuary, on either side of the vengeful greybeard, blood and fire would have been thrown in the tenor's face, hell would have opened, and on a mixture of *Don Juan* and the *Freischütz* I should have lowered my final curtain.'*

Britten didn't forget these words, and shortly afterwards when he contemplated writing another full-scale opera and found his imagination irresistibly kindled by Herman Melville's posthumous novel, *Billy Budd, Foretopman*, it was to Forster as collaborator that he instinctively turned. With characteristic courage, this septuagenarian novelist and essayist agreed to set out on a new and hazardous career as opera librettist. Hitherto, his experience of dramatic writing had been confined to a couple of open-air pageants; but how deep was his love of music could be seen from the part it had played in his novels and essays. (Who, having read *Where Angels Fear to Tread*, could ever forget his account of the performance of *Lucia di Lammermoor* at Monteriano?) The libretto of *Billy Budd* was the joint creation of himself and Eric Crozier; and, as might be expected after his remarks on *Peter Grimes*, it was conscientiously faithful to the spirit and even the letter of the original.

Melville was an old man of sixty-nine when after twenty years' silence as a

* From 'George Crabbe and Peter Grimes' in *Two Cheers for Democracy*. Arnold, 1951.

novelist he began to write his last story. The first draft of the various Billy Budd manuscripts was dated 16 November 1888; the main revision begun on 2 March 1889; and the story finished on 19 April 1891, a few months before Melville's death. F. Barron Freeman has shown* how the initial short story of sixteen sections, *Baby Budd, Sailor*, was expanded into the novel of thirty-one sections generally known as *Billy Budd, Foretopman.*

'An Inside Narrative' Melville called it, going out of his way to suggest that this was the reason for some of its crudities—'The symmetry of form attainable in pure fiction cannot so readily be achieved in a narration essentially having less to do with fable than with fact.' Indeed, it appears almost as if he were bent on a work of rehabilitation, for he quotes a completely distorted account of the events that led to the execution of Budd, purporting to come from a contemporary naval weekly chronicle at the end of the eighteenth century, and explains that so far this had been the only record of this strange affair. But it would appear that the actual events on which *Billy Budd, Foretopman* is based took place, not in the British Navy at the time of the mutinies of Spithead and the Nore which is the period Melville has chosen for the setting of his story, but in the American Navy nearly half a century later; and the intensity of his interest in what came to be known as the Mackenzie Case can be appreciated from the fact that his first cousin, Guert Gansevoort, was one of the lieutenants on board the brig-of-war *Somers* in 1842 at the time of the so-called mutiny.

The Mackenzie Case is specifically referred to in *Billy Budd, Foretopman.* In explaining the difficulty the drumhead court experienced in trying Billy Budd, Melville wrote: 'Not unlikely they were brought to something more or less akin to that harassed frame of mind which in the year 1842 actuated the commander of the U.S. brig-of-war *Somers* to resolve, under the so-called Articles of War, Articles modelled upon the English Mutiny Act, to resolve upon the execution at sea of a midshipman and two petty-officers as mutineers designing the seizure of the brig. Which resolution was carried out though in a time of peace and within not many days sail of home. An act vindicated by a naval court of inquiry subsequently convened ashore. History, and here cited without comment.' Melville's care in explaining the reasons that actuated the captain of the *Indomitable* in giving his evidence and the drumhead court in reaching their verdict seems indirectly to be aimed at vindicating Gansevoort who as the chief aide of Captain Mackenzie against the 'mutineers' on the *Somers* came in for a good measure of subsequent criticism. It is perhaps worth noting that in June 1888, just five months before Melville started to write *Baby Budd, Sailor*, the case was reopened by the publication of an article by Lieutenant H. D. Smith in the American Magazine entitled *The Mutiny on the Somers.* As by then

* *Melville's Billy Budd*, edited by F. Barron Freeman. Harvard University Press, 1948.

Billy Budd: Billy Budd (Theodor Uppman) and Captain Vere (Peter Pears) in the original Covent Garden production of 1951

Gansevoort had been dead for twenty years, Melville must have felt that no time was to be lost if he wished to present the events in their proper perspective.

But this material could be used only after it had been digested and assimilated to its fictional purpose. As Freeman says, 'the "inner" drama of Billy Budd uses the Mackenzie Case in the same way that it uses *The Naval History of Great Britain* by William James and Melville's own *White Jacket*: as a factual source on which to build an "interior" drama of the forces of fate'.*

Here, as in *Peter Grimes*, the grit of actuality—actual persons and actual incidents—was apparently the prime cause of the long process of artistic secretion that built up, first, an independent literary work and, subsequently, an opera; and it would seem that, consciously or subconsciously as far as Britten was concerned, the actual element behind the fictional treatment still retained a powerful germinating force.

The action in *Billy Budd* takes place on the seventy-four HMS *Indomitable* during the summer of 1797. This was the moment when the mutinies of Spithead and the Nore had just occurred. Conditions in the English Navy were particularly brutalizing, cruel and horrible then, and

* F. Barron Freeman, op. cit.

there is little doubt that the men's grievances were justified; but the authorities were naturally appalled by the hint of revolution at a time when every ounce of energy had to be put into the life-and-death struggle with France.

The *Indomitable* is at sea alone, on her way to join the Mediterranean fleet. Like so many of the ships in the Navy at that time, she is short of her full complement of men: so when a passing merchantman named *The Rights of Man* is sighted, a boarding party is sent off, and among others Billy Budd is impressed from her crew. Billy is a handsome, pleasant fellow, sound in heart and limb, whose only physical defect is an occasional stammer. He gets on well with everyone on board ship, and everyone likes him—except the master-at-arms, John Claggart. From the outset Claggart pursues him with hidden but implacable malevolence. Natural depravity is bent on corrupting natural innocence and encompassing its downfall. But in plotting Billy's destruction, he reckons without the ship's captain, Edward Fairfax Vere, a bachelor of about forty, known throughout the Navy as 'Starry Vere'. A cultured, aristocratic man, popular with both officers and men, and a shrewd judge of character, Vere immediately sees through Claggart's vamped up charges against Billy. He confronts the sailor with the master-at-arms in his cabin; but the horror of Claggart's false accusations so staggers Billy that it brings out his lurking defect and his power to answer is momentarily taken from him by his stammer. He stands there, tongue-tied, until a kindly gesture from the Captain releases something inside him, and he strikes Claggart a fierce blow with his naked fist. Claggart falls—dead. Captain Vere immediately summons a drumhead court. Billy is tried under the articles of war for striking and killing his superior in rank and is condemned to be hanged from the yardarm, a sentence that is carried out at dawn the following day.

The most important respect in which Forster and Crozier have departed from Melville's story is by letting Vere live to a ripe old age—according to Melville, he was mortally wounded in a sea-fight a few years later, just before Trafalgar—and introducing him in a Prologue and Epilogue where he appears as an old man ruminating on the past. At first he finds it difficult to recall the details of those early days; but what remains indelibly impressed on his mind is that in the faraway summer of 1797 someone had blessed him, someone had saved him. Who was it? As recollection comes crowding back, he remembers his old ship the *Indomitable* and the strange, sad story of Billy Budd.

This device of a Prologue and Epilogue is important for a number of reasons. In the first place, the sea in *Billy Budd* is an isolating medium, the element on which the all-male microcosm, the crew of the *Indomitable*, depends for its temporary suspension. To see the ship from without, alone in the centre of its circumscribing horizon, it is necessary to provide the

Billy Budd: The full muster on the main deck and the quarter deck before Billy Budd is hanged at the yardarm, in the original Covent Garden production of 1951

audience with a view-point outside the field of immediate action. Secondly, the final scene (the hanging) is so tense and its impact so overwhelming that time is needed for the audience to recover. Thirdly, the fact that the action is seen through the eyes of an old man who calls it to mind after the lapse of many years parallels the case of Melville himself composing the story at the age of seventy a short time before his death. Finally, it places the Captain at the centre of the action, showing him caught on the horns of a cruel dilemma. As sole witness of Claggart's death, he finds fate has thrust on him the power of life or death over a human being of whose essential innocence he is fully convinced. The iron discipline of duty prevails over the dictates of his heart—what Melville calls 'the feminine in men'—and he allows Billy to die. The fact that Billy understands and forgives him may be the means of his ultimate salvation, but cannot completely reassure him, for (as he cries out in the Epilogue) he could have saved him, and Billy knew it.

This focusing on Vere puts him into what Henry James called 'the compositional centre'* of the drama; and the heroic aspect of the character is accentuated by the vocal casting. Vere is a tenor; Claggart, as befits the villain of the piece, a bass; Billy, a baritone. (In this connection it is interesting to note that in his one-act opera, *Billy Budd* (1949), Ghedini cast Vere as bass, Claggart as tenor and Billy as baritone.)

Some of the overtones in Melville's descriptions of the characters have been dropped. For instance, he more than once implies that the relationship

* Cf. p. 116.

of Vere to Budd is like that of father to son—this is particularly stressed when Vere communicates the finding of the court to the condemned sailor, and Melville suggests that at that moment Vere may have 'caught Billy to his heart even as Abraham may have caught young Isaac on the brink of resolutely offering him up in obedience to the exacting behest'*—but Forster and Crozier omit this, and in any case such an implied relationship would be contradicted by the vocal casting.

There certainly appear to be sufficient indications of unconscious or latent homosexuality in Melville's description of Claggart to justify Freeman's statement that 'the psychological key to Claggart's antipathy is not conscious suppression but unconscious repression of a perverted desire for the boy whose downfall he plotted';† but most of these indications are missing from the opera libretto, though Forster and Crozier plumb the depths of Claggart's character in the introspective monologue they give him in Act I, scene iii, '*O beauty, O handsomeness, goodness!*' No such soliloquy occurs in Melville; but there is excellent operatic precedent for it in Iago's Credo in Verdi's *Otello*. Claggart sings, '*If love still lives and grows strong where I cannot enter, what hope is there in my own dark world for me?*' So beauty, handsomeness, goodness, as personified by the Handsome Sailor, must be destroyed. In the libretto the clash between the two men is shown to be one facet of the eternal struggle between the powers of good and evil. As W. H. Auden wrote in his poem *Herman Melville*:‡

Evil is unspectacular and always human,
And shares our bed and eats at our own table,
And we are introduced to Goodness every day,
Even in drawing-rooms among a crowd of faults;
He has a name like Billy and is almost perfect
But wears a stammer like a decoration:
And every time they meet the same thing has to happen;
It is the Evil that is helpless like a lover
And has to pick a quarrel and succeeds,
And both are openly destroyed before our eyes.

One further change made by Forster and Crozier should here be noted. It was necessary for them to include in their libretto both the novice who receives a flogging for dereliction of duty (a passage in *Billy Budd, Foretopman* that is much more reserved and moderate in tone than the comparable passage in *White Jacket* describing the scourging of young Peter of the mizzentop) and the afterguardsman who comes to Billy at night to

* It is worth remembering that the first work Britten composed after *Billy Budd* was his *Canticle II: Abraham and Isaac.*

† F. Barron Freeman, op. cit.

‡ From *Another Time.*

bribe him to join the mutineers. But whereas in Melville these two characters, though rather shadowy, are quite distinct, in the libretto they are fused together. Humiliated and cowed by his experience, the novice is driven by the fear of further punishment to agree to become Claggart's cat's paw and by tempting Billy to compromise and betray him. A minor character admittedly, but one that Forster and Crozier portray 'in the round'.

The *Billy Budd* libretto is written almost entirely in prose. The only exceptions are the words of some of the interpolated shanties, a few free verse passages, Claggart's blank verse denunciation of Billy to the Captain, and the Ballad of Billy in the Darbies, twenty lines chosen from the thirty-two-line poem with which Melville's narrative ends. The realistic treatment of a subject at one or two removes from actual fact seems to have imposed a predominantly prosaic idiom on the librettists. Some of Melville's dialogue has been preserved intact: e.g. phrases like *Handsomely done, my lad. And handsome is as handsome did it, too!—Jemmy Legs is down on you!—A man-trap may be under his ruddy-tipped daisies.—Fated boy, what have you done!—Struck by an angel of God! Yet the angel must hang!* And there are even one or two passages where Forster and Crozier have based their text on some of Melville's discarded drafts. For instance, in the gun-deck scene, Billy tells his friend Dansker of the Chaplain's visit. '*Chaplain's been here before you—kind—and good his story, of the good boy hung and gone to glory, hung for the likes of me.*' This is a direct citation from one of the discarded fragments of the Ballad of Billy in the Darbies:

Kind of him ay, to enter Lone Bay
And down on his marrow-bones here and pray
For the like of me. And good his story—
Of the good boy hung and gone to glory,
Hung for the likes of me.

It might have been thought that the predominance of prose would have tended to make the opera ponderous and heavy; but this is not so. Those prose sections that are dealt with on the near-declamation level proceed quickly and lightly: those that are set as passages of *arioso* or as ensembles take on a lyrical quality. Persons who have not seen the text printed as prose in the libretto would find it difficult to believe that such numbers as the post-flogging trio for the Novice, his friend and a small chorus of sailors with its refrain '*Lost for ever on the endless sea*' (I, i), or the duet between the Sailing Master and the First Lieutenant '*Don't like the French*' (I, ii), or the '*We've no choice*' trio between the First and Second Lieutenants and the Sailing Master at the end of the court-martial (II, ii), or Billy's farewell to life (II, iii) are not written to a definite metrical scheme embellished with rhyme or assonance. The prose is so supple and lissom in texture that it seems to take on some of the attributes of verse; and, in fact, as pointed out above, verse fragments are occasionally to be found embedded in it.

The original version of 1951 was written in four acts, each act being a complete and continuous movement, whether or not it was subdivided into scenes; and Britten was careful to bind Acts I and II closely together, and also Acts III and IV, by arranging almost literal musical joins between the end of Act I and the beginning of Act II, and the end of Act III and beginning of Act IV. But the action falls naturally into two parts—exposition and catastrophe—rather than four; and the impact of the work in its original form was considerably weakened by the necessity to break the action at no fewer than three different points. In 1960 he decided to make a revision (first heard in a BBC broadcast on 13 November 1960) in which the four acts were reduced to two. The main change came at the end of the original Act I, where in the 1951 version there had been a Captain's muster on deck, at the climax of which 'Starry Vere' appeared and harangued his men. In the 1960 version, this is substantially altered. Instead of a muster, the whistles sound for a changing of the watch; and instead of being roused by Vere's rhetorical 'Death or Victory' speech, the men discuss their captain in his absence, their enthusiasm proving so infectious that Billy catches fire and apostrophizes him as 'Star of the morning'—

Starry, I'll follow you . . .
Follow thro' darkness, never you fear . . .
I'd die to save you, ask for to die . . .
I'll follow you all I can, follow you for ever.

This means that Vere does not make his first appearance until the following scene where he is discovered reading Plutarch in his cabin. The other changes in the 1960 version are minimal, consisting mainly of a few cuts in the Vere/Claggart dialogue when the Master-at-arms denounces Billy as a mutineer. The music in each of the two revised acts is continuous; and this is an undoubted improvement. The following table makes these changes clear:

1951 *Version*		1960 *Version*		
	Prologue		Prologue	
Act I		Act I	Scene i	The Main-deck and Quarter-deck
Act II	Scene i		Scene ii	The Captain's Cabin
	Scene ii		Scene iii	The Berth-deck
Act III	Scene i	Act II	Scene i	The Main-deck and Quarter-deck
	Scene ii		Scene ii	The Captain's Cabin
Act IV	Scene i		Scene iii	A bay of the upper gun-deck
	Scene ii		Scene iv	The Main-deck and Quarter-deck
	Epilogue		Epilogue	

II

There is an analogy, though it should not be pushed too far, between the form of this opera and that of a symphony. The first scene of Act I is expository, most of the characters being introduced singly or in groups. The two following scenes are the equivalent of a slow movement—a reflective serenade below deck in two scenes, the first showing the Captain and some of his officers enjoying an after-dinner conversation, during which they hear distant singing from the Berth-deck, and the second showing the sailors singing shanties before slinging hammocks and turning in for the night. The first scene of Act II serves as a scherzo, namely the whole of the chase after the French frigate and the call to action stations. The remainder of the act provides the climax and *dénouement*.

The opposition between what Melville (in a discarded draft) called 'innocence and infamy, spiritual depravity and fair repute' lies at the heart of Britten's score. The opening bar of the Prologue with its quiet rippling movement contains a clash between B flat and B natural which typifies this struggle:

Ex. 50

As the two melodies unfold, they seem to be establishing a bitonality of E flat major and C major; but in reality the clash is much sharper and more powerful—B flat major against B minor—and this is confirmed by another passage in the Prologue where a bitonal B flat major/B minor chord thrice repeated encloses a musical phrase later to be associated with Claggart, the first part of which is related to the first of the two keys and the second part (the descending fourths) to the second.

Ex. 51

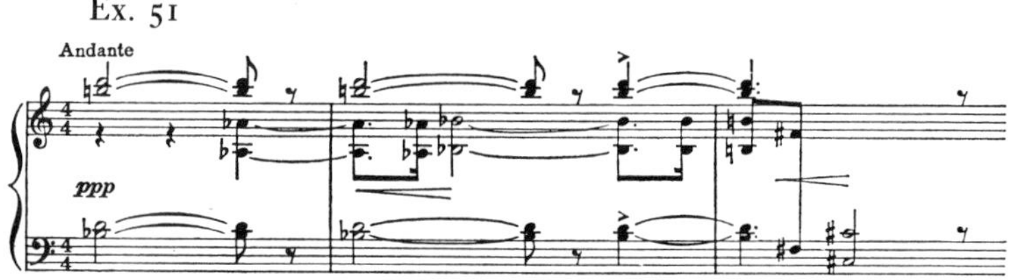

At the beginning of Act I when the lights go up on the *Indomitable* with the men holy-stoning her maindeck, the same notes are there; but now the B flat has suffered an enharmonic change to A sharp and the chord has lost its bitonal implications.

Ex. 52

The bitonal clash between two keys with their roots a semitone apart is closely associated with Claggart's hatred for Budd. Before Claggart's first entry (I, i) the orchestra is playing a theme in G major connected with the boarding party; but as soon as he is addressed by the First Lieutenant, the music clouds over and the key changes to G sharp minor. The same key relationship governs the initial airs of the two characters: Billy's exultant '*Billy Budd, king of the birds*' opens in E major; Claggart's '*Was I born yesterday?*' in F minor. Similarly, the A major fight between Billy and Squeak in the third scene of Act I is interrupted by Claggart's B flat arrival; and a few bars later as the men sling their hammocks in the bays, a sailor (off) sings a shanty '*Over the water, over the ocean*' in E major, while the orchestra is still meditating in F minor on the way Claggart has just lashed out at one of the boys with his rattan. In the following act the temperature of the music drops each time Claggart approaches the Captain in order to denounce Budd, and the key drops too—this time from G minor to F sharp minor, not major.

The enharmonic change from B flat to A sharp that was noted at the beginning of Act I (see Ex. 52 above) occurs in reverse at the end of Act II scene iv just after Billy has been hanged at the yardarm. This is one of the most astonishing and frightening moments in the opera. Melville describes how at that moment an inarticulate noise like 'the freshet-wave of a torrent suddenly swelled by pouring showers in the tropical mountains' burst forth from the men massed on the ship's open deck. In a wordless fugal stretto sung so quickly that they sound like a pack of wild beasts, the sailors seem for the moment to be on the verge of mutiny. (This passage is in E major.) But the officers order all hands to pipe down, and the command is given on B flat.

Ex. 53

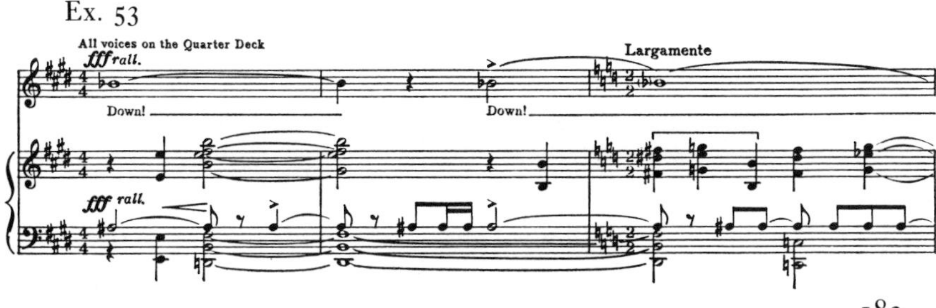

For some bars an attempt is made to assimilate this note enharmonically as an A sharp into the Lydian mode of E: but ultimately force of habit is too much for the men, they obey the command and disperse, and the music resignedly modulates to the key of B flat major. At this point the music pivots on A sharp/B flat as if on the hinge of fate.

The final resolution of this bitonal conflict comes at the end of the Epilogue. Once again the phrase formerly associated with Claggart is enclosed by the bitonal chord (as in Ex. 51); but this time Claggart's descending fourths have disappeared, and in their place there is a fanfare—fanfares in this score are usually associated with Billy Budd—spread over the common chord of B major. At the same time Vere's voice is accompanied by a figure earlier associated with Billy's song of farewell (II, iii), with the result that the final cadence contains a double clash—B major against B flat major, and B flat major against A major—and the ultimate resolution on B flat major comes with all the force and finality of a double resolution:

Ex. 54

Just as there is an occasional enharmonic ambivalence about the music, so there is sometimes an ambivalence between the music and the action, and the music and the words. A problem posited by the action may receive its solution in purely musical terms; and the listener must be prepared to recognize and accept this.

For instance, it is rewarding to examine the musical and psychological metamorphoses of a simple musical phrase of a fifth and a semitone. In the

Prologue, Vere as an old man is bewildered and troubled as he tries to remember what he did in the far-off case of Billy Budd, and why he did it.

Ex. 55

Right at the beginning of Act I the phrase appears in the shanty sung by the sailors holy-stoning the deck:

Ex. 56

When Billy Budd is impressed, he shouts a farewell to his old comrades on *The Rights of Man* and his words fall naturally into the simple tune of the shanty:

Ex. 57

Some of the officers on the *Indomitable*, however, misunderstand this spontaneous greeting of Billy's and take it as an unbecoming reference to the liberal and suspect views expressed by Thomas Paine in his book *The Rights of Man*; and as the chorus echoes Billy's phrase, they order the decks to be cleared. Henceforward this innocuous phrase is associated with the idea of mutiny. The officers, when discussing a glass of wine with the Captain after dinner, identify the phrase with Spithead and the Nore (I, ii):

Ex. 58

The oboes bring it back in sinister guise when the Novice tempts Billy to join the gang which he says is plotting mutiny on the ship (Ex. 50a); the muted trumpets transmute it into glittering guineas to bribe him (Ex. 59b):

Ex. 59a

Ex. 59b

When Claggart confronts Billy before Captain Vere and accuses him of mutiny, the motif has become the skeleton of the phrase:

Ex. 60

Its final appearance, apart from a repetition of Ex. 55 in the Epilogue, is in the scene already mentioned that takes place immediately after the hanging; and there it forms the subject of the wordless fugal stretto:

Ex. 61

It has already been suggested that fanfares and sennets are closely associated with Billy Budd himself. The air is filled with these calls when the boarding party returns from *The Rights of Man* bringing Billy as an impressed man. Simple arpeggio figures usually accompany his songs—e.g. '*Billy Budd, king of the birds!*'; the passage in his duet with Dansker (I, iii) where he sings '*Ay! and the wind and the sails and being aloft and the deck below so small and the sea so wide*'; his duet with the Captain when he thinks he's about to be promoted (II, ii); his Ballad in the Darbies, and his song of farewell (II, iii). All these are obvious instances, so obvious that it would hardly seem worth while mentioning them, were it not for the astonishing transformation of this device at the end of Act II, scene ii.

Billy is in a stateroom at the back of the cabin where the drumhead court has been held, and it is left to Captain Vere to communicate the finding of the court to him. Melville says that 'what took place at this interview was never known'; and Forster and Crozier follow Melville in this, leaving the death sentence to be communicated to him off-stage at the end of the act. Britten could have ignored the problem and allowed the curtain to fall immediately after Vere's exit; but he chose to tackle it musically and keeps the curtain up for over a minute on an empty stage, while slow heavy chords for the whole orchestra, or strings, or woodwind, or brass, or horns, ranging through many gradations of volume, tell of the fatal interview behind the closed door. As can be seen from the few bars quoted, the passage is really a widely spread arpeggio of F major, harmonized with chromatic intensity and so tremendously augmented as to give the effect of a simple signal seen through an extremely powerful telescope—a rainbow of hope:

Ex. 62

Largo

As for the chords themselves, smaller groups of them appear in the following scene to accompany Billy's farewell to the world—'*I'm strong, and I know it, and I'll stay strong, and that's all, and that's enough*'—and also at the end of the Epilogue when Vere sings '*But I've sighted a sail in the storm, the far-shining sail, and I'm content.*'

One further example of ambivalence deserves special mention.

Perhaps the most moving moment in the first act is the compassionate trio after the Novice's flogging:

Ex. 63

The saxophone melody reappears in the second act when Claggart threatens the Novice with a further flogging if he refuses to tempt Billy. After this scene the Novice never reappears; but when at the end of Act II, scene ii

Vere sings '*Beauty, handsomeness, goodness, it is for me to destroy you. I, Edward Fairfax Vere, captain of the "Indomitable", lost with all hands on the infinite sea*', the Novice's phrase reappears in a turbulent orchestral interjection and provides a poignant comment on the brutality of the punishment devised by man for man.

Ex. 64

Any analysis of the score of *Billy Budd*, however penetrating, would fail in its purpose if it gave the impression that the opera is abstruse or difficult to listen to. The scoring is light and transparent throughout. As soon as the lights go up on Act I, the music captures the feeling of a ship at sea: the shrill sound of the wind in the rigging, the bustle of life on deck, and the underlying swell of the ocean. The second and third scenes with their two beautifully interlocked serenades, show first the officers and then the men during the quiet interval between supper and sleep when there is time to relax and meditate. The second act starts with an alarum that is none the less exciting for being in vain. After the exhilaration of the chase after the French frigate, the mood of frustration induced by waiting returns with the mist, and in this atmosphere Vere witnesses the drama of Claggart and Budd unroll before his eyes with the inevitability of fate and is powerless to intervene.

The final scenes are brief, but everything in them is placed with an unerring sense of effectiveness. Billy's Ballad in the Darbies is one of Britten's happiest inventions—a slow, sleepy tune to a low-pitched, sluggish accompaniment that changes its chords reluctantly as Billy sings '*Roll me over fair. I'm sleepy and the oozy weeds about me twist*', and reminds one of Hylas' song in *The Trojans*.

Some critics have suggested that it would have been an improvement if Budd, being the hero of the opera, had been cast as a tenor instead of a baritone; but in that case the setting of this Ballad would undoubtedly have suffered, for the low pitch at which it is written and the tone colour of that particular range of a baritone voice are essential to its effect.

The march to which the whole crew assembles at the beginning of Act II, scene iv to witness the hanging is a fugato mainly for percussion, and its characteristic rhythm containing both triplets and quintuplets spills over into the Epilogue, where its pianissimo roll on the timpani accompanies Vere's recital of Billy's burial at sea and forms the wake of the *Indomitable* as she disappears from view in the minds of the audience.

There is one final comment to be made. When it was known that Britten was writing an opera with an all-male cast, there were some who prophesied failure because they claimed that without women's voices the monotony of tone colour would be unendurable. (Even Méhul in his biblical opera *Joseph* (1807), where there are no female characters at all, decided to entrust the part of Benjamin to a soprano.) After the first performance of *Billy Budd* this particular criticism disappeared because in fact it was discovered that Britten's writing for this all-male cast was extraordinarily varied. Apart from the seventeen individual characters, who include five tenors, eight baritones, one bass-baritone and three basses, he calls for a main-deck chorus of thirty-six, a quarter-deck chorus of fourteen, four Midshipmen, whose voices should appear to be breaking, and ten powder-monkeys, who are not required to sing, but whose shrill chattering voices form an important element in the build-up of the big chorus in Act II, scene i when chase is given to the French frigate.

The verdict on *Billy Budd* must be that between them Forster and Crozier wrote one of the best and most faithful librettos to be based on a literary masterpiece, and Britten created a score of outstanding psychological subtlety. The work rouses a wide range of emotions; but perhaps the dominant one is compassion—compassion for the weak and unfortunate, for those who are homeless, the victims of fate; compassion for suffering in all its forms.

VIII
Gloriana

I

In the past there have been few English dynastic operas and few occasions on which a reigning monarch has played a direct part in supporting opera in this country.

Albion and Albanius was a dynastic opera in honour of what Dryden called 'the double Restoration of Charles II' (Albion). Unfortunately Charles's death delayed its production until 1685, when Dryden introduced some appropriate references to James II (Albanius) and it was produced at the Queen's Theatre in Dorset Garden; but its run was brought to an untimely conclusion by the news of the rising of the Duke of Monmouth in the West. In any case, the music provided by Louis Grabu seems to have been so indifferent that no one regretted the opera's demise. The same criticism seems to have been true of Clayton's setting of Addison's *Rosamond* (1707): but there the dynasty celebrated was that of the Duke and Duchess of Marlborough.

When the Hanoverians succeeded to the throne, Handel gained a considerable measure of royal favour; and both George I and II contributed towards the cost of Italian opera in London between 1722 and 1744, the royal subscription of £1,000 being paid annually to The Royal Academy of Music (Undertakers of the Opera), except in 1734 when it was paid personally to Handel himself and during the three years 1739–41 when it lapsed.* Handel's only attempt at a dynastic opera was *Riccardo Primo, Re d'Inghilterra* (1727) written on the occasion of George II's Coronation.

After Handel's death Royal patronage declined for about a century: but, thanks largely to the musical sensibility of the Prince Consort, Queen Victoria displayed an active interest in opera in the early years of her reign. During her husband's lifetime, she frequently attended performances at Covent Garden and Drury Lane, and in particular gave her patronage to the various Pyne-Harrison seasons of English opera that started in 1857. When

* See 'Finance and Patronage in Handel's life' in *Concerning Handel* by William C. Smith Cassell, 1948.

Wallace's *Lurline* was successfully produced at Covent Garden in 1860, she is reported to have advised Louisa Pyne and William Harrison to make money out of it as long as it would run. The Prince Consort's death in 1861 put an end to her public theatre-going; and although there were occasional command performances at Windsor Castle towards the end of the century, her interest in English opera seems to have been confined to urging Sullivan to drop his operetta partnership with Gilbert in order to write a 'grand' opera, a royal command that led to the production of *Ivanhoe* in 1891.

Queen Alexandra took a keen personal interest in opera. She frequently attended performances at the Royal Opera House during Edward VII's reign; so it is not altogether surprising to find that *La Fanciulla del West* (1910) was dedicated *A Sua Maestà La Regina Alessandra d'Inghilterra—rispettoso omaggio di Giacomo Puccini.* But at this period so few English operas were performed in London that it is doubtful if members of the Royal Family could have seen any of them at Covent Garden, even if they had particularly wanted to.

There was accordingly no precedent for the fact that in May 1952 Her Majesty Queen Elizabeth II gave her approval to the suggestion that Britten should write a Coronation opera on the theme of Elizabeth I and Essex, and that later Her Majesty agreed to accept the dedication of the work and attend its first performance at a special gala on 8 June 1953 in honour of her Coronation.

An English historical subject was something of a novelty so far as English opera was concerned. Different historical periods had often been used as settings for romantic operas; but if historical characters and episodes were introduced, they were usually treated with the same freedom as if they were creations of fiction. It is true that during the Commonwealth Sir William Davenant had evolved a new type of operatic representation based on historical subjects that were then about a century old—*The Siege of Rhodes* (1656), *The Cruelty of the Spaniards in Peru* (1658), and *The History of Sir Francis Drake* (1659)—but his example was not followed up. This lack of initiative was all the more surprising since the Elizabethan playwrights, particularly Shakespeare, had given a strong lead in the writing of English historical plays.

Later on, there was the example of Russian musicians to note. The nationalist school of the nineteenth century frequently chose patriotic themes for its operas, e.g. Cavos's *Ivan Susanin* (1815), Glinka's *A Life for the Czar* (1836), Rimsky-Korsakov's *The Maid of Pskov* (1873), Mussorgsky's *Boris Godunov* (1874), and Borodin's *Prince Igor* (1890). A similar tendency might easily have been observable in nineteenth-century Italy, had not local censorship proved so sensitive over the political implications of historical subjects that frequently places, names and dates had to be changed.

The twentieth century has produced new standards of historical accuracy and new methods of historical research. Invention and fancy are at a discount: it is selection that counts—and presentation.

Just as Pushkin based his tragedy of *Boris Godunov* on Nicolai Karamsin's *History of Russia*, so William Plomer went to J. E. Neale and Lytton Strachey for his sources. *Elizabeth and Essex* was in fact the starting-point for the libretto of *Gloriana*. Strachey had tried to outline this episode of Elizabeth's old age—'a tragic history' he called it—with something of the detachment and self-sufficiency of a work of art; but the bewildering richness of life in Elizabethan England seems to have defeated him. He himself confessed that 'the more clearly we perceive it, the more remote that singular universe becomes'.* The Elizabethans were more paradoxical, elusive, ambiguous and irrational than the Victorians; and profound social changes in the intervening period had left Strachey little or nothing to debunk. *Elizabeth and Essex* is not a completely successful book; but it contains numerous dramatic cues, and it was this aspect of it that appealed so strongly to Britten and Plomer.

In the process of selection, a number of important persons and episodes had to be discarded. Of the persons, perhaps the most notable was Sir Francis Bacon. His character was too subtle, complex and compelling, and would have demanded too much attention in the opera. But it must be admitted that his total disappearance—and there is no mention of him in the libretto—seriously weakens Essex's character. For a considerable time he loomed like a grey eminence in the background, and many of Essex's squabbles with the Queen seem to have been concerned with her unwillingness to listen to his pleas that Bacon should be granted preferment. Yet when the final crisis came and Essex was arraigned for high treason, Bacon acted without scruple or hesitation as counsel for the prosecution, and by his handling of the case helped to bring his former benefactor to the block on Tower Hill.

A less important person who was omitted was Elizabeth's godson Sir John Harington. In *Portraits in Miniature*, Strachey described one of Sir John's adventures as follows: 'He was summoned by Essex to join his ill-fated expedition to Ireland, in command of a troop of horse. In Ireland, with a stretch of authority which was bitterly resented by the Queen, Harington was knighted by the rash Lord Deputy, and afterwards, when disaster came thick upon disaster, he followed his patron back to London. In fear and trembling, he presented himself before the enraged Elizabeth. "What!" she cried, "did the fool bring you too?" The terrified poet fell upon his knees, while the Queen, as he afterwards described it, "chafed much, walked fastly too and fro, and looked with discomposure in her visage". Then suddenly

* Lytton Strachey, *Elizabeth and Essex*.

rushing towards him, she caught hold of his girdle. "By God's Son", she shouted, "I am no Queen, and that man is above me!" His stammering excuses were cut short with a "Go back to your business!" uttered in such a tone that Sir John, not staying to be bidden twice, fled out of the room, and fled down to Kelston, "as if all the Irish rebels had been at his heels".' Plomer ignored this intensely dramatic material.*

There was also the celebrated scene in the Council Chamber, when Essex, obstructed by the Queen in the matter of the Irish appointment, lost his temper and turned his back on her. Crying 'Go to the devil!' she boxed his ears, whereat he clapped his hand to his sword and shouted 'This is an outrage that I will not put up with. I would not have borne it from your father's hands.' Plomer did not use this episode either, though he allowed Essex, to make a brief, though hardly noticeable, reference to it in Act II, scene iii.

Cuffe appears in the libretto as a minor character, a feed to Essex. More extended treatment is given to Cecil, Raleigh and Mountjoy, though the result is still somewhat perfunctory when their operatic characters are compared with historical reality. The two women—the Countess of Essex and Penelope, Lady Rich (Essex's sister)—emerge more successfully, partly because less is actually known about them, and the librettist has had a freer hand accordingly. Many facets of Essex's character are shown: the proud and tetchy nobleman; the headstrong lover; the romantic advocate of the simple life; the ambitious courtier; the sullen conspirator; the unsuccessful general. But he disappears completely after his return from Ireland; and although his final act of treason—his march through the City of London and call to insurrection—is referred to obliquely in Act III, scene ii, he himself is not shown at the head of his followers, nor does he appear in connection with his trial and condemnation.

So far it would seem as if the historical picture presented by the opera is a partial and incomplete one. But one character remains—Elizabeth herself—and as soon as she is considered, the whole perspective of the opera changes and everything seems to fall into focus. It is then clear that the episode of Essex has been used only in so far as it helps to place in relief her character as a Queen and a woman who, though ageing, is still at the height of her intellectual powers; and it is here that Britten and Plomer have scored their most incontrovertible success. Even a scene like the Masque at the Norwich Guildhall (II, i), which ostensibly has nothing to do with the plot, is vital to the opera, since it shows that it was an important part of the Sovereign's functions to accept graciously the ceremonial that inevitably accompanied her public progresses through her kingdom.

* It is true that in the original version of the opera Sir John Harington made a brief unexplained appearance in the epilogue where his participation in the Irish expedition was specifically mentioned, but this was omitted in the 1966 revision.

Elizabeth first appears (I, I) leaving a tilting ground after a tournament. It is one of her public appearances, and she is accompanied by a retinue and preceded by trumpeters. Her pompous entry disturbs a brawl between Essex and Mountjoy, whom she has just honoured for his prowess in the tiltyard with the gift of a golden queen from her set of chessmen. She summons her subjects to hear her judgment and forbids Essex and Mountjoy to continue their private quarrel. A feature of this scene is the loyal chorus:

Green leaves are we,
Red rose our golden Queen,
O crownèd rose among the leaves so green!

The following scene (I, ii) is laid in one of her private apartments at Nonesuch. First, she discusses public and private business with Cecil, whose precepts on government give the impression of wheels moving within wheels. Essex arrives. Dismissing Cecil, she abandons herself to the pleasure of his company, well aware of the weakness of his character as well as the lure of his charm. After singing two lute songs to entertain her, the second of which is a setting of a poem '*Happy were he*' actually written by the original Earl of Essex, he urges his claim to be sent to Ireland to conquer the rebel Tyrone; but she easily evades giving an answer. Left alone, she soliloquizes:

If life were love and love were true,
Then could I love thee through and through!
But God gave me a sceptre,
    The burden and the glory—
I must not lay them down:
    I live and reign a virgin,
        Will die in honour,
Leave a refulgent crown!

In the second act she is shown on two ceremonial occasions: the first at Norwich, where she receives the homage of the citizens and is entertained with a rustic masque; and the second at the Palace of Whitehall, where she enjoys an evening of dancing. These are separated by a short scene in the garden of Essex House where Mountjoy's secret tryst with Lady Rich is interrupted by the appearance of Essex complaining to his wife of his treatment by the Queen. Lady Rich, Essex and Mountjoy discuss the possibility of seizing the reins of State, while Lady Essex counsels caution.

During the dancing at the Palace of Whitehall (II, iii), there is an episode that shows how spiteful Elizabeth could be, particularly to women who were closely connected with men she was interested in. Noticing that Lady Essex is dressed with special magnificence, she gets hold of her dress through a stratagem and puts it on herself. It is a gross misfit, and the effect is grotesque. She parades in it before the Court to the extreme confusion of Lady Essex. In all this the librettist has kept fairly close to historical accuracy, his only major change being to transfer the affair of the dress from Lady Mary Howard, whom the Queen actually suspected of an intrigue with Essex, to Lady Essex herself. The attack on Lady Essex is so savage and wilful that when the Queen sweeps off stage, the feelings of the group of would-be conspirators (Lady Rich, Essex and Mountjoy) are roused to fury. First they seek to comfort Lady Essex—'*Good Frances, do not weep*'—and then Essex bursts out with his bitter taunt, '*Her conditions are as crooked as her carcass!*' Suddenly Elizabeth returns in state with her councillors and announces she has appointed Essex Lord Deputy in Ireland. The moment is brilliantly chosen. At a stroke Essex's heart empties of all rancour. He accepts the honour and charge, and assures his Sovereign '*With God's help I will have victory, and you shall have peace.*'

Vain words! The campaign is a calamity; Tyrone and his Irish kerns are unvanquished. Essex, seeing the extent of his failure, panics and, leaving his troops in the lurch, returns hurriedly, unannounced, to England. He breaks in on the Queen early in the morning at Nonesuch, while she is at her toilet 'in a dressing-gown, unpainted, without her wig, her grey hair hanging in wisps about her face, and her eyes starting from her head'.* Surprised though she is by his sudden irruption, not for one moment does she lose command of the situation. Essex talks of forgiveness, babbles of foes who beset him in England, reminds her of his love—but all to no purpose. Elizabeth knows instinctively he has failed her trust, and after he has left her presence, her view is confirmed by Cecil. She makes up her mind. Essex must be kept under surveillance lest he and his followers prove a danger to the realm. To Cecil she confesses:

I have failed to tame my thoroughbred.
He is still too proud,
And I must break his will
And pull down his great heart.
It is I who have to rule.

Nevertheless, Essex and his followers break out in an abortive attempt to rouse the citizens of London, the rising goes off at half-cock, and Essex is proclaimed a traitor (III, ii).

The final scene (III, iii) begins after Essex's trial for treason, when he has been found guilty and condemned to death. The verdict is communicated to the Queen, who for the moment hesitates to sign her favourite's death warrant. Then she grants an audience to Lady Essex and Lady Rich, who

* Lytton Strachey, op. cit.

Gloriana: Lord Mountjoy (Geraint Evans), Lady Essex (Monica Sinclair) and Penelope, Lady Rich (Jennifer Vyvyan) plead for the life of the Earl of Essex with Queen Elizabeth I (Joan Cross) in the original Covent Garden production of 1953

both beg for his life. To Lady Essex she is gracious, promising protection for his children. She is antagonized, however, by Lady Rich with her obstinate, insolent importuning. The Queen sees that further delay would be fatal. Summoning up all her fortitude, she signs the warrant.

At this point in the opera, the stage darkens, the Queen is left alone, and there is an epilogue during which time and place become of less and less importance. This is a passage that is always likely to excite controversy. Whereas Strachey ended *Queen Victoria* with a virtuoso coda in which he drew together many of the varied strands of Victoria's life in a long last flashback, in *Elizabeth and Essex* he was content with a final section depicting the gradual stages of Elizabeth's final dissolution. This has been used by Britten and Plomer as basis for a preview of six brief episodes that were to occur after Essex's beheading and before Elizabeth's death. A fully orchestrated version of Essex's second lute-song '*Happy were he*' accompanies these episodes. Many of the words in this epilogue are based on actually recorded speech. Only three phrases are actually sung by Elizabeth, two of them echoes of Essex's lute-song:

In some unhaunted desert . . .
There might he sleep secure . . .
Mortua, mortua, sed non sepulta . . .

Otherwise the dialogue is melodramatic, the music being interrupted to admit speech over sustained tremolo strings, wind, or percussion. The procedure may be unorthodox, but it is undeniably effective in the theatre. Nearly all the words—particularly Elizabeth's speech to the audience, which is derived from her Golden Speech to Parliament—are given maximum clarity; and the lute-song itself rings out nobly in its full orchestral apotheosis, cracked though it be by the melodramatic interruptions.

The whole opera ends with an off-stage repeat of the chorus '*Green leaves are we*' that dies away into deepest silence.

It should be added that a few revisions were made to the score at the time of its revival at Sadler's Wells Theatre in 1966. These affected mainly the Queen's Soliloquy and Prayer (I, ii) and the Epilogue (III, iii).

II

Gloriana is the only through-composed opera of Britten's in which the acts are not unbroken musical entities. Each of the eight scenes, which make up the opera's three acts, is complete in itself and has attached to it a brief orchestral prelude that is played before the curtain rises. The result is that, while the opera lacks the cumulative musical flow of *Peter Grimes*, or *The Rape of Lucretia*, or *The Turn of the Screw*, it provides a succession of vivid self-contained tableaux.

The prelude to Act I, scene i, which is more extended than any of the others, repeats a device originally used in *Peter Grimes*. It gives a graphic musical description of the jousting in the lists, with each percussive charge introduced by a lively sennet on the brass; and when the curtain rises, the same music is repeated quietly to accompany Cuffe's running description of the tournament that is taking place offstage. After the victor (Mountjoy) has

Ex. 65

been presented with a golden prize by the Queen, the crowd turns to her and acclaims her in a solemn hymn.

This is one of Britten's most genial inventions. Its slowly moving intervals, especially the 6ths, 7ths and 9ths, unfold like the petals of a cinquefoil Tudor rose, and the sensation that they overlap each other is enhanced by the movement of the parts within the 5/4 tempo. The chorus is repeated in Act II, scene i and Act III, scene iii; and it is not surprising to find it associated in other ways with the course of the opera. Its theme has already been used as the bass for one of the clanking episodes in the jousting prelude to Act I, scene i:

Ex. 66

it provides an introductory flourish for the different phrases of Elizabeth's Soliloquy (I, ii):

Ex. 67

and there are momentary references to it in Act III, scenes i and iii.

There is a motif associated with the Queen's favour that deserves special attention. It is based on the notes of the triad and appears when Essex is appointed Lord Deputy in Ireland (Ex. 68a), having already occurred in Act I, scene i during the quarrel between Essex and Mountjoy (Ex. 68b):

Ex. 68a

Ex. 68b

With an altered coda, it forms the theme of the trio (II, iii) '*Good Frances, do not weep*' (Ex. 69a) and also of Lady Rich's pleading for Essex's life (III, iii), which so exasperates the Queen by its obstinate persistence (Ex. 69b):

Ex. 69a

Ex. 69b

and it is related to the '*Victor of Cadiz*' chorus in the Whitehall Palace scene (II, iii), the theme of which is taken over by the orchestra at the end of the scene, when it is played by the orchestra in the pit, the crescendo of its rising phrases gradually overwhelming the Coranto being played by the Court band on the stage.

Much of the score is sparse and muscular. Sometimes monody is sufficient for Britten's purpose, as is the case with the first part of the unaccompanied song of the Country Girls in the Masque (II, i) '*Sweet flag and cuckoo flower*' with its characteristic Lydian fourth, and the flute solo accompanied by a tabor for the Morris Dance (II, iii) which recalls the earlier *Metamorphoses after Ovid*.

At the same time there are finely constructed passages, such as the Ensemble of Reconciliation (I, i), the whole sequence of intimate lyrical ensembles in Act II, scene ii (duet, double duet, and quartet), and the particularly beautiful Dressing-Table Song (III, i) sung by the Lady in Waiting with a chorus of Maids of Honour.

Equally beautiful are the masquers' *a cappella* choruses in Act II, scene i; and the Courtly Dances in Act II, scene iii, succeed in capturing much of the genuine Elizabethan idiom with their cross-rhythms, false relations, crazy filigree ornamentation, and heavy bounding basses.

There are numerous happy touches of musical characterization. For instance, although the Recorder of Norwich has only eight bars in Act II, scene i, he is nevertheless so firmly drawn that he remains as vividly in one's memory as if he had been a character in Crabbe's *The Borough*; and the statesman's mind of Cecil is depicted in all its curious intricacy and ultimate bathos.

But in the end it is through the imaginative presentation of the Queen, who gave her name to the age and was its chief ornament and glory that the opera triumphs. The fanfares accompanying her entrance and retirement in the opening scene at the tournament (I, i) give her a truly majestic setting, and she leads the Ensemble of Reconciliation with characteristic firmness. In the following scene (I, ii) she is depicted first as a politician with her minister Cecil, then as a woman being wooed by Essex, and lastly as a Queen alone with God. This soliloquy and prayer form perhaps her noblest musical utterance in the whole opera. (The number was slightly revised for the revival of *Gloriana* at Sadler's Wells Theatre in 1966.) In the second act she shines mainly by reflection: first she is seen on royal progress in Norwich (II, i), where she receives the loyal homage of the Norfolk masquers; and later (II, iii) in her palace at Whitehall she participates with her courtiers in a strenuous series of dances. In the last act, the irruption of Essex into her dressing room (III, i) where he discovers her in undress, is the cue for a very moving duet. After this, her hesitation before signing Essex's death warrant (III, iii) leads directly into the epilogue with its recession towards old age, death and dissolution. Her final words sung during the recapitulation of the second lute-song (now scored for full orchestra) '*mortua, mortua, sed non sepulta*', recall Essex's words to her in his earlier song:

> *Where, when he dies, his tomb might be a bush*
> *Where harmless robin dwells with gentle thrush.*

An unfulfilled woman maybe; a devious statesman; but undoubtedly a great Queen.

IX
The Turn of the Screw

I

Henry James's novella, *The Turn of the Screw*, was published in 1898 and immediately established itself as a masterpiece of its *genre*—a melodramatic thriller, a ghost story dealing with innocence and corruption, possession and exorcism.

The fact that the main protagonists are two young orphans, Miles aged about eleven and his sister Flora aged eight, was likely to prove an incentive rather than a discouragement from Britten's point of view; the Essex setting of the story in the country house at Bly (distant cousin perhaps to Borley) brought it into close East Anglian focus; and the deployment of the action on two planes—the natural and the supernatural—was an added attraction. Small wonder that Britten wanted to turn it into an opera if possible. But some critics were doubtful of the chances of success, feeling that James's strength lay in his ability to heighten tension through impression and ambiguity, and in his strategy of avoiding the direct confrontations of vital points at issue by recounting the indirect reactions of the characters concerned, so that visual presentation in stage terms might render it difficult to maintain the special atmosphere he created so inimitably in the telling of the story. They need not have worried. Despite reservations natural to his temperament and times, James was more explicit in *The Turn of the Screw* than many people were prepared to allow.

What, for instance, was the nature of the suspect relationship between Miles and Peter Quint, who before his death served as valet to Miles's uncle and guardian? James says quite clearly: 'there had been matters in his life—strange passages and perils, secret disorders, vices more than suspected', and the fault was 'Quint was much too free'—too free with Miles, too free with everyone. Freedom of this kind might bring sexual licence in its train; and a substratum of sexual implications spreads like a secret poison through the layers of the story. In some ways, Miles in his prepuberty is too young to be corrupted by this relationship whether with Quint the man or Quint the ghost; but the essence of the corruption is in the deliberate cultivation of an element of precocity, and the tragedy lies in the struggle for possession of the child by an adult (or adults) on adult terms.

The parallel relationship between Flora and Miss Jessel, her former governess, is rather shadowy and serves merely as confirmation of the crucial importance of the Miles/Quint axis.

It is the new Governess who (as narrator) provides the central emotional reference point. Apart from her, Bly seems to be a closed community, shut off from the world outside. Not only has she come from Hampshire via London to this lonely spot in Essex, but in London she has met and fallen in love with the children's uncle and guardian. This is the absentee master of Bly, who is the mainspring of the situation, though he stands outside the action and ducks his responsibilities. She admits to being carried away at her original interview with him in Harley Street; and when she reaches Bly and makes friends with the housekeeper, Mrs Grose, there is a significant misunderstanding in the course of their conversation.

> 'What was the lady who was here before?'
>
> 'The last governess? She was also young and pretty—almost as young and almost as pretty, miss, even as you.'
>
> 'Ah, then I hope her youth and her beauty helped her! He seems to like us young and pretty!'
>
> 'Oh, he *did*. It was the way he liked every one!'

The governess is thinking of the guardian uncle; Mrs Grose of Quint. The ambivalence continues as far as Quint's first materialization on the tower of the house at Bly. The Governess is exploring the grounds, meditating how charming it would be if someone (clearly she has in mind the master of Bly) would appear at the turn of a path, stand before her, smile and approve. 'He did stand there!' she writes, 'but high up, beyond the lawn and at the very top of the tower.' After this shock of surprise, there is a second shock which reveals that the apparition is not the master of Bly at all, but a figure who is later identified as the ghost of the master's body-servant, Quint. This was certainly a traumatic emotional experience for the Governess; but afterwards there are no further examples of transference between the master and the servant. Gradually an alternative outlet for her emotions appears—Miles himself. There is an occasion when, nervous and restless, she listens outside her charge's bedroom door at night. Miles realizes she is there and calls her in. Their poignant midnight talk leads to the point where she is so moved that she throws herself upon the boy in bed, embracing him in what she conceives to be the tenderness of her pity. 'My face was close to his, and he let me kiss him, simply taking it with indulgent good-humour.' The mystic union is clinched a little later when, after Mrs Grose has taken Flora away from Bly, the Governess is left alone with Miles. They take their meals together; and in her story she recalls how they continued silent while the maid was with them—'as silent, it whimsically occurred to me, as some young couple who, on their wedding-journey, at the inn, feel shy in the presence of the waiter. He turned round only when the waiter had left us. "Well—so we're alone!" ' It is the crowning irony of the story that finally it is the Governess who, actuated by the strongest though not necessarily the most innocent motives, wrestles with Quint's ghost for the possession of the boy; and when she thinks she has won, '*I* have you,' she cries, 'but he has lost you for ever!' At that moment Miles has a convulsive reaction and is about to fall, when the Governess catches him; and the final words of her narrative are: 'I caught him, yes, I held him—it may be imagined with what a passion; but at the end of a minute I began to feel what it truly was that I held. We were alone with the quiet day, and his little heart, dispossessed, had stopped.'

So ends the Governess's story,* which Henry James presents as being read to a group of listeners (by a man called Douglas) years after it had been written.

As his librettist, Britten chose Myfanwy Piper. Her husband, John Piper, had been involved in the designs for *The Rape of Lucretia*, *Albert Herring*, *Billy Budd* and *Gloriana*, so she had had numerous opportunities of attending rehearsals of these operas and thereby of learning 'the kind of language that sounded natural and inevitable' in opera, and also 'what to avoid—though not always how to avoid it'.†

At an early stage in the planning, composer and librettist decided to construct the libretto in two acts instead of three, and to have a multiplicity of scenes so as to reinforce the impression (so powerfully conveyed in James's story) that the action covered a considerable period of time and that there were long stretches of normality between the occasional supernatural appearances of the phantoms. John Piper had been chosen as designer, and it was understood that transparencies would play an important part in presenting the ghosts on the stage and in fading out from one scene and into another. The scenario took fifteen scenes from the story—there are twenty-four numbered sections in James's novella—and it became clear that even with the benefit of elaborate lighting effects, these would have to be linked with each other by orchestral interludes (later called Variations). Compression and brevity would have to be the order of the day, since a scene with its orchestral prelude could average only about eight or nine minutes. The eight scenes of the first act provided a complete exposition of the characters and the situation. 'At the end of the act, the Governess, though still not

* An interesting suggestion has been made by J. Purdon Martin, MD, FRCP (in 'Neurology in Fiction: *The Turn of the Screw*', *British Medical Journal*, 22 December 1973) that the Governess shows signs of suffering from temporal lobe epilepsy.

† 'Some Thoughts on the Libretto of *The Turn of the Screw*' by Myfanwy Piper, from *Tribute to Benjamin Britten*. Faber and Faber, London, 1963.

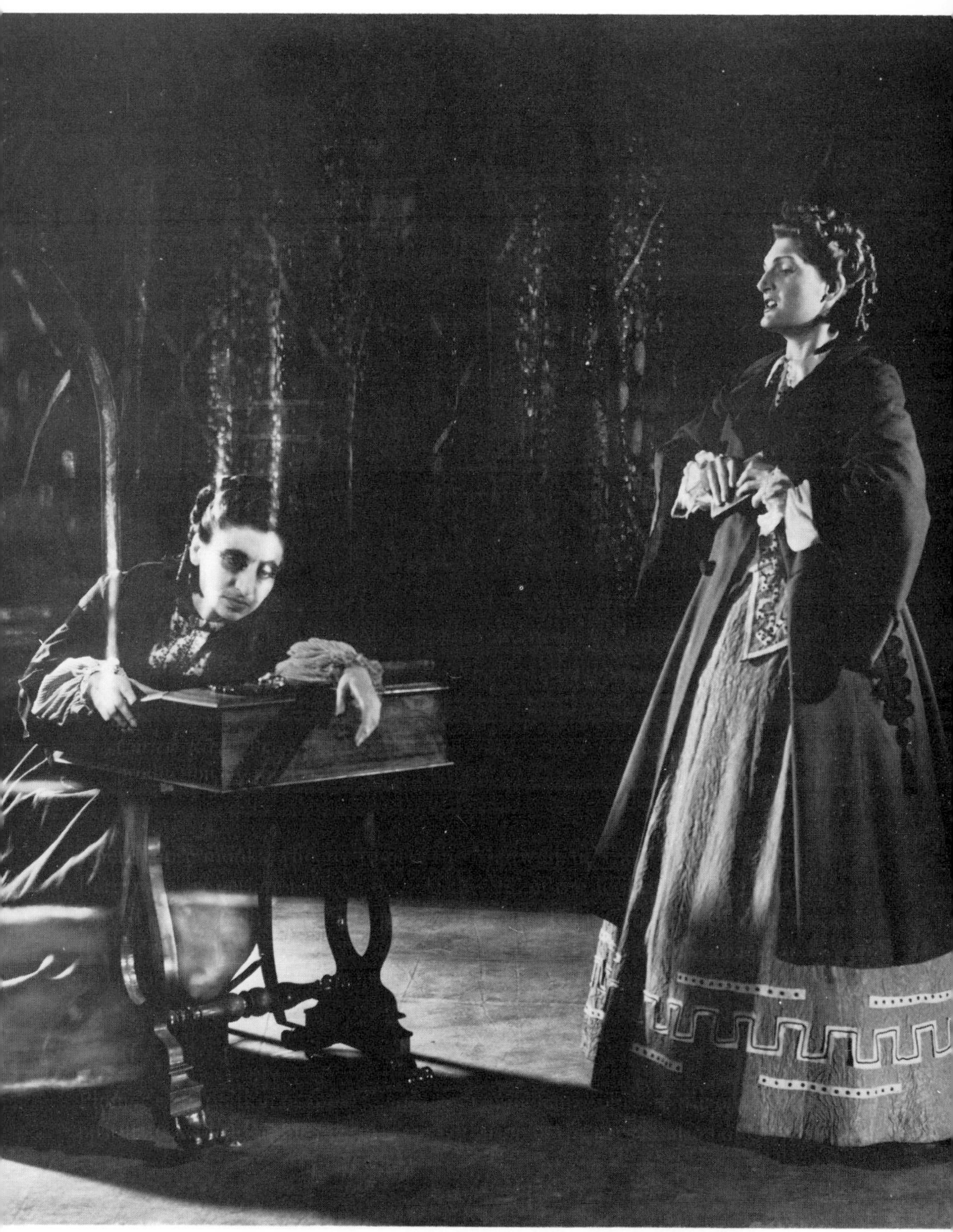

The Turn of the Screw: The ghost of Miss Jessel (Arda Mandikian) confronts the Governess (Jennifer Vyvyan) in the original 1954 production by the English Opera Group

active, was in possession of all the facts.'* The first scene of the second act, in which the ghosts of Peter Quint and Miss Jessel come together is an invention of the librettist's for which there is no textual authority in James. The remaining seven scenes of that act keep quite close to James's story and show the build-up of the crisis as precipitated by the Governess's interference.

Two late changes seem to have been made in constructing the libretto. 'After the first three scenes had been completed,' writes Myfanwy Piper,† 'it was decided, for musical reasons, that there must be a prologue, and several quite different prologues were written before we were both satisfied. Much later, although we had decided to leave out the whole episode of the letter to the guardian in Act II, it suddenly seemed essential and had to be written and inserted.' Both scenes are in fact essential—the prologue because without it the motivation of the situation at Bly is unexplained, the relationship between the master and his dead valet difficult to apprehend, and the life-line between Bly and the ordinary world outside not established; the letter scene because it enables the Governess to give free rein to her emotions in writing to someone outside Bly and because the theft of the letter by Miles is crucial to the climax.

There is a considerable amount of dialogue in James's story, and much of this could be usefully adapted for the libretto; but not a single word is spoken by either of the ghosts, and this posed a particularly daunting problem, for Britten decided it was essential for the opera that the ghosts should sing 'and sing words (no nice, anonymous, supernatural humming or groaning)'.‡ Two lucky *trouvailles* came to the librettist's assistance in this wellnigh impossible task: from a comment by James himself on Miss Jessel in one of his prefaces, she culled the phrase 'lost in her labyrinth'; and W. B. Yeats's line, 'The ceremony of innocence is drowned', provided a clinching refrain for the Colloquy between the two ghosts in Act II, scene i.

As for the children, one of James's striking sentences—*The lake was the sea of Azof*—was sufficient cue for some of the school-room tags and mnemonics. Nursery songs also played their part. In order to establish Miles's character musically, Britten needed an important but simple song and selected some doggerel dealing with the different meanings of the Latin word *Malo* which he found in an ancient Latin grammar belonging to Myfanwy Piper's aunt.

Malo, Malo, *I would rather be*
Malo, Malo, *in an apple tree*
Malo, Malo *than a naughty boy*
Malo, Malo *in adversity.*

* Myfanwy Piper, op. cit.
† Myfanwy Piper, op. cit. ‡ Ibid.

It was the librettist's idea that this song should be sung also by the Governess at the end of the opera when she discovers that Miles is dead.

The last scene of Act I was a crucial spot. In James's story, there occurs at this point the celebrated 'double-take' scene where late at night the Governess creeps into an empty room in a lower storey of the tower at Bly to look out of the window unobserved and sees Miles in the courtyard below gazing up at someone she cannot see on the top of the tower, but whom she instinctively knows to be the ghost of Quint. This was hardly capable of realization in terms of the theatre or of opera, even with the help of transparencies on the stage (though it could undoubtedly provide a magnificent scene in a film). Instead, Myfanwy Piper planned a confrontation between all the six characters—the only sextet in the whole opera, and in fact the only time when the two adults, the two children, and the two ghosts are on the stage together.

The complete scenario of the opera runs as follows:

ACT ONE

Prologue
Theme
Scene i: *The Journey*
Variation I
Scene ii: *The Welcome*
Variation II
Scene iii: *The Letter*
Variation III
Scene iv: *The Tower*
Variation IV
Scene v: *The Window*
Variation V
Scene vi: *The Lesson*
Variation VI
Scene vii: *The Lake*
Variation VII
Scene viii: *At Night*

ACT TWO

Variation VIII
Scene i: *Colloquy and Soliloquy*
Variation IX
Scene ii: *The Bells*
Variation X
Scene iii: *Miss Jessel*
Variation XI
Scene iv: *The Bedroom*
Variation XII
Scene v: *Quint*
Variation XIII
Scene vi: *The Piano*
Variation XIV
Scene vii: *Flora*
Variation XV
Scene viii: *Miles*

II

There are only six characters in *The Turn of the Screw*—seven if one includes the anonymous part in the prologue, which is written for tenor and can be doubled with Quint—and of these, two are children, the one a girl supposed to be about eight years old, and the other her elder brother whose voice is still unbroken. With the children playing key roles, it seemed inevitable that this should be planned as a chamber opera; and Britten decided to write the score for more or less the same orchestra as in *The Rape of Lucretia* and *Albert Herring*.

It has already been shown that the construction of the opera called for sixteen orchestral interludes. Britten decided that these should consist of a theme and fifteen variations. The theme is based on the following note row:

Ex. 71a

(Curiously enough a similar row was used by Stravinsky a few years later in *The Flood* to build up the chord of Chaos with which the Prelude opens.) Britten uses the row tonally rather than serially; and it should be noted how the theme (Ex. 71b) falls into three assymmetrical phrases and how some of the semiquavers owe allegiance to the previous double dotted crochets, while others anticipate the following notes:

Ex. 71b

The intervals of the note row can be construed as a series of six ascending fourths or six descending fifths, and because of this it might be thought that the first note of each pair would carry a dominant and the second note a tonic implication. This, however, is not the case. The first note in each case is a tonic and the second a subdominant. For instance, the theme as quoted above is in A, and not in D.

The tonal suggestions of a theme like this are obvious; and it might also be thought that they would dictate the key structure—a cycle of key changes each of which would represent, as it were, a further turn of the screw. But this is not so. The key structure of the opera is based on other, and in some ways subtler, considerations. For instance, in Act I the main keys of the interludes and scenes are, in ascending sequence, as follows:

Theme and Scene i	A minor
Variation I and Scene ii	B major
Variation II and Scene iii	C major
Variation III and Scene iv	D major (modulating to G minor)
Variation IV and Scene v	E major (modulating to E minor)
Variation V and Scene vi	F major (modulating to F minor)
Variation VI and Scene vii	G major
Variation VII and Scene viii	A flat major

From this table it will be seen that the first seven scenes are in all the seven white-note keys of the octave, and these cover the *natural* aspects of the exposition. The first black-note key appears in the last scene of the act, when for the first time the two ghosts are heard.

The identification of the *supernatural* world with flat keys and flattened notes is important to the score. On Quint's first apparition (in scene iv), an E flat chord is inserted in the prevailing D major texture:

Ex. 72

His first sung phrase is in scene viii—a call to Miles on E flat, followed by free-flowing melismata:

Ex. 73a

And Miles answers 'I'm here—O I'm here!' also on a high E flat. In fact, this E flat becomes so surcharged with supernatural overtones that later in the opera its appearance is sufficient to evoke an immediate change of mood.

Act II has four black-note keys as against one in Act I; and with one exception the keys are in descending sequence:

Variation VIII and Scene i	A flat major (modulating to G sharp minor)
Variation IX and Scene ii	F sharp major (modulating to an unestablished F sharp minor)
Variation X and Scene iii	F major (modulating to F minor)
Variation XI and Scene iv	E flat minor
Variation XII and Scene v	E major
Variation XIII and Scene vi	C major
Variation XIV and Scene vii	B flat major
Variation XV and Scene viii	A major (modulating to A flat major)

In the opening Colloquy between the two ghosts, Quint's call (Ex. 73a) is altered to fit the refrain 'The ceremony of innocence is drowned':

Ex. 73b

The other ghost (Miss Jessel) is not so strongly characterized as Quint. Her appearances are frequently underpinned by a sombre, brooding, slowly spread chord:

Ex. 74

Of special interest is the scene (II, iii) where the Governess finds her in the schoolroom sitting at the desk. Part of the sombre, brooding chord has spread into the accompaniment, which pins down the melodic line and prevents it from taking wing:

Ex. 75

This little scene would not be so striking musically were it not for the fact that it provides an exquisite foil for the Governess's letter writing episode that follows. This is treated as a miniature scene within a scene and has a quick instrumental prelude (while the letter to the children's guardian is being written) followed by a quieter section (while she reads aloud what she has written). The musical illustrations show (*a*) the first phrase of the letter as written and (*b*) the same phrase as read aloud:

The sequel to this scene, where the ghost of Quint tempts Miles to intercept the letter before it is posted, brings a melodramatic passage where Quint has three spoken phrases—'What has she written?' 'What does she know?' 'Easy to take.' Each of these is given different accentuations, which echo a side drum phrase, e.g.:

Ex. 77

As has been mentioned above, some of the children's musical material in the early scenes is based on nursery songs—a straightforward rendering of *Lavender's blue* in the third scene of Act I; and *Tom, Tom, the Piper's Son*, with slightly more extended treatment in scene v. In the schoolroom scene Miles sings his 'Malo' song. This is one of Britten's most touching inventions. Like the Governess's letter song (quoted above), the tune is basically formed out of interlinked thirds. Its apparent simplicity is deceptive, for there is considerable subtlety in the way the melodic line avoids symmetry, and in its harmonization. Quite apart from one or two

Ex. 78

literal repetitions later on, this little tune makes a number of altered appearances. It provides a theme for Variation VI. Played by the horn in a quick and light tempo, it forms a bass to the accompaniment of Quint's short song at the beginning of Act II ('I seek a friend, obedient to follow where I lead'). Played by the cor anglais in its normal rhythm, it is heard at the end of the bedroom scene (II, iv); and immediately afterwards a diminished form is played by the pizzicato strings quickly and urgently as a kind of miniature fugato in Variation XII. It provides an expressive coda to scene v of Act II. And at the end of the opera the theme is sung by the despairing Governess (in the key of A) as she lays Miles's body on the ground.

As is Britten's usual custom, the music is continuous within the acts, and the orchestral interludes and their following scenes are cunningly interwoven. Occasionally the scenes are extremely short—Act II, scene v, for instance, is only twenty-seven bars long. In comparison a scene like The Window (I, v) seems long and moves through a series of different episodes and narrations.

The scenes that have most definite musical unity of their own are perhaps The Bells (II, ii) and The Piano (II, vi). In the former, the sound of the church bells provides a framework for Miles and Flora, as they chant their own Te Deum on their way to Church, diversifying the sacred words with occasional interjections from the schoolroom.

> . . . *O ye rivers and seas and lakes:*
> *Bless ye the Lord.*
> O amnis, axis, caulis, collis,
> Clunis, crinis, fascis, follis . . .

The bells, with their clear timbre and different changes, emphasize the sinister atmosphere of the scene. The scene called The Piano is constructed on the lines of a miniature piano concerto. A Diabelli-like theme makes its appearance in Variation XIII; and when the lights go up on the schoolroom Miles is seen sitting at the piano, playing. The theme is varied, particularly with repeated notes and scale passages that are played with sufficient virtuosity to justify the comments of the Governess and Mrs Grose 'O what a clever little boy!' Miles starts a second piece and then begins to show off with occasional glissandi. Under cover of his showmanship, Flora slips away to her forbidden tryst with Miss Jessel; and when the Governess and Housekeeper rush off to bring her back and the scene slowly fades, Miles is left playing a triumphant kind of toccata which becomes Variation XIV.

In the final scene (II, viii), the climax between the Governess and Miles and Quint* is played out as a passacaglia over a ground bass built up cumulatively from the basic theme (Ex. 71b). Finally the white-note keys triumph over the black-note keys. Quint's farewell melismata are a semitone higher than in Ex. 73a. The spell is broken; Miles is dead; and all that remains is the altered 'Malo' lament sung by the Governess:

> . . . Malo, Malo *than a naughty boy.*
> Malo, Malo *in adversity.*

* An interesting note on revisions carried out by Britten on this scene before the vocal score was actually published is to be found in 'Britten's Revisionary Practice: Practical and Creative' by Donald Mitchell. *Tempo*, Autumn/Winter 1963.

X
Noye's Fludde

Sooner or later it seemed inevitable that Britten would want to write a dramatic or semi-dramatic work for church performance. In 1957 he found the subject he required in one of the medieval miracle plays and chose from the Chester Cycle the episode of Noye and his family, the building of the ark, and the flood. Formerly it had been the custom for each separate play in these cycles to be performed by one of the Guilds on a cart known as a pageant, which moved about the town so that several complete performances of the cycle could be given at different spots. As the Introductory Note to Britten's score makes clear: '*Noye's Fludde*, set to music, is intended for the same style of presentation—though not necessarily on a cart. Some big building should be used, preferably a church—but not a theatre—large enough to accommodate actors and orchestra, with the action raised on rostra, but not on a stage removed from the congregation. No attempt should be made to hide the orchestra from sight.'

The action of *Noye's Fludde* made it possible to cast most of the parts for children. Adults are needed only for the Voice of God (spoken), and for Noye (bass-baritone) and his wife (contralto). Sem, Ham and Jaffett and their wives should be played by boys and girls between the ages of eleven and fifteen, though Jaffett (the eldest) may have a broken voice. Mrs Noye's Gossips should be older girls, with strong voices, especially in the lower registers. The animals are played by children. Forty-nine different species are referred to in the Chester Miracle play, of which thirty-five (in pairs) subdivided into seven groups were used in the first production of *Noye's Fludde*, viz.:

I Lions, Leopards, Horses, Oxen, Swine, Goats, Sheep;
II Camels, Asses, Buck and Doe;
III Dogs, Otters, Foxes, Polecats, Hares;
IV Bears, Wolves, Monkeys, Squirrels, Ferrets;
V Cats, Rats, Mice;
VI and VII } Herons, Owls, Bittern, Peacocks, Redshanks, Ravens, Cock and Hen, Kites, Cuckoos, Curlews, Doves, Duck and Drake (six pairs in each group).

Noye's Fludde: Noye (Owen Brannigan), Mrs Noye (Sheila Rex) and the animals in the ark

The total cast consists of three adults and ninety children (including four boys who are used as property men).

It now remained to be seen how far the make-up of the orchestra should be influenced by the great preponderance of children in the cast. Britten boldly decided to opt for a large number of young amateur players as well as some professionals. The professional group consists of solo string quintet (Vl I and II, Vla, Vcl, DB), solo treble recorder, piano (four hands), organ, and timpani: the amateur group of strings ripieni (Vl I, II and III, Vle, Vcl I and II, DB), descant recorders in two parts and treble recorders, bugles (in B flat) in four parts, twelve handbells (in E flat), and a specially large collection of percussion, viz.:

Bass Drum	Whip
Tenor Drum	Gong
Side Drum	Chinese blocks
Tambourine	Wind machine
Cymbals	Sandpaper
Triangle	Slung mugs

The score is tempered to the abilities of the young amateur players. For instance, the Introductory Note specifies: 'There are three sorts of amateur *Violins*: the *Firsts* should be capable players, not however going above the 3rd position, and with the simplest double-stops. The *Seconds* do not go out of the first position, while the *Thirds* are very elementary, and have long stretches of just open strings. The *Violas* need to be as accomplished as the *1st Violins*, as do the *1st Cellos*, while the *2nd Cellos* have only the simplest music. The *Double Bass* is very simple.' Similar instructions are given for recorder players and bugles.

As regards the percussion, most of the instruments specified are the stock orchestral ones, with the exception of the Sandpaper and Slung Mugs. The former consists of two pieces of sandpaper attached to wooden blocks and rubbed together: the latter are mugs or cups of varying thickness and size chosen so as to make a rough kind of scale and slung on string by their handles from a wooden stand and hit with a wooden spoon. The total orchestra numbers a minimum of sixty-seven players, of whom ten are professionals and fifty-seven amateurs.

This would seem to imply that no fewer than a hundred and fifty-six actors and instrumentalists are needed to mount a performance of *Noye's Fludde*; but the total forces involved are even larger, for at three points Britten decided to call on the whole congregation to join in singing three hymns that are built into the score—'*Lord Jesus, think on me*'; '*Eternal Father, strong to save*'; and '*The spacious firmament on high*'.

Noye's Fludde begins with the congregation singing four verses of the first of these hymns, at the end of which Noye walks through the congregation on to an empty stage, where he kneels, and God's Voice is heard accusing mankind of sin, prophesying destruction, and promising to save Noye and his family because of Noye's righteousness. After this revelation, Noye summons his family to help in the building of the ark; and the tail-rhyme of the text (stanzas rhyming aaabcccb) is handled so that the triple rhymes (a and c) are set to a simple syncopated tune, while the end rhymes (b) are treated like a refrain from a non-syncopated hymn tune. This refrain varies from verse to verse; but the one that is most characteristic and sticks longest in the mind is Noye's '*At the coming of the flood*':

Ex. 79

The entry of the animals into the ark shows Britten's invention at its most genial. The text's eight half-stanzas (of four lines each) are treated as variations on a basic pattern, consisting of (a) preludial bugle calls, (b) songs by various callers, and (c)—this is Britten's own invention: there is no authority for it in the Chester pageant—a chattering series of repetitions of the phrase '*Kyrie eleison*' sung by the animals themselves as they pass through the congregation to enter the ark:

In the Chester pageant, Noye's wife appears as a perverse and cantankerous character. According to A. C. Cawley,* this comic tradition is at least as old as the picture of Noah's Ark in the Junius manuscript (*c.* A.D. 1000), which shows her standing at the foot of the gangway, while one of her sons tries to persuade her to go on board. Britten takes full advantage of this scene and finds admirably comic variants of the various tunes for Noye's wife and her gossips. The final *coup*, when the three sons bodily carry her, protesting, into the ark and Noye gets his ears boxed for his welcome, leads directly to the storm.

* *Everyman and Medical Miracle Plays.* Ed. A. C. Cawley. J. M. Dent (Everyman Edition) London, 1956.

This is a large-scale instrumental movement composed as a passacaglia. The ground bass consists of pairs of ascending minor thirds rising generally by whole-tone steps. These pass through all twelve notes of the chromatic scale (a reminder of the processes recently used in *The Turn of the Screw*) and are tonally anchored by a strong repeated G. At the outset of the storm, when the first raindrops are heard, the slung mugs impart just the right quality of sound to depict extra-large single raindrops plopping on to hot dry earth:

Ex. 81

The different variations depict rain, more rain, wind, thunder and lightning, more wind, waves, yet more wind, flapping rigging, great waves, ship rocking, panic of the animals; and then at the height of the storm everyone in the ark sings the first verse of '*Eternal Father, Strong to Save*', the congregation joining in the second verse. The storm then gradually subsides, while the orchestra plays fragments of the variations in reverse order, interspersed with fragments of the hymn tune.

The storm is over, but the flood remains.

Noye sends out a Raven, which does not return to the Ark; and the Raven is followed by the Dove. Here graceful use is made of flutter-tonguing for the solo recorder (Ex. 82a). The bird flies off to a lively little waltz tune (Ex. 82b); and when it returns with an olive branch in its beak, the tune is reversed (Ex. 82c), and as it alights on the Ark the opening chords are reversed too (Ex. 82d):

Ex. 82a

Ex. 82c

Noye blesses God for this sign of peace; and the Voice of God is heard authorizing Noye to allow his family and all the animals to leave the Ark. The animals troop out to a crescendo of Alleluias:

Ex. 83

God's Voice is heard again, promising that the rainbow shall serve as a covenant that in future He will never try to wreak similar vengeance on mankind. This is the cue for the actual appearance of the rainbow accompanied by a peal of handbells (in E flat major); and the final hymn (in G major), '*The spacious firmament on high*', begins. Between the first, second, third, and fourth verses, the Sun, the Moon, and the Stars also appear. The congregation joins in for the fifth verse; and in the sixth Tallis's tune is treated as an eight-part canon at the unison, or octave. At the end, the Voice of God is heard, blessing Noye tenderly. The handbells appear in augmentation; and there is a final dying call from the bugles.

XI
A Midsummer Night's Dream

I

Music was certainly in Shakespeare's mind when he wrote *A Midsummer Night's Dream*, whether the occasion of the first performance was a wedding celebration or a public performance by the Lord Chamberlain's Servants. '*Fairies sing*' is the quarto stage direction before 'You spotted snakes with double tongue'. Bottom sings 'The ousel cock so black of hue' to keep up his spirits; and before his 'exposition of sleep', he calls for 'the tongs and the bones'. The fairies oblige—'*Musicke Tongs, Rurall Musicke*' is the folio direction. A little later, when Oberon wakes Titania, they both call for music—the direction '*Musicke Stille*' appears in the folio—and Oberon invites her to dance:

> *Come, my queen, take hands with me,*
> *And rock the ground whereon these sleepers be.*

When Theseus and Hippolyta enter with their train to hunt, there is a folio direction '*Winde hornes*'.* The second time the horns sound (also marked by a special stage direction), their call awakens the sleeping lovers, who all start up. At the end of the play, just before the Epilogue, Oberon sings a Song (so specified in the text)—'Now until the break of day'.

After the Restoration many of Shakespeare's plays were adapted for the new London patent theatres by producing them with 'Singing, Dancing and Machines interwoven, after the manner of an Opera'. The turn of *A Midsummer Night's Dream* came in 1692, when the text was rearranged, under the title of *The Fairy Queen*, and masques inserted in Acts II, III, IV, and V. The author of this baroque semi-opera is not known, though it is generally thought to have been Elkanah Settle. The music of the masques was written by Henry Purcell. That the production by Thomas Betterton at the Queen's Theatre in Dorset Garden was popular is evident from the fact that it was revived the following year with additional numbers and a second

* Singular in the quarto instead of plural.

edition of the libretto called for; that it was extravagant is attested by the stage directions and by the passage in the preface where the author confesses that little material advantage was likely to accrue to the promoters 'considering the mighty Charge in setting it out, and the extraordinary expence that attends it every day 'tis represented'.

(In 1967 a new concert version of *The Fairy Queen* was devised by Peter Pears and edited by Benjamin Britten and Imogen Holst. This was given at the Maltings Concert Hall, Snape, during the 1967 Aldeburgh Festival. The material was arranged in four parts: I. Oberon's Birthday, II. 'Night and Silence', III. 'The Sweet Passion', IV. Epithalamium. In this version, the musical shape of the key-sequences is preserved, and optional wind parts have been added to some of the dances and choruses.)

After Purcell's *The Fairy Queen*, the next operatic version was Richard Leveridge's *The Comick Masque of Pyramus and Thisbe* (1716), where the action was confined to the mechanicals and their play, and the music 'composed in the high stile of Italy', meaning that it was a satire on the prevailing craze for Italian opera in London. Nineteen years later Leveridge's libretto was used for a similarly titled work with music by John Frederick Lampe.

A new operatic version called *The Fairies* was made by John Christopher Smith in 1755. In this case, David Garrick, who presumably wrote the libretto, completely omitted the mechanicals and their 'tedious brief scene' of Pyramus and Thisbe. This was produced at Drury Lane. Sixty years later a further operatic version—this time to a libretto by Frederick Reynolds with music by Henry Bishop, supplemented with songs by Arne and Smith—was produced at Covent Garden.

Other operatic versions were made abroad in the nineteenth century—by G. Manusardi, and F. von Suppé—but all of these pale into insignificance in the light of Felix Mendelssohn and his achievement in writing deliciously appropriate incidental music for the play. As a young boy of seventeen he had seen *A Midsummer Night's Dream* in Berlin and read it in the Schlegel-Tieck translation, and in his resulting enthusiasm he composed a piano duet in classical sonata form for himself and his sister Fanny to play. The following year he orchestrated the piece, and it was first performed as a concert overture at Stettin in 1827. In 1843 he followed up the Overture by composing a full set of incidental numbers, the only difficulty being that this music was written for full orchestra and demanded the utmost care and accuracy in performance, something that few theatre orchestras were capable of achieving.

There were numerous features in Shakespeare's play that were likely to attract Britten as a composer. The contrast between the natural and supernatural elements was something he had already tackled with conspicuous success in *The Turn of the Screw*. The pungent timbre of the

A Midsummer Night's Dream: Oberon (Alfred Deller) and Tytania (Jennifer Vyvyan) with their attendants in the original 1960 production by the English Opera Group

boy fairies' unbroken voices made a special appeal to him; and the nocturnal quality of the action 'following darkness like a dream' called for the exercise of imaginative powers similar to those already displayed in the *Nocturne*. Above all, the delicious native freshness of Shakespeare's lyrical poetry will have put him on his mettle.

It takes a bold man to turn one of Shakespeare's plays into an opera, and it takes an even bolder man to decide to set Shakespeare's own words. This is precisely what Britten decided to do. In collaboration with Peter Pears, he set about shortening and adapting Shakespeare's text. The 2,136 lines of the original were cut to about half, and the action simplified by starting, not at the Court of Theseus in Athens, but in the wood with the quarrel between Oberon and Tytania.* The opera is laid out in three acts, all of which are set in the wood, except for a transformation scene to Theseus' Palace in Act III. Shakespeare's material has been rearranged as follows:

* In the opera Britten preserves the quarto spelling, 'Tytania', which affects the pronunciation of the name.

Britten	*Shakespeare*
Act I	passages from Act II, i; I, i; II, i; I, ii; II, ii
Act II	III, i; IV, i; III, ii
Act III	IV, i; IV, ii; I, i; IV, i; V, i

This means that the first act introduces the various groups of characters who are wandering in the wood, the second act shows the effect on them of Oberon's magic spell, and in the third act, first Oberon undoes the spell, and then the scene is changed to Theseus' Palace so that Theseus and Hippolyta together with the two pairs of lovers can be wedded and the mechanicals can present the play they've been rehearsing as an appropriate nuptial entertainment.

The changes made to Shakespeare's text are minute. One line—'*Compelling thee to marry with Demetrius*'—has been invented in order to explain 'the sharp Athenian law' that Lysander and Hermia are trying to evade. And Britten and Pears make one significant addition. Whereas Shakespeare mentions four young fairies by name—Peaseblossom, Cobweb, Moth and Mustardseed—and all four are featured when they first appear (in III, i), Moth gets omitted in the later scene (IV, i). Britten and Pears manage to adjust the position somewhat in his favour by reinstating him in the later scene, though without giving him fresh dialogue. There are naturally a number of minor adjustments. Some of Puck's verse is given to the chorus of fairies. Occasionally lines are re-apportioned among the speakers. The time sequence is adjusted so that the action seems to take place within two consecutive nights, instead of the four happy days mentioned by Theseus at the opening of the play as the waiting period before his nuptials with Hippolyta.

II

The first thing Britten had to decide was how to cast the opera. The quartet of lovers does not predominate, but is central to the action. Helena and Hermia are cast as soprano and mezzo-soprano; Lysander and Demetrius as tenor and baritone. High voices were chosen for the supernatural characters. Cobweb, Peaseblossom, Mustardseed and Moth are boy trebles; and the chorus of fairies, trebles or sopranos. Tytania is a coloratura soprano; and Oberon a counter-tenor (or contralto). Puck posed a special problem; and ultimately Britten, recalling some Swedish child-acrobats gifted with extraordinary agility and powers of mimicry whom he had recently seen in Stockholm, decided to cast Puck as a boy-acrobat with a speaking role. The mechanicals are at the other end of the scale: Flute and Snout are tenors, Starveling baritone, Bottom a bass-baritone, and Quince and Snug basses. Theseus and Hippolyta, who only come upon the scene halfway through the last act, are bass and contralto respectively.

The choice of counter-tenor for Oberon posed a problem. There is no doubt that the rarified vocal quality (still a taste to be acquired by some music-lovers) suits the part; but there are tricky problems of balance to be solved, particularly in relation to his duet passages with Tytania.

The score is written for a medium-sized orchestra, larger than the usual English Opera Group chamber ensemble. There are six woodwind (two flutes, oboe, two clarinets, bassoon), four brass (two horns, trumpet, and trombone), two percussion players, two harps, harpsichord and celesta (one player), and strings. There is also a stage band of recorders, small cymbals and wood blocks for the 'tongs and bones' music. It is characteristic of the score that different kinds of texture and orchestral colour are associated with different groups of characters. For instance, the fairies are characterized by harps, harpsichord, celesta and percussion; the lovers, by woodwind and strings; the mechanicals by the lower brass and bassoon.

The first act opens in a wood at night. It is clear that Britten expects the ear like the eye to travel up and down the tall tapering trunks with the shafts of moonlight falling through. As an introduction he has chosen a series of common chords played tremolo by the strings with alternate upward and downward *portamenti* between the chords, giving an impression of the unequal breathing of the slumbering wood:

Ex. 84

It will be seen that these chords are sometimes presented in their root position and sometimes in their first or second inversions, and that their roots (G, F sharp, D, E, A, C sharp, G sharp, E flat, C, B flat, F, B) cover all twelve notes of the chromatic scale. The initial slide from G to F sharp is a step that characterizes much of the fairy music; but the note row itself does not receive such intensive treatment as that of the theme in *The Turn of the Screw* (Ex. 71b). Instead, the episode is used as prelude to Act I and three times as interludes to break up the *a-b-c-b-a* scene construction of the first act (where *a* stands for the fairies, *b* for the lovers, and *c* for the mechanicals). In what should have been the fourth interlude (between scenes iv and v), the chromatic chord sequence becomes the accompaniment to Tytania's air '*Come, now a roundel, and a fairy song*'.

These chromatic chords are found in an altered form in the introduction to the initial meeting of Oberon and Tytania in Act I, where the fairies sing

Oberon is passing fell and wrath,
Because that she, as her attendant, hath
A lovely boy stolen from an Indian King,
And jealous Oberon would have the child

above an accompaniment that contains first inversions of the chords of E, G, B, D, C sharp, F, G sharp, C, E flat, F sharp, B flat, the twelfth chord (of A major) being held back for the confrontation of Oberon and Tytania with their simultaneous cry of '*Ill met by moonlight*'.

There is a kind of tart flavour about the music for the fairies. Britten was very conscious that *his* fairies were 'very different from the innocent nothings that often appear in productions of Shakespeare'. He went on to say:* 'I have always been struck by a kind of sharpness in Shakespeare's fairies: besides, they have some odd poetry to speak . . . [They] are, after all, the guards to Tytania: so they have, in places, martial music. Like the actual world, incidentally, the spirit world contains bad as well as good.'

In the fairies' opening chorus there is a curious feature of alternative syllabic accentuation:

Ex. 85

But the 6/4 metre has barely had time to establish itself, in this smoothly flowing line, and in the event the dislocation of the accents is stronger to the eye reading the score than to the ear when listening to a performance. A spikier effect is obtained by more obvious syncopations in a later chorus '*You spotted snakes with double tongue*':

Ex. 86

* From 'A New Britten Opera' by Benjamin Britten. *The Observer*, 5 June 1960.

For Oberon's spell Britten has had recourse to the same sort of tone colour (celesta) that he used to accompany the appearances of the ghosts in *The Turn of the Screw*; but the harmonies are denser and the melody more convoluted. (Note the way the second phrase of the melody is nearly, but not quite, an inversion of the first phrase.)

Ex. 87

This passage provides a lead-in for Oberon's baroque air '*I know a bank where the wild thyme blows*'. The air consists of a number of short contrasting

Ex. 88a

episodes. In the flowers section, the harps trail brief scalic passages like tendrils, which are lengthened for the section where '*the snake throws her enammel'd skin*'. Oberon's reference to Tytania brings a deceptively simple, tartly harmonized tune:

Ex. 88b

The organization and tone quality of this number occasionally call to mind the Second Lute Song in *Gloriana*.

Puck's spoken lines are generally accompanied by trumpet and drum; and these trumpet arpeggios are not unlike the sennets that herald some of the hero's appearances in *Billy Budd*.

For the two pairs of lovers, Britten was faced by the problem of how to dissolve so much wordy sparring into music. He decided that, speed being essential, the dialogue should for the most part be set as freely flowing accompanied recitative. The key to the greater part of the lovers' declarations and protestations is contained in Lysander's opening questions to Hermia in Act I:

Ex. 89

The long declamatory line can usually be broken up into motifs where four adjacent notes in a diatonic scale are arranged in different patterns. This of course would provide a close fit for the setting of four beat octosyllabic verse; but as the lovers speak in blank verse or rhyming couplets, the two extra syllables in each line frequently make it necessary to prolong the melody by adding two notes to every couple of four-note phrases. This accompanied recitative is treated very freely; but occasionally there are nodal points where some sort of ensemble is built up. There is one instance in Act I where Hermia and Lysander sing a duet built on the phrase '*I swear to thee . . .*' The most intricate example is the fugato quartet in Act III, where each lover proclaims that he (she) has found his (her) loved one '*like a jewel, mine own, and not mine own*':

Ex. 90

The scalic opening of this phrase recalls the hymn-like tune sung by the Male and Female Chorus in *The Rape of Lucretia* and also the final sextet in that opera.

In the middle of Act I the mechanicals meet to discuss the little play they are planning to present at court. When asked what the play treats on, Quince replies, 'Marry, our play is the most lamentable comedy and most cruel death of Pyramus and Thisby.' And this cadence, as echoed by Flute, Snout, Starveling and Snug, becomes a kind of musical epigraph:

Ex. 91

Act II contains only two scenes as against five in Act I: these are (a) the mechanicals rehearsing (which leads to the 'translation' of Bottom) and (b) the lovers wandering through the mazy wood which leads to their final state of enchanted exhaustion. The act starts with a succession of four chords containing all twelve notes of the chromatic scale—the first chord (using three notes) is scored for muted strings, the second (four notes) for muted brass, the third (three notes) for woodwind, and the fourth (two notes) for harps and percussion—typifying the drowsy effects of Oberon's magic spell:

Ex. 92

In the orchestral prelude to the act, some of the notes of the chords are used as starting points for melodic development, but these lines always return to their starting point to reconstitute the original chords. There are three complete variations on the four chords. A fourth is started, but interrupted, as soon as the second chord is reached, by the entry of the mechanicals. At the end of their scene, the four chords return as accompaniment to the doped Tytania's apostrophe to Bottom, '*O how I love thee! how I dote on thee!*' and three further instrumental variations in quickening tempo follow by way of orchestral interlude. In this case the last (fourth) chord heralds the appearance of Puck and Oberon and the lovers straying through the wood, towards the end of which scene each of the four chords is used in turn as Puck leads, first Lysander, then Demetrius, next Helena, and finally Hermia, to the different spots where they lie down and fall asleep. The act ends with the fairies singing a benison '*On the ground sleep sound*' which is harmonized by the four chords:

Ex. 93

Like the second act, the third is divided into two scenes: but these mark a complete transition—from the Wood to the Court. A diatonic prelude for strings establishes the natural mood of day in contrast to the chromaticism of the supernatural night. This scene brings the reconciliation of Oberon and Tytania, who dance together to the tune of a beautiful Saraband, where the melody (cor anglais) is repeated in a mirror-like inversion by the clarinet:

Ex. 94

The reconciliation of the two pairs of lovers follows, in a quartet which has been referred to above (see Ex. 90). The sound of the Duke's hunting horns is heard, at first off-stage as the lovers awake, and later as the main substance of the orchestral interlude before the transformation scene to the Court of Theseus:

Ex. 95

This final scene starts with a noble introduction for Theseus and Hippolyta, who appear for the first time: a broad, sweeping tune—in fact, one of the most flowing and sustained in the whole opera:

Ex. 96

When the time comes for the mechanicals to present their entertainment in honour of the threefold nuptials, they oblige with what is virtually a little *opera buffa*. (Shade of Leveridge!) The comedy of Pyramus and Thisbe is so amusing in itself that any adequate production of the play is bound to elicit much laughter from the audience. This is the case too when Britten's *opera buffa* is performed; and as at the moment of laughter part of the music is likely to be blacked out, not all listeners may realize how complex and tightly integrated is this little opera within the main opera. Accordingly it is worth while drawing attention to its organization in some detail. There are fourteen numbers in all:

1. Introduction, *Pomposo*. 'If we offend.' (Sextet *a cappella*)
2. *Andante pesante*. 'Gentles, perchance you wonder at this show.' (Prologue)
3. *Lento lamentoso*. 'In this same interlude.' (Wall)
4. *Moderato ma tenebroso*. 'O grim-looked night.' (Pyramus)
5. *Allegretto grazioso*. 'O wall, full often.' (Thisby)
6. Duet, *Allegro brillante*. 'My love thou art.' (Pyramus and Thisby)
7. *Lento lamentoso* (see no. 3). 'Thus have I, Wall?' (Wall)
8. *Allegro giocoso*. 'You ladies.' (Lion)
9. *Andante placido*. 'This lanthorn.' (Moon)
10. *Allegretto grazioso* (see no. 5). 'This is old Ninny's tomb.' (Thisby)
11. *Presto feroce*. 'Oh!' (Lion)
12. (*a*) *Lento*. 'Sweet Moon, I thank thee.' (Pyramus)
    (*b*) *Allegro disperato*. 'Approach, ye Furies fell.' (Pyramus)
13. (*a*) *Allegretto grazioso* (see no. 5). 'Asleep, my Love?' (Thisby)
    (*b*) *Lento*. 'These lily lips.' (Thisby)
14. Bergomask, *Ruvido*

These brief numbers are separated from each other by recitative interjections from Theseus, Hippolyta, and the four lovers, including a particularly involved recitative ensemble for six voices just before the Prologue, laid out on similar lines to the 'chatter' recitatives in *Albert Herring*. As is implicit in the Italian directions,* the music satirizes the style of nineteenth-century romantic opera. The illustrations give an extract from Pyramus' air (no. 4), and the instrumental introduction (note the *flauto obbligato* part!) to Thisby's air (no. 5):

The Bergomask is a jolly dance in two parts—the first moves intermittently between 3/4 and 6/8 (equal quavers); and the second is a very quick rumbustious 2/4, with rushing semiquaver passages and slightly irregular bar-groupings.

It sounds midnight. The epigraph of the Pyramus and Thisby play (see Ex. 91) recurs fortissimo in the orchestra. It subsides; the mortals retire to bed; and the fairies return to a tintinnabulation of instruments simulating the midnight chimes at different pitches and different speeds—thirty-five such chimes in all. The fairies' little tune is deceptively simple, but metrically irregular:

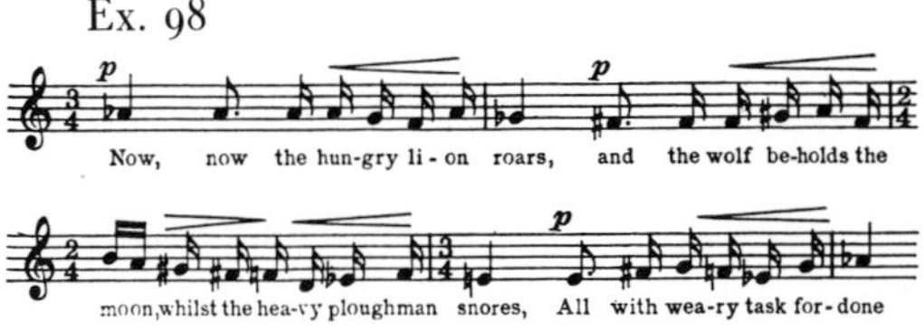

* It is amusing to note that Britten's directions throughout the rest of the score are in English.

The fairies still have a musical trick in reserve; and again it is a metrical one. Britten features a Scotch snap in the slow and solemn setting of the chorus '*Now until the break of day*'. It is a bold stroke to make the weak verse beats

Ex. 99

three times the length of the strong ones, even though the accentuation is not displaced; but it comes off in a fresh and striking fashion. A scherzo passage for Puck brings the opera to a close with gay elusive trumpet calls.

A Midsummer Night's Dream succeeds as an opera, partly because the subject matter is obviously congenial to Britten's temperament, and also because the work is supremely well organized. The differentiation between the natural and supernatural worlds and the characterization of the four groups of persons are so well established musically that the numerous transitions can be made with ease and speed, and no time wasted. It is true that there are moments such as the long stretches of near-recitative dialogue between the two pairs of lovers, where the music seems thin: but this is doubtless deliberate, for whenever the action reaches a climax, the musical tension tightens, drawing in the slack. Throughout the score Britten shows an unerring sense of proportion, and nowhere is this more evident than in the last act where the transformation to the Court of Theseus lifts the opera on to a different level, outside the dream-world of the enchanted wood, and the play within the play turns out to be a miniature opera within the opera proper, with a complex internal organization of its own.

As for the poetry of the original, this has in no way been harmed. Britten himself has confessed* that he did not 'find it daunting to be tackling a masterpiece which already had a strong verbal music of its own', since its music and the music he had written for it were at two quite different levels.

Whereas formerly the only fully satisfactory Shakespeare operas could be said to be Verdi's *Macbeth*, *Otello* and *Falstaff*, now Britten's *Dream* must be added to that short but distinguished list.

* Ibid.

XII
Curlew River

I

Britten's wish to bring some form of operatic entertainment into the church was certainly stimulated by the success of *Noye's Fludde*. He decided, however, that what he next wrote would be for fully professional performers, without an admixture of amateurs, and that the congregation would be an audience in the normal sense, and would not participate in the action. He needed also a new type of convention to obtain a really satisfactory form of presentation.

When casting round for a suitable myth or fable, he recalled one of the Noh plays he had seen on his visit to Japan in February 1956, and which had made a deep impression on him at the time. The occasion was vividly described in the travel diary of Prince Ludwig of Hesse and the Rhine.* 'Before the entrance of an actor through a door at the left a coloured curtain is swept back in an impressive way. The stage itself has a little low door back right, through which stage-hands, chorus etc. enter and depart, bent double; no scenery, except a stylized painting of a pine tree on the back wall of the stage. In the middle, against this back wall, two drummers sit. They let off sudden bursts of clacking and gonging drum-sounds with their hands. To these drummings they recite in strained voices, like people about to vomit. The choir which accompanies the play makes the same kind of sound but sometimes suddenly breaks into chanting song, liturgical and impressive . . . Everything on the stage happens in retarded motion. The actors move with the slowest of steps, artfully lifting the toes of their white-socked feet before setting them down with care and precision. The white feet and the magnificent costumes are reflected clearly by the polished floor of stage and passage. Most of the costumes are obviously historical, made of the most splendid silks and brocades. It seems that the more important a character, the finer his apparel must be, regardless of the appropriate dress

* From 'Ausflug Ost 1956', printed in *Tribute to Benjamin Britten*. Faber, 1963.

for the rôle he is acting. With the finest clothes go the wonderful masks which can change their expression by a tilt of the head.'

To this description of the characteristic style of Noh play production should be added one or two words of explanation. The stylized pine tree at the back of the stage is a symbol that is closely associated with Noh drama in general and in particular with the popular Noh play *Takasago*, which deals with the spirits of the pine tree. As for the musicians, a full complement would be four, consisting of three drummers playing a *taiko* (a flat drum set in a wooden stand on the floor), an *otsuzumi* (an elongated drum held on the knee), and a *kotsuzumi* (an hour-glass-shaped drum held on the shoulder). In addition, there would be a player of the *fue* (flute).

One of the Noh plays that Britten and his party saw in Tokyo was *The Sumida River* (Sumidagawa); and in fact he was lucky enough to attend two performances of the same play in the course of a week or so. A detailed description of the action is given in the Prince of Hesse's travel diary:

'The ferryman is waiting in his boat, a traveller turns up and tells him about a woman who will soon be coming to the river. The woman is mad, she is looking for her lost child. Then she appears and the ferryman does not wish to take a mad person, but in the end he lets her into his boat. On the way across the river the two passengers sit behind each other on the floor as if in a narrow boat, while the ferryman stands behind them, symbolically punting with a light stick. The ferryman tells the story of a little boy who came this way a year ago this very day. The child was very tired for he had escaped from robbers who had held him. He crossed the river in this boat, but he died from exhaustion on the other side. The woman starts crying. It was her son. The ferryman is sorry for her and takes her to the child's grave. The mother is acted by a tall man in woman's clothing with a small woman's mask on his face. Accessories help you to understand what is going on: a bamboo branch in the hand indicates madness, a long stick is the ferryman's punting pole, a very small gong is beaten for the sorrowing at the graveside. As soon as these props are no longer necessary, stage-hands who have brought them to the actors take them away again. The sorrowful declamations of the mother rising and subsiding in that oddly pressed voice, the movement of her hand to the brim of her hat as if to protect her sadness from the outside world, the small "ping" of the little gong which she beats at the child's grave, become as absorbing as does the sudden foot-stamping which emphasizes important passages. The play ends in the chanting of the chorus.'

The memory of this extraordinary theatrical performance had never been far from Britten's mind in subsequent years, for he felt that in some ways it offered a new kind of operatic experience and wondered what could be learned from it. 'The solemn dedication and skill of the performers were a lesson to any singer or actor of any country and any language. Was it not possible to use just such a story—the simple one of a demented mother seeking her lost child—with an English background (for there was no question in any case of a pastiche from the ancient Japanese)? Surely the Medieval Religious Drama in England would have had a comparable setting—an all-male cast of ecclesiastics—a simple austere staging in a church—a very limited instrumental accompaniment—a moral story?'* Accordingly he approached his friend William Plomer and invited him to adapt *Sumidagawa* as a parable for church performance. Plomer was an excellent choice as librettist, for he had spent several years in Japan and was fully conversant with the Noh drama and its conventions. His main job was to anglicize the action of *Sumidagawa*, which had been written by Motomasa in the first part of the fifteenth century; and in this adaptation the Sumida River became the Curlew River, the scene being changed from the province of Musashi to a church by a Fenland river. The medieval period remained. In the Noh play, the incidental music was the ancient Japanese music that has been jealously preserved by successive generations. For *Curlew River*, this was scrapped; but to preserve the medieval atmosphere Britten decided to start his opera with the plainsong hymn *Te lucis ante terminum*, and from it, as he says,† 'the whole piece may be said to have grown'.

The difficulty of this work of adaptation should not be underrated. It is not that the action is particularly complicated; but the text of *Sumidagawa*, like that of all Noh plays, is impregnated with Buddhistic teaching. 'In this the main theme is the transitoriness of human life, and at the same time is presented a view of all the pain and misery people may endure when they are not rendered superior to it by a recognition of the higher philosophy that teaches that the whole universe is a dream, from whose toils the freed spirit can escape.'‡ To translate this into Christian terms was no easy task; but Plomer showed great discretion in the way he solved the problem. Two examples may be of interest.

Shortly after the arrival of the Madwoman, the Chorus comments—

A thousand leagues may sunder
A mother and her child,
But that would not diminish
Her yearning for her child.

(*Curlew River*)

In *Sumidagawa*, the Chorus continues in the following Buddhistic vein—

* From a note by the composer printed on the jacket of the libretto of *Curlew River*. Faber, 1964.

† Ibid.

‡ From *Plays of Old Japan: The No* by Marie C. Stopes. London, 1912.

The nature of the bond is transient,
The bond is transient in this world, and yet
Parent and child are destined not to live
In loving union even this short while.
But, like the four birds in the fable old,
*Between the cruel separation lies.**

(*Sumidagawa*)

This passage is missing from *Curlew River*.

The second example comes from the climax of the play, when the spirit of the child is first heard within the tomb, singing with the chorus, and then is heard solo. In *Sumidagawa*† the passage runs as follows:

CHILD: *I adore thee, O Eternal Buddha.*
I adore thee, O Eternal Buddha.
CHORUS: *The voice is heard, and like a shadow too*
Within, can one a little form discern.
[The Spirit of the Child appears.]
MOTHER: *Is it my child?*
CHILD: *Ah! Mother! Is it you?*
[The Spirit disappears.]

Here is the parallel passage from *Curlew River*—

ALL (except MADWOMAN and SPIRIT):
Hear his voice!
See, there is his shape!
[The SPIRIT of the BOY appears in full view above the tomb.]
MADWOMAN: *Is it you, my child?*
[The SPIRIT circles slowly round the MADWOMAN, who appears transformed.]
SPIRIT (off): *Go your way in peace, mother.*
The dead shall rise again
And in that blessèd day
We shall meet in Heaven.
God be with you all.
God be with you, mother.
MOTHER and THE REST:
Amen.
SPIRIT: *Amen.*

Plomer added a double framework. At the beginning of the action, a party of monks and acolytes with their Abbot walk in procession to the acting area,

* Translated by Marie C. Stopes. † Ibid.

Curlew River: Peter Pears as the Madwoman in the original 1964 production by the English Opera Group

where those monks who are to play the Madwoman, the Traveller and the Ferryman are ceremonially robed. At the end of the action, those who have played the three characters resume their monks' habits, and the Abbot leads the recession away from the acting area. (This device of procession and recession had already been used by Britten in *A Ceremony of Carols.*)

II

Plomer's adaptation of *Sumidagawa* kept sufficiently close to the original to postulate a considerable measure of stylization in the presentation of *Curlew*

River. The cast is all-male, the part of the Madwoman being sung by a tenor. As for the orchestra, Britten abandoned the characteristic layout of the English Opera Group chamber orchestra in favour of a new type of ensemble. From the traditional music associated with the Noh plays, he accepted the need for extended percussion and wrote parts for five small untuned drums, five small bells and one large tuned gong. He likewise accepted the flute as an essential solo instrument and added parts for horn, viola, double-bass, harp and chamber organ.

As is made clear in Colin Graham's notes attached to the rehearsal score, the production of *Curlew River* 'created a convention of movement and presentation of its own'. Graham goes on to suggest that 'movement and production details should be as spare and economical as possible . . . Every movement of the hand or tilt of the head should assume immense meaning and, although formalized, must be designed and executed with the utmost intensity.' The ritualistic nature of the actors' movements was of course intensified by the use of masks for the acting of the story.

The effect of this stylization was to isolate the players within their parts. Seeing this, Britten accepted the consequential implications—that the singers were as much a chamber music ensemble as the instruments and that a conductor was no longer a necessity.

The abolition of the conductor was a momentous step. It meant that each of the vocal parts must be given a measure of freedom that might include an element of rhapsody, and that some way would have to be found in the score of specifying which part (whether vocal or instrumental) had precedence at any particular moment, and, accordingly, who should lead and who should follow in the different episodes of this new musical democracy. The necessary time adjustments could be made with the help of certain rhapsodical effects which could be repeated *ad libitum*; and here Britten found it necessary to invent a new pause mark, which he called the 'curlew'.

According to Imogen Holst's introduction to the rehearsal score, 'the curlew sign over a note or rest shows that the performer must listen and wait till the other performers have reached the next barline, or meeting-point—i.e. the note or rest can be longer or shorter than its written value'. These aids to synchronization (reinforced by continuously cued parts for the players) enabled the singers and instrumentalists to 'conduct' the performance of the opera themselves; and this inevitably meant that, despite careful musical signs and directions, there were more variable factors affecting performances of the work than would be the case in a work relying on the services of a conductor.

Something of the flexibility of the musical style can be gauged from the following passage. The non-alignment of the Madwoman's part, the flute solo, and the harp ostinato shows (in the words of Imogen Holst) that 'their closely linked counterpoint has the freedom of independence':

Ex. 100a

The curlew theme just quoted is later built up into an ensemble by canonic imitation (Ex. 100b); and here the interrelation of the parts is only approximate. It will be seen that the elastic texture of such an ensemble in some ways resembles the 'chatter' recitatives in *Albert Herring* and *A Midsummer Night's Dream.*

Ex. 100b

Another aspect of this non-alignment is provided by the non-synchronized movements of different parts at the unison or the octave. For instance, the opening processional is a plainsong chant:

Ex. 101a

When a little later the monks are ceremonially robed for the play, the chant is taken over by the instruments in an altered guise. The harmonic implications of this asynchronous heterophony are important, for the notes of the melody begin literally to create the notes of the harmonies. Britten

Ex. 101b

accepted this; and if the score of *Curlew River* is compared with that of *Billy Budd* or *A Midsummer Night's Dream*, it will be seen that the new linear supremacy has led to the abandonment of most of the old triadic procedures with their polytonal implications. A simple example of this process is found in the Ferryman's opening music. Note how the horn enunciates the Ferryman's musical theme and how the viola and double-bass provide an accompaniment that usually follows, but occasionally anticipates the theme:

Ex. 102

The effect is sometimes that of underlining, sometimes that of shadowing, but always indicative of subservience. The result is invariably to exalt the musical line at the expense of independent harmony—heterophony in the place of polyphony.

Many of the harmonies in this score are note-clusters fed by prolonging the notes of the melodic line. This can be conveniently observed in the handling of the organ part in various parts of the score. A good example comes when the Spirit of the Boy addresses his mother:

Ex. 103

Beautiful though the curlew theme may be with its rising and falling lilt (Ex. 100), the Madwoman's most memorable moment is her initial cry (off-stage) of '*You mock me! You ask me whither I go.*' The Madwoman appears

Ex. 104

on the stage, and the same strange cry becomes '*Let me in! Let me out! Tell me the way!*' The asperities of her agonized search are assuaged only when at the climax of the action her repetition of the curlew theme is ultimately absorbed in the Dorian mode of the plainsong chant *Custodes hominum*, and her thanksgiving of *Sanctae sit Triadi* is echoed by the Spirit of the Boy from inside the tomb—a true resolution to the curlew quest:

Ex. 105

XIII
The Burning Fiery Furnace

Britten's second parable for church performance, *The Burning Fiery Furnace*, followed so closely on the first that it seemed natural for it to be made to more or less the same measure as *Curlew River*. The same convention was used whereby a group of monks led by their abbot, after entering the church in procession, proceed ceremonially to don the necessary costumes for the action, which is then presented in stylized fashion on an open circular-shaped stage, while the monks who are the instrumentalists form a conductorless chamber-music ensemble.

Once again Britten picked William Plomer as his librettist: but this time there was no question of turning a Noh play into a Christian parable. Instead, the two collaborators chose the Old Testament story of the three Jewish exiles (best known by the Babylonian names of Shadrach, Meshach, and Abednego) whom Nebuchadnezzar, at the request of Daniel, appointed as governors of the province of Babylon. Although these three Jews were prepared to accept office under Nebuchadnezzar, they refused to defile themselves with the eating and drinking customs of the country they were living in, or to worship the golden image that Nebuchadnezzar caused to be set up, thereby incurring his stern displeasure. As a punishment he commanded that the strongest soldiers in his army should bind the three of them in their coats, their hose, their hats, and their other garments and cast them into a furnace heated to seven times its usual temperature. This furnace was in fact so fiery that the task force of soldiers was instantly killed by the great heat; but the three Jews survived, praising, glorifying and blessing Jehovah in the furnace, where an Angel in the likeness of the Son of God joined them and protected them from the heat, so that when the king commanded the three of them to be brought out, it was found that they were completely unharmed, not even a hair of their heads having been singed. Nebuchadnezzar was so impressed by this miracle that he made a public proclamation affirming the power of the Jewish deity and restored Shadrach, Meshach, and Abednego to their former position as rulers of the province.

Whereas the action of *Curlew River* had been bisected by the episode of

The Burning Fiery Furnace: Nebuchadnezzar (Peter Pears) challenges the three young men in the original 1966 production by the English Opera Group

the actual crossing of the river with its swirling currents depicted by slow glissandi first on the strings and later on the harp, in *The Burning Fiery Furnace* the central point is provided by the sound of 'the cornet, flute, harp, sackbut, psaltery, dulcimer, and all kinds of music' which preludes the dedication of the image of gold set up by Nebuchadnezzar. This passage provided two cues which Britten followed up. In the first place, he added an alto trombone to the group of instruments he had already used in *Curlew River*; secondly, he used these instrumentalists to lead a procession of courtiers through the Church preparatory to the raising of Nebuchadnezzar's golden image—a bold and highly dramatic stroke.

The climax to the work is naturally provided by the miracle of the furnace and its non-destroying flames; but in order to provide a point of contrast, a divertissement is introduced in the early part of the opera, where in the course of Nebuchadnezzar's feast, two boy singers and a tumbler provide a light entertainment. The words of the acolytes are riddling:

The waters of Babylon,
The flowing waters,
All ran dry.
Do you know why?
. . . .
The reason the waters all ran dry
Was that somebody had monkey'd with the water supply;
The reason the gardens grew like mad
Was because of all the water they'd had.

The cocky little tune, with its flute and wooden blocks accompaniment, recalls Bottom's 'tongs and bones' music in *A Midsummer Night's Dream.*

How closely the framework follows the style of *Curlew River* can be seen from comparing the following quotations from the opening plainsong chant and the robing ceremonial with Exs. 101a and 101b above.

Ex. 106a

Ex. 106b

And how closely this plainsong is woven into the music of the three Jewish youths can be seen from the passage where they are left alone after the Astrologer has denounced them to Nebuchadnezzar:

Ex. 107

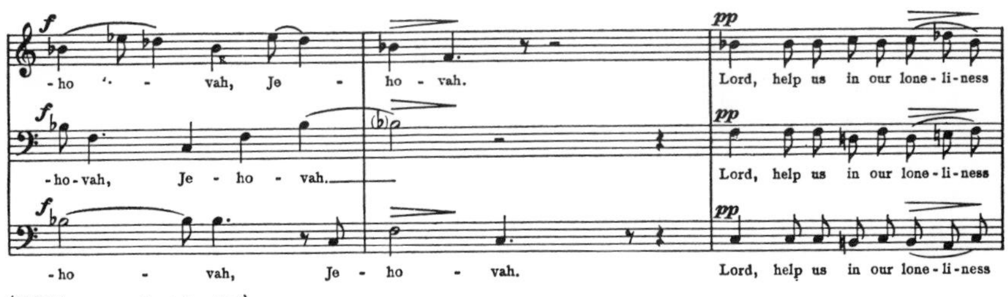

(*N.B.* The accompaniment is omitted)

After a herald has announced Nebuchadnezzar's decree that an image of gold shall be set up and worshipped, the instrumentalists 'warm up' their instruments for the forthcoming procession, while the three isolated Jewish youths continue to pray. These are the eight key phrases.

Ex. 108g

Ex. 108h

For the actual procession, each tune is lengthened to fill five bars of 4/4 tempo; and the following combinations are used for the different five-bar episodes: (i) horn and Babylonian drum, (ii) horn, trombone, and Babylonian drum, (iii) flute, trombone, viola, and Babylonian drum, (iv) glockenspiel, flute, viola, small cymbals and Babylonian drum, (v) glockenspiel, little harp, and small cymbals, (vi) little harp, horn, and Babylonian drum, (vii) horn, trombone, viola, and Babylonian drum, (viii) glockenspiel, little harp, flute, trombone, and small cymbals, (ix) little harp, flute, horn, viola, and Babylonian drum, (x) glockenspiel, little harp, flute, horn, trombone, viola, small cymbals and Babylonian drum. As can be seen from this scheme, each instrumental combination contains at least one instrument that has appeared in the immediately preceding combination, and towards the end the combinations become cumulative.

This processional march is one of the most original and effective strokes in the whole parable.

The D major/E flat minor polytonality of the march, with its ambivalent F sharp/G flat third, is prolonged by glissandi and tremolandi that greet the raising of the image of gold and the following chorus '*Merodak! Lord of Creation, we bow down before you*'. Melodically it reaches its apogee when the three young Jews are brought before Nebuchadnezzar, who accuses them of refusing to serve the god of gold. (Here the key has modulated to E major/F minor.)

Ex. 109

The appearance of the Angel in the fiery furnace recalls the miracle of the appearance of the Spirit of the Boy in *Curlew River*, and the Angel's voice is used to prolong some of the phrases of the Song of the Three Children by augmentation and imitation.

Ex. 110

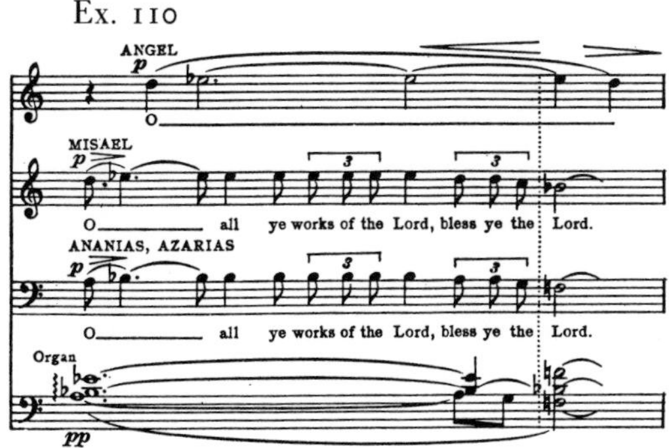

When the performance of the parable is over, the monks help the various characters to disrobe and resume their monks' habits. The Abbot reminds the congregation:

Friends, remember!
Gold is tried in the fire,
And the mettle of man
In the furnace of humiliation.

and then the plainsong chant, *Salus aeterna*, is used as a recessional.

The Burning Fiery Furnace marks a further step in the development of the technique of open-stage opera production.

XIV
The Prodigal Son

I

The libretto for the third of Britten's church operas, like those of the earlier two, was written by William Plomer; and this time the choice of subject fell on a New Testament parable. As Plomer himself wrote, on the jacket of the published libretto:* 'Of all the parables in the New Testament, none has had quite such a universal and ever-renewed appeal as that of the Prodigal Son . . . With its unforgettable climax of reward and rejoicing being lavished not upon virtuous correctness but upon a sinner, this parable celebrates the triumph of forgiveness. The story seems to bring into the clearest possible focus the Christian view of life.'

Once again the action is set within the convention of a group of monks, acolytes and lay brothers, who enter a church in procession and proceed to the acting area where the monks and acolytes are ceremonially robed for their parts, the lay brothers becoming the instrumentalists. The conductorless orchestra of eight is almost identical with that of *The Burning Fiery Furnace*, the only exceptions being that the flute has been replaced by an alto flute, the trombone by a trumpet in D, and the percussion omits the Babylonian drum that added special colouring to the processional march in *The Burning Fiery Furnace*, but introduces a gourd that underlines the 'walking music' of the Younger Son's journey to and from the great City.

Whereas *Curlew River* and *The Burning Fiery Furnace* are both divided in half—the first by the crossing of the river, and the second by the procession through the church prior to the erection of the image of gold—in *The Prodigal Son* the action requires an A B A change of scene, for the Younger Son is shown leaving his pastoral home to journey to the City and returning home after the Parasites have stripped him of his substance. This is ingeniously accomplished by a kind of panoramic effect, the Younger Son trudging round the circular acting area, while his Father, Elder Brother and their servants recede from view, and later, after the Prodigal has succumbed

* Faber, 1968.

The Prodigal Son: Peter Pears as the Tempter in the original 1968 production by the English Opera Group

to the temptations of the city, the return journey taking place in reverse.

To those who were familiar with the conventions established by *Curlew River* and *The Burning Fiery Furnace*, *The Prodigal Son* brought an unexpected surprise. Whereas in the two earlier church parables the monks were headed by their abbot in the initial procession, in *The Prodigal Son* the abbot is absent—for the very good reason that he plays the part of the Tempter and makes a surprise entrance through the congregation as soon as the procession of monks has reached the acting area in the church.

This character is an invention of Plomer's and is used to make explicit the motivation of the action:

> *Ah—you people, listening here today,*
> *Do not think I bid you kneel and pray.*
> *I bring you no sermon,*
> *What I bring you is evil.*
> . . .
> *Here you will see them!*
> *Father, servants who obey*

His least command,
Two sons, the elder stern,
The younger full of life,
He is the one I'll use
To break this harmony.
What perfect harmony!
See how I break it up.

The scene where the Tempter comes forward and confronts the Younger Son has disquieting undertones. The Younger Son is startled and asks by what right this stranger questions and examines him. The answer comes:

I am no stranger to you,
You know me very well,
I am your inner voice, your very self.

The Tempter proceeds to urge him to act out his secret desires, rather like Nick Shadow addressing Tom Rakewell in *The Rake's Progress*; and the analogy between Plomer's libretto for Britten and the libretto written by W. H. Auden and Chester Kallman for Stravinsky is strengthened when one reaches the Prodigal Son's three temptations in the city. This commentary by the Tempter (spoken recitative) might almost refer specifically to Mother Goose's brothel. '*Your senses have been freed by the pleasures of wine, but you have not yet begun to learn what pleasure means. Now you are offered the delights of the flesh, what you have been praying for. My boy, indulge yourself! Show yourself to be a man.*' But there is no special musical relationship between the two operas. Possibly the device of repetition and fragmentation when the Tempter decides to shatter the idyllic harmony of this Judaean country pastoral:

See how I break it up!
See how I break it up!
See how . . .
See how . . .

recalls the treatment of other similar passages from Britten's operas, such as the scene in *The Turn of the Screw* where Quint tempts Miles to steal the letter (see Ex. 77):

What has she written?
What has she written?
. . .
What does she know?
What does she know?
. . .

Easy to take,
Easy to take,
. . .
Take it!
Take it!

and the scene in *Billy Budd* where Vere suddenly becomes conscious of Claggart's villainy:

John Claggart, John Claggart,
Beware! beware!

The other characters follow closely the lines laid down by the parable in the Bible—the patriarchal Father, the Elder Son with his feeling that he has been unfairly treated, and the servants with their various pastoral pursuits.

II

Like the other two church parables, *The Prodigal Son* opens with a plainsong, *Jam lucis orto sidere*, whose *Amen!* is an ambivalent cue for the

Ex. 111a

Tempter's appearance:

Ex. 111b

It will be seen that the *Amens* of the plainsong as echoed by the Tempter diminish into a lively and insinuating tune with a strange enharmonic twist whereby the penultimate F natural becomes an E sharp. Mention of the country pastoral about to be disclosed pulls the tonality towards B flat; but before that key can be established, the robing ceremony takes place to the same sort of oriental dressing-up of the processional plainsong as was characteristic of *Curlew River* and *The Burning Fiery Furnace* (see Exs. 101b and 106b).

This leads immediately to the discovery of the Father seated under a tree, with his two sons and his servants gathered around him; and the pastoral tonality is established with a warm B flat major chord. The alto flute adds a mellow rhapsodic line to the Father's opening air '*The earth is the Lord's*':

Ex. 112a

The four notes of the singer's initial phrase are used in different combinations to introduce or close most of his subsequent phrases. Twenty-four permutations of this four-note phrase are possible; and nine of them occur in the Father's air:

Ex. 112b

A little later the phrase is expanded by the Father when he agrees to hand over the Younger Son's portion:

Ex. 112c

And as the Younger Son is robed to indicate his assumption of his share of the inheritance, the four-note theme is harmonized by the harp (later the organ) in a way that recalls similar procedures in *Billy Budd* (see Ex. 62) and elsewhere:

Ex. 112d

When the Prodigal succumbs to the threefold temptations of the City, he is successively stripped of portions of his inheritance. The stripping of the first portion is accompanied by a variant of the chordal version (Ex. 112d above); the stripping of the second portion by the phrase reduced to its basic four notes, but in the remote key of E major;

Ex. 112e

the stripping of the last portion by a bare skeleton outline from the drums. When after repenting his sins the Prodigal decides to return home, his Father greets him with a moving phrase, where only two notes of the original four remain, the other two having been absorbed into the accompanying chord.

Ex. 112f

This is a cadence of true forgiveness.

One of the most exciting features of the score of *The Prodigal Son* is the relationship between the Tempter and the Younger Son, which starts with the scene where the Tempter persuades the Younger Son to act out his desires. At this point the independence of the two vocal parts is complete. (Note how the trumpet takes over the Tempter's earlier exhortation to the people in the audience—see Ex. 111b.)

Ex. 113

On their journey to the City, however, the two voices become more closely related, though the Tempter's still has precedence. (Note how cleverly the Tempter leads the Younger Son into the temptation theme—see Exs. 111b and 113.)

Ex. 114

The part of the Elder Son is less important than those of the Father, the Younger Son and the Tempter. Nevertheless he is vividly characterized in the score. His incredulity and lack of sympathy, varied with sudden outbursts of jealousy and impetuosity, are depicted by the use of wide leaping intervals in the vocal line. When he hears that his Father has decided to give his Younger Brother his portion, he breaks out in rising anger:

Ex. 115

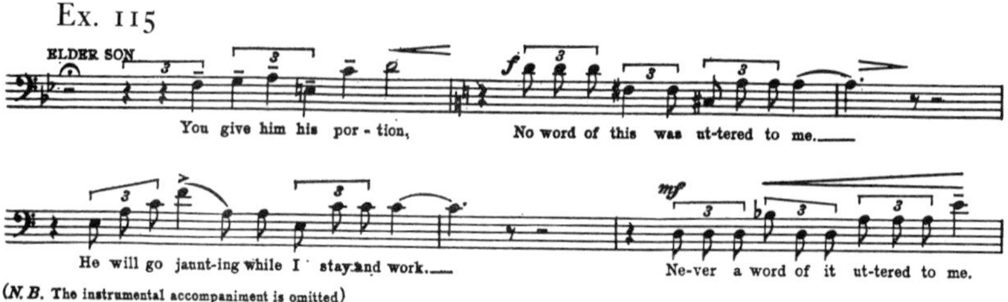

The members of the chorus have a more varied and more important part to play in *The Prodigal Son* than in either of Britten's earlier church operas.

In the first place, they are the servants in the household of the Father and his two sons. (There is no mention in the parable of a wife, or daughter or daughters.) In the City they are the Parasites who urge the Younger Son to excess in drinking, whoring and gambling, and also the Beggars who are starving because of the local famine. In the final scene they become the servants again.

The early choruses in the first part of the opera are composed on the lines of 'chatter' choruses ('*To the fields we go*', etc.) and this makes it easier for them to be faded out, as the servants move off to the fields, or to be faded in later as they return. ('*It is work that keeps*', etc.) In the City section, there are nine different choruses:

- I A quick and rumbustious 9 (2+2+2+3)/8 Parasites' Chorus of welcome. '*Welcome, welcome stranger!*'
- II Siren Voices (off-stage) offering wine.
- III A lively 6/8 Parasites' Drinking Chorus with brilliant whooping trumpet accompaniment, '*Come and try*'.
- IV Siren Voices (off-stage) offering '*nights of ecstasy*'.
- V A slow and heavy 6/8 Parasites' Chorus, '*Nights are days, days are nights.*'
- VI Siren Voices (off-stage) offering gold.
- VII A lively and rhythmic 3/4 Parasites' Gambling Chorus, with two wood blocks featured in the accompaniment, '*Never mind your gold is short*'.
- VIII Siren Voices (off-stage) asking for pity.
- IX Beggars' Chorus in 3/2 slow march time over a ground bass, '*We are starving*'.

This is quite a complex scheme considering that the scene in the City takes little more than a quarter of an hour to perform. When the Prodigal returns home, his Father summons the servants and orders them to bring robe, ring and shoes for his Younger Son to put on, to prepare the fatted calf for banquet, and to take part in a song and dance of welcome. They chant '*O sing unto the Lord a new song*', while dancing a round to the accompaniment of a heavy and sustained ground-bass consisting of an alternately rising and sinking scalic passage, the bars of which fall into an irregular 7+6 grouping:

Ex. 116

(N.B. The vocal parts for the Younger Son & Father, and the other instrumental parts, are omitted)

This dance is interrupted by the return of the Elder Son and his expostulation at his Father's extravagance in lavishing more money on his wastrel brother. But his Father reassures him and invites him (and all those present) to share his joy, '*for thy brother was dead, and is alive again, was lost, and is found*'. This is followed by the ceremonial disrobing ceremony, after which the Abbot leads the monks, acolytes and lay brothers in the recessional, *Jam lucis orto sidere* (Ex. 111a).

The Prodigal Son completes, not a trilogy, but a triptych of one-act operas for church performance, each lasting just over an hour and written to a common formula, though using different themes: a Japanese Noh play, an Old Testament story, a New Testament parable. In each case the initial plainsong chant grounds the opera firmly in the traditional context of the Christian Church, and from it grows and proliferates the music that accompanies the acted play—a convention within a convention. The instruments are closely related to the dramatis personae and give each opera its characteristic tone colour: flute in *Curlew River*, alto trombone in *The Burning Fiery Furnace*, trumpet and viola in *The Prodigal Son*. Singers and players form their own self-governing ensemble; and the lead passes from one voice to another, from one instrument to another, as action and music dictate. Despite the economy of means employed, these one-act operas exhibit great variety of musical texture and tension, and the impression they create is indeed full-scale.

XV
Owen Wingrave

I

For many years Britten had been chary of involving himself in television opera. He particularly objected to the fact that in an orthodox television studio, singers and orchestra had to be in different rooms. But at the beginning of 1969, John Culshaw, head of BBC television music programmes, peruaded him to conduct a BBC2 colour production of *Peter Grimes* by taking singers, supers, orchestra and production staff to the Snape Maltings where the concert hall was adapted to form a temporary television studio. The result was so satisfactory that the BBC decided to try to commission him to write a new opera specially for television. At first Britten hesitated. But in some ways he may have felt that the special restrictions inherent in the medium constituted an almost welcome challenge, and ultimately he consented. By the autumn of 1969 the new opera was well under way.

As subject he chose a short story by Henry James called *Owen Wingrave*. This had originally been published in the Christmas number of *The Graphic* for 1892 and reprinted in an American collection of James's tales entitled *The Wheel of Time* and in a British collection entitled *The Private Life*, both published in 1893. Britten had read it in the early 1950s or even earlier—certainly prior to his setting of *The Turn of the Screw*—and had found that its theme made a special appeal to his pacifist sensibilities, for it showed the viciousness and futility of the wargame as revealed by the history of a family of professional soldiers. 'Wingrave' is the family surname; 'Wingrave' is the story's epigraph—a rare instance in James's writings of a surname being manufactured to reveal a person's dominant characteristics, almost like the naming of humours in the old comedies of masks.

In the preface to the volume in the New York edition of Henry James's works entitled *The Altar of the Dead* which included *Owen Wingrave*, James wrote movingly of the moment of vision which led to the conception of this story 'one summer afternoon many years ago, on a penny chair and under a great tree in Kensington Gardens'. His imaginative process seems to have been awakened by the fact that while he sat there 'in the immense mild summer rustle and the ever so softened London hum a young man should have taken his place on another chair within [his] limit of contemplation, a tall quiet slim studious young man, of admirable type, and have settled to a book with immediate gravity'. James then speculates at what point the young man on the spot became the character in the story, but decides that such questions are answerless:

> My poor point is only that at the beginning of my session in the penny chair the seedless fable hadn't a claim to make or an excuse to give, and that, the very next thing, the pennyworth still partly unconsumed, it was fairly bristling with pretexts. 'Dramatise it, dramatise it!' would seem to have rung with sudden intensity in my ears. But dramatise what? The young man in the chair?

And so the idea of Owen Wingrave was conceived, the young scion of a military family, destined for an army career from birth, but now, just at the moment when he was being coached for Sandhurst, beginning to read for himself, think for himself, and rebel against a choice of career that had been imposed on him by his family, and which he now felt to run counter to his innermost personal convictions.

To get the right compositional focus in his story, James decided to put the professional coach, at whose establishment Wingrave and his friend young Lechmere are being 'crammed', into the centre of the action. Spencer Coyle is a kind and friendly person, through whose eyes and ears the reader follows the story; and in this role he is supported by his sympathetic wife. The characters at Paramore, the Wingraves' ancestral seat—old Sir Philip Wingrave (Owen's grandfather), Miss Jane Wingrave (Owen's aunt), and Mrs and Miss Julian (a widowed mother and her daughter Kate, who are friends of the family)—are seen as if from the outside by the Coyles who are invited to spend part of a weekend at Paramore. Owen takes the visitors round the house and shows them the family portraits. One of these—a double portrait depicting father and son—is the subject of a family legend. Apparently the father killed his son in a fit of anger, because he failed to take up another boy's challenge to fight. Shortly afterwards the father was himself discovered dead on the floor of the same room; and since then Paramore has been haunted by the apparitions of the old man and the boy. This tragedy now repeats itself. Kate Julian, who thinks she's in love with Owen, taunts him with cowardice; and he, to prove his courage, agrees to sleep in the haunted room. He does so and is discovered dead there the following morning.

The cry 'Dramatise it, dramatise it!' continued to ring in James's ears even after *Owen Wingrave* had been completed and published as a story; and in 1907 he decided to turn it into a one-act play, which he called *The Saloon*,

Owen Wingrave: The Paramore set by David Myerscough Jones at Snape Maltings

using the word 'salon' in its old form. When it was finished, he was persuaded to submit it to the Incorporated Stage Society; but the Society rejected it at a meeting on 12 January 1909, when Bernard Shaw agreed to write to James about it. He did so, and his letter sparked off a lively correspondence between the two writers* Shaw deplored James's use of the supernatural, and James put up a characteristically subtle defence. Shaw's argument was summarized in a letter he wrote on 21 January:

> My dear Henry James,
>
> You cannot evade me thus. The question whether the man is to get the better of the ghost or the ghost of the man is not an artistic question; you can give victory to one side just as artistically as to the other. And your interest in life is just the very reverse of a good reason for condemning your hero to death. You have given victory to death and obsolescence. I want to give it to life and regeneration. . . .

James's reply was comparatively succinct (for him!):

> There was only one question to me, that is, that of my hero's within my narrow compass, and on the lines of my very difficult scheme of compression and concentration, getting the *best of everything*, simply;

* This correspondence is printed in full in Leon Edel's Foreword to *The Complete Plays of Henry James*. Rupert Hart-Davis, 1949.

Owen Wingrave: Miss Wingrave (Sylvia Fisher), Sir Philip (Peter Pears), Kate (Janet Baker) and Mrs Julian (Jennifer Vyvyan) in the original 1970 BBC television production

> which his death makes him do by, in the first place, purging the house of the beastly legend, and in the second place by his creating for us, spectators and admirers, such an intensity of impression and emotion about him as must promote his romantic glory and edifying example for ever. I don't know what you could have more. He wins the victory—that is he clears the air, and he pays with his life. The whole point of the little piece is that he, while protesting against the tradition of his 'race', proceeds and pays exactly like the soldier that he declares he'll never be.

In the event James did not rewrite *The Saloon* as Shaw had urged him to; and it was ultimately produced in London on 17 January 1911 as a curtain-raiser to Cicely Hamilton's *Just to Get Married*. From contemporary notices it appears that the final scene was played (against the author's advice) in far too melodramatic a style, and the play was not a success.

As had been the case with *The Turn of the Screw*, Britten invited Myfanwy Piper to be his librettist. Looking at the available material, she decided to ignore *The Saloon* as being not to her purpose, and concentrated on the story. From the outset she felt herself free to fill out some of James's half-suggestions and to invent new business, particularly when such treatment seemed likely to suit the medium of television. In her hands the action fell into two acts and was presented as follows:

ACT I

Prelude A series of portraits of Owen's military ancestors

Scene 1: The study at Coyle's military establishment (Owen, Coyle, Lechmere)

Interlude I Regimental banners wave brilliantly

Scene 2: Owen in Hyde Park, alone, sitting reading—crosscut with Miss Wingrave and Coyle in her lodgings in Baker Street

Interlude II A sequence of old faded tattered flags

Scene 3: A room at the Coyles' establishment (Mr and Mrs Coyle, Lechmere, Owen)

Interlude III Paramore

Scene 4: Mrs Julian, Kate Julian, Miss Wingrave, and Sir Philip Wingrave receive Owen with deep disfavour at Paramore

Scene 5: A week passes during which Owen is under constant attack from his family

Scene 6: The hall at Paramore. The Coyles and Lechmere have arrived as guests and are received by Owen

Interlude IV The Preparation of Dinner

Scene 7: The serving of dinner (full cast)

ACT II

Prologue Ballad (sung by a Narrator)

Scene 1: The hall at Paramore one evening, and the gallery outside the haunted room

Scene 2: The Coyles' bedroom later that night; and subsequently the gallery outside the haunted room

It looks as if these two acts were planned to serve somewhat different purposes. Act I with its seven different scenes deals primarily with war—the implications of training for war, action in the field, death in battle, glory after death—and offers a background for Owen's violent reaction against his family and its military tradition, whereas Act II is virtually one continuous scene, which presents the legend of the ghosts in ballad form (prologue):

There was a boy, a Wingrave born,
A Wingrave born to kill his foe.
Far away on sea and land,
The Wingraves were a fighting band.
Trumpet blow, trumpet blow,
Paramore shall welcome woe.

This act moves swiftly to its climax where Owen, taunted with cowardice by

Kate Julian, elects to be locked up in the haunted room for the night* and is found dead the next morning.

The difference between the acts is reflected also in a slight shift of focus where Coyle is concerned. At the beginning of Act I, particularly in scenes i, ii and iii, he is shown in his professional capacity as a coach, with Owen and Lechmere as his pupils. From Act I scene vi to the end of Act II he appears in a different capacity as a sympathetic friend of Owen's. The two roles are, of course, closely related: but Coyle's position in the compositional centre of the story means that when he is absent (as is the case in scenes iv and v of Act I) the remaining characters have a tendency to verge on caricature.

The greater part of the libretto is written in a kind of heightened prose, broken into irregular line lengths; the Ballad of the Wingrave Boy makes a good attempt to reproduce true ballad idiom; and some fragments of poetry are specially featured in the second Interlude of Act I when Owen is discovered reading in the Park, not (as James suggested) from a book of Goethe, but (as Myfanwy Piper has decided) from Shelley's *Queen Mab*. It is interesting to find that whereas most of Myfanwy Piper's heightened prose has been set by Britten as air, arioso, or recitative, the Shelley quotations are merely declaimed by Owen at fixed pitches but without exact indication of note lengths or rhythm.

II

Though designed for the intimacy of the television screen, *Owen Wingrave* is not a chamber opera like *The Turn of the Screw*—the score is written for about the same-sized orchestra as Britten's Symphony for Cello and Orchestra. Owen is a baritone; Coyle a bass-baritone; and Lechmere and Sir Philip Wingrave tenors. Three of the women (Miss Wingrave, Mrs Julian, and Mrs Coyle) are sopranos; and Kate Julian is a mezzo-soprano. The ballad is sung by a narrator (tenor). This casting is significant. The choice of middle range takes Owen out of the heroic tenor category with its bravura implications; and it may be recalled that in *Billy Budd* a similar problem was solved in a similar way, Billy being cast as a baritone, with Vere as tenor and Claggart as bass.

The opera opens with an instrumental prelude, which immediately establishes two factors—that the action is concerned with military matters and that for generations past the Wingrave family has been dedicated to the pursuit of war. In the first three bars, the twelve notes of the chromatic scale

* At this point Myfanwy Piper has made an important alteration to James's story. According to James, when Kate taunted Owen and dared him to sleep in the haunted room, he told her he'd already spent the previous night there, to which she retorted 'whether he'd care if he should know she believed him to be trying to deceive them', and so at his express request he was taken by Kate to spend a second night there, and this time she locks him in. This over-subtlety is (rightly) rejected in the opera, where Owen tries only once to sleep in the haunted room—with fatal results.

are split up into three chords forming a martial percussive theme that recalls the sharp sizzling clashes of swords and scimitars:

Ex. 117

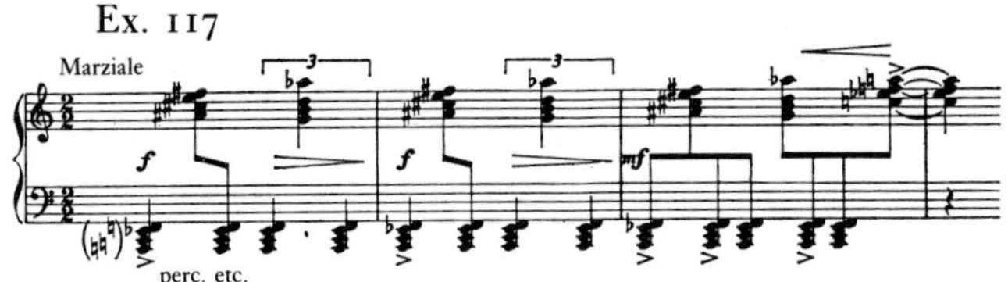

This is immediately followed by a series of eleven musical portraits of Owen's military ancestors as they hang on the gallery and stairs of the family mansion at Paramore. Each portrait is a musical cadenza, usually for a solo instrument; and as each portrait is introduced a fresh note is added to a held chord so that with the eleventh portrait (which is Owen's dead father) the chord contains eleven different notes of the chromatic scale. It is then withdrawn, and the missing twelfth note (D natural) becomes the bass for Owen's personal appearance after his father's portrait has been presented. The structure of this scheme can be gathered from the following example, which shows, first, the eleven-note chord underpinning the portrait of Owen's father (entrusted to woodwind and brass) followed by the martial percussive theme, leading to Owen's actual appearance, where a horn solo is supported by a low D pedal. It should be noted that many of the intervals in Owen's theme are thirds, particularly minor thirds, and where two minor thirds follow each other they imply the existence of a diminished triad. In fact, the solo themes depicting the Wingrave ancestors are riddled with minor thirds, and the military atmosphere seems favourable to the diminished triad. Musically, the diminished triad might be thought to be hesitant, ambivalent, unable to make up its mind: but in this particular context it seems to stand for a constitutional inability to face the ethical and philosophical implications of a system geared to war and aggression as a normal way of life:

Ex. 118

Scene i of the opera follows without pause; and here it will be seen that the notes of the diminished triad occupy an important position in the accompaniment to Coyle's lecture on military tactics:

Ex. 119

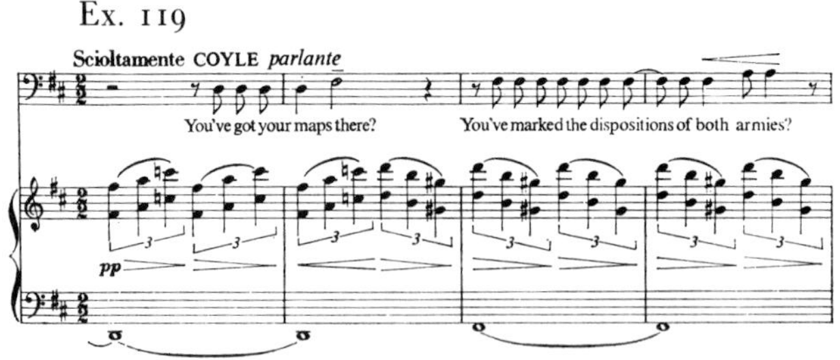

It should be noted that the deployment of the twelve notes of the chromatic scale in Examples 117 and 118 leads to no special serial development. As far as Owen is concerned, the score illustrates his continuing preoccupation to establish himself as a man of peace on a broad diatonic basis; and in this he resembles Billy Budd. To the sensitive listener it is clear that in *Owen Wingrave* Britten has tapped areas of deep feeling that were common also to *Billy Budd*. But whereas in *Budd*, owing to the special limitations of that character, these feelings were not always articulate—indeed, Billy's stammer was an outward indication of his occasional inability to express himself, particularly under stress—in *Owen Wingrave* librettist and composer succeeded in exploring Owen's thoughts and motivation in depth. This is particularly true of Owen's affirmation of belief—'In peace I have found my image, I have found myself'—which comes halfway though Act II. This is close in tonality, feeling and certain aspects of compositional treatment to Billy's moving 'farewell to ye, old Rights o'Man!' which followed immediately on his Ballad in the Darbies. Here is the opening of Owen's air:

Ex. 120

Donald Mitchell has made a most perceptive comparison between the two men's songs:*

> If one compares the actual sound of [these two airs], there is one subtle and significant aspect of the sonority of the 'peace' aria in *Wingrave* that immediately strikes one. Whereas the chords in the *Budd* excerpt are dropped like great anchors into and against the quaver flow of piccolo and harp, in *Wingrave* it is the percussion orchestra which sustains the quaver figuration into which the chords of affirmation are injected. Up to this point in the opera, the percussion has been associated, through the opening pulsation, with the idea of war and violence, with the mailed fists of the Wingraves. Now, however, the percussion orchestra (*plus* vibraphone, *minus* drums) functions in quite a different role, as the very opposite of aggression: as a shimmering radiance, no less, surrounding and decorating the chordal affirmations of Owen's resolve.

The analogy between Owen and Billy can be pursued further still. In *Budd*, after the drumhead court has been held, it is left to Vere to communicate the court's findings to Billy, and he does so behind a closed door in a room off-stage, while the stage itself is left empty, and the unheard communication is accompanied by a slow procession of common chords, instrumented for different sections of the orchestra, or (exceptionally) for full orchestra. In the second act of *Wingrave*, Sir Philip Wingrave summons Owen to an interview. The talk that leads to his disinheritance takes place behind a closed door, while Miss Wingrave, Mrs and Miss Julian, and Mr and Mrs Coyle wait outside in the hall. But this interview is more explicit than the one in *Budd*, since during it Sir Philip's voice is heard from the room off-stage where the interview is taking place, though his words are only half audible, and Owen's part in the discussion is taken over by a horn solo played behind the scenes.

The ballad that forms the Prologue to Act II plays the same sort of role in

* From 'Owen Wingrave and the Sense of the Past', printed in the sleeve note to the recording issued by Decca in 1971.

Ex. 121

the second half of this opera as that of the plainsong chants that frame Britten's three Church Operas. Particularly skilful is the way it is altered to form an eerie pianissimo ostinato that ticks its way through the penultimate scenes of Act II, when Owen has been locked in the haunted room and the Coyles are passing a sleepless night in the guest chamber. And

Ex. 122

even here one is still pursued by the *Billy Budd* analogy when one recalls the prominent part played in that opera by the motif of a rising fifth followed by a rising semitone (see Exs. 55–61). The climax comes when three notes of the theme coalesce to form the chord that accompanies Kate's cry as she finds Owen dead on the floor of the haunted room.

Although the work is fully viable in the opera-house, it must be remembered that it was originally written for television. This has led in places to a compressed style of presentation—bridge passages were shortened, transitions speeded up, scenes mixed. For instance, the scene where Owen is shown sitting alone in the Park, reading from a book that turns out to be a collection of Shelley, is cross-cut with a scene showing Coyle interviewing Miss Wingrave in her London lodging; and at one point all three characters share a common vision of the Horse Guards* trotting by, with what Owen calls 'that rippling, sweet, obedient well-being'. This is a passage that proves to be remarkably successful in television terms. So too in the original BBC 2 production were the colour effects of some of the interludes, particularly the contrast between the clean, brilliant colours of the regimental banners in Interlude I and the old tattered flags with faded colours like smouldering jewels that accompanied Owen's reading from *Queen Mab* (Interlude II). The television production scored a good point too for the way it used what appeared to be an old-fashioned silent film in monochrome as visual accompaniment to the Narrator's Ballad. The intimacy imposed by the small screen was particularly successful in the dinner party scene at the end of Act I. Not only could the cameras give a general view of the dinner party in progress, but they could also focus on each character individually as occasion arose and, if necessary, allow them to reveal their unspoken thoughts.

The television production was seen by millions of viewers when it was broadcast by BBC 2 on 16 May 1971. Two years later the first stage performance was given by the Royal Opera at the Royal Opera House, Covent Garden, on 10 May 1973. There, during its first season, *Owen Wingrave* was seen by audiences numbering several thousands. In future it is to be hoped there will be occasions when the original television production with its admirable cast can be revived. It will always be interesting to compare it with whatever happens to be the most recent 'live' production in an opera-house.

* Actually the officers and men of the Royal Military Police Mounted Troop (Aldershot) were filmed for these scenes.

XVI
Death in Venice

I

Britten's close friendship with Peter Pears had led in the course of time to the creation of much music which had been written with the special qualities of his friend's tenor voice in mind. This was true of all the operas after *Paul Bunyan*. The title roles in *Peter Grimes* and *Albert Herring* were specially written for Pears; so too was that of the Earl of Essex in *Gloriana*. In *Billy Budd* Pears was cast as Captain Vere; and this undoubtedly influenced Britten's decision to make the eponymous hero a baritone. Pears gave powerful character interpretations as the Male Chorus in *The Rape of Lucretia*, Quint in *The Turn of the Screw*, the Madwoman in *Curlew River*, Nebuchadnezzar in *The Burning Fiery Furnace*, and the Tempter in *The Prodigal Son*. His only minor character parts had been as Flute in *A Midsummer Night's Dream* and Sir Philip Wingrave in *Owen Wingrave*. Quite an extensive roll-call! When the latter opera was completed, Britten decided to choose for his next opera a subject which would give Pears a major part to play, by way of celebrating a partnership that had lasted for nearly a third of a century.

In the past, when searching for suitable opera subjects, he had occasionally gone to prose texts for his material; and so it was in this case. In Thomas Mann's novella *Der Tod in Venedig*, he found what he was looking for—a particularly rich part for the chief character, Gustav von Aschenbach. In this story Aschenbach appears in a double capacity—as a successful author, or artist, who is presented as if he were a projection of the actual author of *Der Tod in Venedig*, of Mann himself; and also as the chief actor in this story of corruption and death. The elderly man becomes obsessed with Tadzio, a Polish boy of thirteen. Tadzio's part is a silent one in the sense that although he obviously chatters like any normal boy to his boy friends and the members of his family, who are staying at the same hotel on the Lido as Aschenbach, he never says anything to Aschenbach, nor is he reported as saying anything to anyone else who is featured in the story. A dumb part—but not one that was likely to deter Britten, as would be obvious to those who remembered the silent but vital contribution made by Grimes's apprentice boy to the two scenes in the second act of *Peter Grimes*. From the outset it was obvious that if *Der Tod in Venedig* was to be turned into an opera, its success would stand or fall by the composer's ability to provide a convincing part for Aschenbach (who would have to be on the stage for virtually the whole of the action), and by the singer's ability to give an outstanding performance.

Britten had worked before with Myfanwy Piper, who had supplied the librettos for two of his operas based on prose texts by Henry James—*The Turn of the Screw* and *Owen Wingrave*. He now asked her to give Thomas Mann's novella similar treatment. She condensed the action into seventeen scenes; and the composer added an impressionist overture entitled 'Venice' between scenes ii and iii. The opera was to contain about 145 minutes of music: so it was clear that the average length of a scene would be about eight minutes, and the composer would have to arrange his score so that the music moved with swiftness and ease, and the scenes dissolved and flowed into each other without interruption. Indeed, at certain points it might be necessary for the composer to use a kind of musical shorthand in order to maintain the speed necessary to tackle a subject that featured so many complex issues—psychological, philosophical, and mythical.

Aschenbach, one is told, is a successful elderly writer, who since the death of his wife and the marriage of his only daughter has become increasingly insecure and solitary. In the novella Mann described him with so much sympathy and understanding that at times an autobiographical element seemed to creep in. In the opera, as Myfanwy Piper pointed out, there is no narrator, but 'essential information and comment is given by Aschenbach himself in prose (recitative accompanied by the piano), as distinct from the shaped recitative and the songs and lyrical passages.'* Indeed, *Death in Venice* restores recitative—whether dry, accompanied, or near-arioso—to the supreme position it used to hold in the early years of Italian opera, particularly in Venice at the beginning of the seventeenth century. The dry recitative is especially interesting. Here Britten follows a technique he had tried out in the second interlude of *Owen Wingrave* where the pitches are exactly notated, but not the time values of the notes, the implication being that the words are to be given the loose conversational rhythm imposed by the ordinary speaking voice. There are ten such passages in *Death in Venice*. The voice is usually accompanied by the piano, and Aschenbach marks these recitatives by taking from his pocket a small notebook 'the symbol of his novelist's trade'.

In Mann's novella, Aschenbach meets a number of characters—the

* From the programme note by Myfanwy Piper for the original English Opera Group performances. Subsequent Myfanwy Piper quotations come from the same source.

Traveller, the Elderly Fop, the old Gondolier, and the Leader of the Strolling Players—who guide him on his journey to what proves to be his death. In her programme note, Myfanwy Piper says:

> Nowhere does Mann suggest that they have supernatural powers, or that they are one and the same person, but he links them by endowing each with the snub nose and grin of death, and the broad-brimmed hat and staff of Hermes, conductor of the dead across the Styx. For dramatic and musical reasons they are all sung by the same performer, and we have extended Mann's list to include the Hotel Manager, the Barber, and the god Dionysus, whose voice is heard by Aschenbach in a dream.

A remarkable feat of doubling!

A major problem was posed by Tadzio, the Polish boy. His beauty catches Aschenbach's eye, and the writer becomes obsessed with this image of perfection; but he fails to establish any sort of contact with the boy, except the occasionally intercepted glance, and remains solely an onlooker and unsuccessful pursuer. Myfanwy Piper comments:

> In the book he has no verbal contact with Tadzio, or his family and friends: nor does he in the opera, and we have emphasized this separateness by formalizing their movements into dance.

Although the seventeen scenes of the opera form a single stream of narrative, for theatrical purposes it was necessary to divide them into two acts. The caesura comes after scene vii, which is entitled 'The Feasts of the Sun'. Watching Tadzio and his boy friends playing on the beach, Aschenbach allows his fancy to stray to ancient Greece:

> He hears the voice of Apollo, turns the children's games into myths and the beach into Socratic Greece, with Tadzio as the olive-crowned victor of the boys' pentathlon. . . . Tadzio smiles at him and Aschenbach realizes that what he feels is love.

This is the climax and end of Act I.

Shortly before the end of the novella, Mann gives a lurid account of a dream Aschenbach suffers one night, an orgy of frenzy associated with the arrival of 'the stranger god', who is presumably Dionysus. In the opera, this nightmare is made more explicit by introducing Apollo in opposition to Dionysus. Mann's exaggerated Bosch-like imagery of frantic females shrieking and clutching snakes, and of horned and hairy males beating on brazen vessels and drums is not followed up in the opera; but his graphic description of the mad rout yelling a cry 'with a long-drawn U-sound at the end' provides the cue for a dionysiac chorus in which the singers vocalize on 'Aa-oo' sounds. The same vowels are echoed in the cries of '*Tadziù!*' called

Death in Venice: The Games of Apollo with Robert Huguenin as Tadzio in the original 1973 production by the English Opera Group

by his friends on the Lido beach, and the gondoliers' cry of '*Aou*'*!*' on the lagoon.

Death in Venice is like a long operatic narration. The following summary of the action is combined with a commentary on the music.

II

Scene 1: A Cemetery in Munich

The opera opens with an accompanied recitative for Aschenbach, which is based on the twelve notes of the chromatic scale. But although the blockage

Ex. 123

of which he sings ('*no words come*') is fundamental to the subsequent action he takes, no attempt is made by the composer to erect this musical series into a compositional system. What is musically important, however, is the emphasis on the minor third—in the above example contoured as F natural to G sharp, G sharp to B natural, B natural to D natural, and C natural to E flat. This recalls Britten's earlier preoccupation with the intervals of the diminished triad in *Owen Wingrave* (see particularly Exs. 118 and 119). An unknown traveller appears on the steps of a mortuary chapel and sings about the marvels of exotic climes, urging Aschenbach to travel to the south. For an instant the two voices combine. Then the traveller disappears; and Aschenbach makes up his mind. A fortissimo major third (F sharp and A sharp) issues from the trombones like a ship's siren—and he is on his way to Venice.

Scene 2: On the Boat to Venice

The boat sets out from Pola; and the beat of the engines is emphasized by a rhythm played on the side drum with brushes. A group of youths on board shout to the girls on shore, and out of this exchange of ribaldries arises the two-part chant of their destination:

Ex. 124

An elderly fop starts a popular song, '*We'll meet in the Piazza*', which is taken up by the youths on board. After the boat has arrived in Venice and the passengers have disembarked, the overture follows.

Overture: Venice

This is the most extended instrumental number in the score. Its initial theme is a kind of barcarolle with a lazily lapping and overlapping motif of ripples (threes against fours). This is based on the '*Serenissima*' phrase and is capable of considerable variation. Out of this barcarolle rises

Ex. 125

an open-air brass fanfare, the same tune being presented at four different pitches, subject to slight rhythmic changes:

Ex. 126

This Gabrieli-like fanfare alternates with a brazen clangour of bells. And by these simple musical means, the composer's impressionist evocation of Venice with her towers, domes. and palaces rising from the waters of the lagoon is complete.

Scene 3: The Journey to the Lido

Aschenbach takes a gondola from Venice to the Lido, and is rowed by an old Gondolier, who gruffly asserts his independent spirit, somewhat to Aschenbach's discomforture. On the way over, they pass a boatload of boys and girls singing an unaccompanied song '*Bride of the sea . . .*' with a choral refrain of '*Serenissima . . .*' (founded on Ex. 124) which helps to establish a special dimension of distanced sound on the lagoon. On arrival at the Lido quayside, Aschenbach is greeted by the hotel staff, while the old Gondolier is found to have disappeared without being paid. This prompts Aschenbach to a sombre soliloquy—'*Mysterious gondola . . . How black a gondola is—black, coffin black, a vision of death itself and the last silent voyage.*'

Scene 4: The first evening at the hotel

On his arrival at the hotel Aschenbach is welcomed by the Manager and shown to his room—a room with a specially fine view:

Ex. 127

The wide sweep of this panorama recalls the moment in Bartók's *Bluebeard's Castle* when Judith flings open the fifth door to reveal a vast, magnificent landscape. But here it is a lagoonscape instead of a landscape that meets Aschenbach's gaze. The musical motif with its dropping thirds underpinned by a sequence of rising triads is one of Britten's most characteristic

Death in Venice: Peter Pears as Gustav von Aschenbach in the original 1973 production by the English Opera Group

hallmarks. The hotel guests now assemble for dinner. There is a buzz of polyglot conversation, like one of the chatter-choruses in *Albert Herring*; and Aschenbach sees Tadzio for the first time—'*a beautiful young creature, the boy*'—with the other members of his Polish family. This is the cue for a Lydian melody played by the vibraphone, which henceforward is closely associated with Tadzio:

Ex. 128

Scene 5: On the Beach

Aschenbach is on the beach, with various other hotel guests. A strawberry seller passes by. In view of the comparative rarity of female characters in this opera, the high tessitura of her soprano cry is particularly appealing, though the accompaniment is somewhat equivocal:

Ex. 129

Tadzio comes out on to the beach and sits with his family. At first Aschenbach does not know his name, but when his friends call to him to join in their games, they cry '*Adziù!*' and this is echoed '*Ah-oo!*' From

Ex. 130

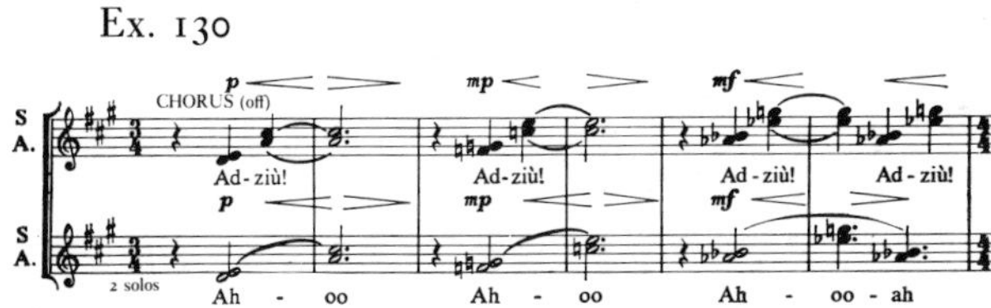

this Aschenbach deduces that the boy's proper name is Tadzio, short for Thaddeus. Tadzio and his friends play games on the beach, which are characterized by the sounds of xylophone, marimba, and glockenspiel. Aschenbach watches and listens, entranced.

Scene 6: The Foiled Departure

Aschenbach crosses to Venice from the Lido (variant of Ex. 125), and the Gondolier's strange cry '*Aou'!*' emphasizes the melancholy of the lagoon. The sirocco is blowing, and Venice is hot and uncomfortably crowded. Aschenbach is depressed and decides to leave. He returns to the Lido by gondola, accompanied as before by a variant of Ex. 125 and the gondoliers' cries of '*Aou'!*' but his departure is foiled by a stupid mistake over the registration of his luggage at the station, and presently he finds himself returning to the Lido, to the hotel he had so recently left. The Manager welcomes him back and shows him into the room he had vacated a few hours previously. The view is virtually unchanged (a slight variant of Ex. 127). Aschenbach sees Tadzio and some of his friends playing on the beach. His spirits revive and he realizes what it was that had made it so hard for him to leave. This leads to a moment of resignation and acceptance that recalls similar moments in other operas by Britten, such as the '*Goodnight!*' scene in *Owen Wingrave*. This particular cadence contains a feeling of impending doom, despite its resolution each time on a major triad:

Ex. 131

Scene 7: The Feasts of the Sun (The Games of Apollo)

This scene allows the framework of the opera to be extended so as to project the boys' beach games into the antique Olympian world and to provide an important ballet diversion. The greater part of the music consists of a succession of four-part choral hymns, but at several points the solo voice of Apollo (counter-tenor) is heard off-stage, announcing that '*He who loves beauty worships me*'. The chorus elevates Tadzio so that he is equated with Phoebus, and he is given a formal dance solo. This is followed by the feasts of the sun. The boys compete in a variety of sports—running, long jump, discus throwing, javelin throwing, and wrestling—and in each of these Tadzio is the winner. Aschenbach is so excited by this display of skill that he feels he must speak to Tadzio to congratulate him, but as the boy passes him, he fails to do so. Tadzio smiles at him: and when it is too late to respond, Aschenbach bursts out, '*Ah! don't smile like that! No one should be smiled at like that.*' An eight-part upward surge in the orchestra, passing from pianissimo to fortissimo, helps Aschenbach to realize exactly what has happened to him, and he sings the words 'I love you' to an empty stage just before the curtain falls.

The music of the second act starts exactly where the music of the first act left off—a device that Britten had already used in the original version of *Billy Budd*. An extensive passage of dry recitative for Aschenbach, '*So, it has come to this*', leads to—

Scene 8: The Hotel Barber's Shop (i)

Aschenbach is having his hair trimmed. The snipping instrumental accompaniment to the Barber's chatter role paints as vivid a picture as some of the character vignettes to be found in an opera like *Albert Herring*.

Scene 9: The Pursuit

Aschenbach crosses to Venice (variant of Ex. 125). There are posters in the streets advising citizens to take precautions against infection. The foreign newspapers feature rumours of an outbreak of cholera in Venice. The Polish family turns up, and Aschenbach starts to trail them. The pursuit is accompanied by a restless bass *ostinato*. They all reach the Piazza

Ex. 132

and a café orchestra starts to play, led by a violinist who shows off his double-stopping. The Polish family moves on; and Aschenbach follows them into the Cathedral of San Marco, where the choir is singing a *Kyrie Eleison* punctuated by the pealing of bells. This pursuit leads to the point where the Polish family takes to a gondola, followed by Aschenbach also in a

Britten's composition sketch for the end of Act I and the beginning of Act II of *Death in Venice*

gondola, while the two gondoliers' cries of '*Aou*'!' attract the cry of a third gondolier in the distance.

Scene 10: The Strolling Players

Back in the hotel after dinner, Aschenbach attends a light entertainment given by a small company of strolling players on the terrace, consisting of:

I. Waltz (duet for a boy and a girl) '*O mio carino*'
II. Popular Song (the Leader) '*La mia nonna*'
III. Laughing Song (Leader and chorus) '*Fiorir rose in mezzo al giasso*'

Scene 11: The Travel Bureau

Aschenbach visits a travel bureau, which is being besieged by a number of tourists anxious to leave Venice because of the threat of plague. When they have gone, the clerk speaks to Aschenbach in an open, uninhibited way. His long prose speech, '*In these last years Asiatic cholera has spread from the delta of the Ganges . . .*', set as accompanied recitative, is one of the most moving numbers in the score. Its climax unequivocally reveals the presence of the plague:

Ex. 133

Scene 12: The Lady of the Pearls (*i.e.* Tadzio's mother)

Aschenbach decides to warn Tadzio's mother of the danger she runs in allowing herself and her family to linger on at the Lido while the plague is tightening its grip, and to urge her to depart. But when an opportunity occurs, he cannot bring himself to speak.

Scene 13: The Dream

In his despair he falls asleep. The voices of Dionysus ('*Receive the stranger god*') and Apollo ('*No! reject the abyss!*') are heard epitomizing the struggle in his mind. The followers of Dionysus appear, singing their orgiastic cry of '*Ah-oo!*' and this leads to a dionysiac dance, one of the few *allegro molto* passages in the score, based mainly on the Tadzio theme (see Ex. 128).

Scene 14: The empty beach

Aschenbach, shocked by the revelations of his recent nightmare, goes down to the beach and watches Tadzio and his friends, who are playing about in a desultory fashion.

Scene 15: The Hotel Barber's Shop (ii)

To the same sort of accompaniment as before, Aschenbach sits in the Barber's chair to have his greying hair and moustache tinted, and his ageing features made up.

Scene 16: The Last Visit to Venice

In the first flush of his rejuvenation, Aschenbach sings an altered version of the song '*We'll meet in the Piazza*', which was sung by the youths on the boat bound for Venice in scene ii. His pursuit of the Polish family is resumed as in scene ix; and in the excitement of the chase the bass ostinato (Ex. 133) is inverted and treated fugally. At the climax, Tadzio detaches himself from his family and waits for Aschenbach to pass, deliberately looking him full in the face as he does so. But Aschenbach turns away; the Polish family disappears from view; and the strawberry seller reappears with her characteristic cry (Ex. 129). Aschenbach buys some fruit, but finds it musty to his taste. He sits down wearily by a well-head and is appalled by the chaos and sickness that seem to have overtaken him. He apostrophizes himself bitterly; and this leads to the most moving and most extended of all the recitative passages in the opera. In his dilemma he recalls the wisdom of Socrates and the argument in the *Phaedrus* about beauty and its ability to mediate between sensuous man and the world of the spirit—'*Does beauty lead to wisdom, Phaedrus?*' The musical setting recalls the beautiful *Hölderlin Fragments* for tenor and piano that Britten composed in 1958, and which Pears and himself performed so memorably at many of their recitals. Here Aschenbach is accompanied by flourishes from harp and piano, giving

Ex. 134

the singer the simplest cues; and the final notes of each cadence are prolonged by string harmonics. At the end of this deep, tranquil meditation there is a vigorous fugato passage for brass and woodwind based mainly on the landscape theme (Ex. 127)—strings are added at the climax. This is one of the most vigorous musical statements in the score.

Scene 17: The Departure

The Polish family decides to leave and Aschenbach sees their baggage waiting in the hall. He goes out on to the deserted beach, where presently Tadzio appears with some of his friends. The boy has a scrap with one of his friends and a chorus of voices (off-stage) calls '*Adziù!*' (see Ex. 130). Left alone, Tadzio makes a clear gesture towards Aschenbach; but the writer is unable to respond. The boy strolls down the beach towards the distant sea, his vibraphone theme (Ex. 128) soaring higher and higher, becoming increasingly attenuated, and ultimately dying away, while at the moment of death the writer remains slumped in his chair. This orchestral postlude is Britten's most searing Mahlerian *adagio*, bringing to a close his final opera, his farewell to the operatic stage, on a note of pain and passion. It also brings to a close a career in the opera house that spanned more than thirty years.

In a personal tribute to Britten, broadcast on BBC Radio on the day of the composer's death (4 December 1976), Michael Tippett summed up one of Britten's greatest achievements thus:

> [after *Peter Grimes*] he was now willing in himself, and, indeed, determined to be, within the twentieth century, a professional opera composer. That in itself is an extraordinarily difficult thing to do; and one of the achievements for which he will always be remembered in musical history books is that, in fact, he actually *did* it.

Appendix A
Chronological List of Published Compositions*

Key to Publishers:

B. & H. = Boosey & Hawkes Ltd.
F.M. = Faber Music Ltd.
A.C.B. = A. & C. Black Ltd., The Year Book Press.
N. = Novello & Co.
O.U.P. = Oxford University Press.
P.P.U. = Peace Pledge Union.

1925

FIVE WALZTES (WALTZES); for piano, composed between 1923 and 1925: edited by the composer 1969 F.M.

1929

THE BIRDS: song for medium voice and piano (words by Hilaire Belloc)—revised in 1934 B. & H.

A WEALDEN TRIO: Song of the Women (words by Ford Madox Ford); for women's voices (SSA) unaccompanied: edited by the composer 1967 F.M.

1930

A HYMN TO THE VIRGIN: anthem for mixed voices unaccompanied (words anon.)—revised in 1934 B. & H.

THE SYCAMORE TREE: for unaccompanied mixed chorus SATB (words traditional): edited by the composer 1967 F.M.

* This list does not include folk song arrangements and Purcell realizations. Those withdrawn or unpublished works that were published posthumously are listed separately at the end of Appendix A.

APPENDIX A

1931

TIT FOR TAT: five settings from boyhood of poems by Walter de la Mare, composed between 1928 and 1931: edited by the composer 1968 F.M.

SWEET WAS THE SONG: for contralto solo and chorus of female voices (from an unpublished Christmas Suite called *Thy King's Birthday*): edited by the composer 1966 F.M.

STRING QUARTET IN D MAJOR: edited by the composer 1975 F.M.

1932

THREE TWO-PART SONGS: for boys' or female voices and piano (words by Walter de la Mare) O.U.P.

SINFONIETTA: for chamber orchestra, op. 1 B. & H.

PHANTASY QUARTET: for oboe, violin, viola and cello, op. 2 B. & H.

1933

A BOY WAS BORN: choral variations for mixed voices unaccompanied, op. 3 (words selected from *Ancient English Christmas Carols* and the *Oxford Book of Carols*)—revised in 1955 O.U.P.

TWO PART SONGS: for mixed voices and piano—1. I Lov'd a Lass (words by George Wither); 2. Lift Boy (words by Robert Graves) B. & H.

1934

SIMPLE SYMPHONY: for string orchestra or string quartet, op. 4 O.U.P.

HOLIDAY DIARY: suite for piano, op. 5 B. & H.

FRIDAY AFTERNOONS: twelve songs for children's voices and piano, op. 7 (words selected from *Tom Tiddler's Ground* by Walter de la Mare and from other sources) B. & H.

MAY: unison song with piano (words anon.) A.C.B.

1935

SUITE: for violin and piano, op. 6, republished (B. & H. 1976) in a shorter version as *Three Pieces* for violin and piano (I March II Lullaby III Waltz) B. & H.

TE DEUM IN C MAJOR: for choir and organ O.U.P.

CHRONOLOGICAL LIST OF PUBLISHED COMPOSITIONS

1936

OUR HUNTING FATHERS: symphonic cycle for high voice and orchestra, op. 8 (text devised by W. H. Auden) B. & H.

SOIRÉES MUSICALES: suite of five movements from Rossini for orchestra, op. 9 B. & H.

1937

VARIATIONS ON A THEME OF FRANK BRIDGE: for string orchestra, op. 10 B. & H.

ON THIS ISLAND: five songs for high voice and piano, op. 11 (words by W. H. Auden) B. & H.

TWO BALLADS: for two sopranos and piano—1. Mother Comfort (words by Montagu Slater); 2. Underneath the Abject Willow (words by W. H. Auden) B. & H.

FISH IN THE UNRUFFLED LAKES: song for high voice and piano (words by W. H. Auden) B. & H.

MONT JUIC: suite of Catalan Dances for orchestra, op. 12—written with Lennox Berkeley B. & H.

PACIFIST MARCH: unison song with accompaniment (words by Ronald Duncan) P.P.U.

1938

PIANO CONCERTO in D, op. 13—revised in 1945 B. & H.

ADVANCE DEMOCRACY: chorus for mixed voices unaccompanied (words by Randall Swingler) B. & H.

1939

BALLAD OF HEROES: for high voice, chorus and orchestra, op. 14 (words by W. H. Auden and Randall Swingler) B. & H.

VIOLIN CONCERTO op. 15—revised in 1958 B. & H.

LES ILLUMINATIONS: for high voice and string orchestra, op. 18 (words by Arthur Rimbaud) B. & H.

CANADIAN CARNIVAL (KERMESSE CANADIENNE): for orchestra, op. 19 B. & H.

APPENDIX A

1940

SINFONIA DA REQUIEM: for orchestra, op. 20 B. & H.

DIVERSIONS ON A THEME: for piano (left hand) and orchestra, op. 21—revised in 1954 B. & H.

SEVEN SONNETS OF MICHELANGELO: for tenor and piano, op. 22 B. & H.

INTRODUCTION AND RONDO ALLA BURLESCA: for two pianos, op. 23, No. 1 B. & H.

1941

PAUL BUNYAN: operetta (libretto by W. H. Auden): revised by the composer in 1975 and given the opus number 17 F.M.

MATINÉES MUSICALES: second suite of five movements from Rossini for orchestra, op. 24 B. & H.

MAZURKA ELEGIACA: for two pianos, op. 23, No. 2 B. & H.

STRING QUARTET: No. 1 in D, op. 25 B. & H.

SCOTTISH BALLAD: for two pianos and orchestra, op. 26 B. & H.

1942

HYMN TO ST. CECILIA: for mixed voices unaccompanied, op. 27 (words by W. H. Auden) B. & H.

A CEREMONY OF CAROLS: for treble voices and harp, op. 28 (words by James, John and Robert Wedderburn, Robert Southwell, William Cornish, and from anonymous sources) B. & H.

1943

PRELUDE AND FUGUE: for eighteen-part string orchestra, op. 29 B. & H.

REJOICE IN THE LAMB: festival cantata for choir and organ, op. 30 (words by Christopher Smart) B. & H.

SERENADE: for tenor, horn and strings, op. 31 (words by Cotton, Tennyson, Blake, anon., Ben Jonson and Keats) B. & H.

THE BALLAD OF LITTLE MUSGRAVE AND LADY BARNARD: for male voices and piano (words anon.) B. & H.

CHRONOLOGICAL LIST OF PUBLISHED COMPOSITIONS

1944

A SHEPHERD'S CAROL: for unaccompanied voices (words by W. H. Auden)—written for the BBC programme 'A Poet's Christmas' N.

CHORALE (AFTER AN OLD FRENCH CAROL): for unaccompanied voices (words by W. H. Auden)—written for the BBC programme 'A Poet's Christmas'*

1945

PETER GRIMES: opera, op. 33 (libretto by Montagu Slater) B. & H.

FESTIVAL TE DEUM: for choir and organ, op. 32 B. & H.

THE YOUNG PERSON'S GUIDE TO THE ORCHESTRA: variations and fugue on a theme by Purcell, op. 34 B. & H.

THE HOLY SONNETS OF JOHN DONNE: for tenor and piano, op. 35 B. & H.

STRING QUARTET: No. 2 in C, op. 36 B. & H.

1946

THE RAPE OF LUCRETIA: opera, op. 37 (libretto by Ronald Duncan)—revised in 1947 B. & H.

AN OCCASIONAL OVERTURE IN C: for orchestra, op. 38—[*withdrawn*]

1947

ALBERT HERRING: comic opera, op. 39 (libretto by Eric Crozier) B. & H.

PRELUDE AND FUGUE ON A THEME OF VITTORIA: for organ B. & H.

CANTICLE I: for tenor and piano, op. 40 (words by Francis Quarles) B. & H.

A CHARM OF LULLABIES: for mezzo-soprano and piano, op. 41 (words by Blake, Burns, Robert Greene, Thomas Randolph and John Philip) B. & H.

1948

SAINT NICOLAS: cantata for tenor, mixed voices, string orchestra, piano, percussion and organ, op. 42 (words by Eric Crozier) B. & H.

THE BEGGAR'S OPERA: a new realization of John Gay's ballad opera, op. 43 B. & H.

* Published in *The Score*, No. 28, January 1961.

1949

SPRING SYMPHONY: for soprano, alto and tenor soli, mixed chorus, boys' choir and orchestra, op. 44 (words from various sources) B. & H.

THE LITTLE SWEEP: opera for young people, op. 45 (libretto by Eric Crozier) B. & H.

A WEDDING ANTHEM (Amo Ergo Sum): for soprano and tenor soli, choir and organ, op. 46 (words by Ronald Duncan) B. & H.

1950

FIVE FLOWER SONGS: for unaccompanied mixed chorus, op. 47—1. To Daffodils (words by Robert Herrick); 2. The Succession of the Four Sweet Months (Robert Herrick); 3. Marsh Flowers (George Crabbe); 4. The Evening Primrose (John Clare); 5. Ballad of Green Broom (anon.) B. & H.

LACHRYMAE—Reflections on a song of Dowland: for viola and piano, op. 48 also arranged for viola and strings by the composer in 1975 (op. 48a) B. & H.

1951

SIX METAMORPHOSES AFTER OVID: for oboe solo, op. 49—1. Pan; 2. Phaeton; 3. Niobe; 4. Bacchus; 5. Narcissus; 6. Arethusa B. & H.

BILLY BUDD: opera, op. 50 (libretto by E. M. Forster and Eric Crozier) B. & H.

1952

CANTICLE II—Abraham and Isaac: for alto, tenor and piano, op. 51 (text from the Chester Miracle Play) B. & H.

1953

GLORIANA: opera, op. 53 (libretto by William Plomer) B. & H.

WINTER WORDS: for tenor and piano, op. 52 (lyrics and ballads by Thomas Hardy) B. & H.

1954

THE TURN OF THE SCREW: opera, op. 54 (libretto by Myfanwy Piper after Henry James) B. & H.

CANTICLE III—'Still falls the rain': for tenor, horn and piano, op. 55 (words by Edith Sitwell) B. & H.

CHRONOLOGICAL LIST OF PUBLISHED COMPOSITIONS

1955

ALPINE SUITE: for recorder trio B. & H.

SCHERZO: for recorder quartet B. & H.

HYMN TO SAINT PETER: for mixed-voice choir with treble solo and organ (words from the Gradual of the Feast of St Peter and St Paul), op. 56a B. & H.

1956

ANTIPHON: for mixed-voice choir and organ (words by George Herbert) op. 56b B. & H.

THE PRINCE OF THE PAGODAS: ballet, op. 57 B. & H.

1957

SONGS FROM THE CHINESE: for high voice and guitar (words by Chinese poets, translated by Arthur Waley), op. 58 B. & H.

NOYE'S FLUDDE: the Chester Miracle Play set to music, op. 59 B. & H.

1958

EINLADUNG ZUR MARTINSGANS: eight-part canon composed for Martin Hürlimann's Sixtieth Birthday.

NOCTURNE: for tenor, seven obbligato instruments and string orchestra (words by Shelley, Tennyson, Coleridge, Middleton, Wordsworth, Owen, Keats, and Shakespeare), op. 60 B. & H.

SIX HÖLDERLIN FRAGMENTS: for tenor and piano, op. 61 B. & H.

1959

CANTATA ACADEMICA—CARMEN BASILIENSE: for soprano, alto, tenor, and bass solos, chorus and orchestra (Latin text from the charter of the University of Basle and from older orations in praise of Basle), op. 62 B. & H.

FANFARE FOR ST EDMUNDSBURY: for three trumpets B. & H.

MISSA BREVIS IN D: for boys' voices and organ, op. 63 B. & H.

1960

A MIDSUMMER NIGHT'S DREAM: opera, op. 64 (libretto by Benjamin Britten and Peter Pears after William Shakespeare) B. & H.

1961

SONATA IN C: for cello and piano, op. 65 — B. & H.
JUBILATE DEO: for mixed-voice choir and organ — O.U.P.
FANCIE: for unison voices and piano (words by Shakespeare) — B. & H.
WAR REQUIEM: for soprano, tenor and baritone solos, chorus, orchestra, chamber orchestra, boys' choir and organ (text: *Missa pro Defunctis* and poems by Wilfred Owen), op. 66 — B. & H.

1962

PSALM 150: for two-part children's voices and instruments, op. 67 — B. & H.
A HYMN OF SAINT COLUMBA—Regis regum rectissimi: for mixed voice choir and organ — B. & H.

1963

SYMPHONY FOR CELLO AND ORCHESTRA, op. 68 — B. & H.
CANTATA MISERICORDIUM: for tenor and baritone solos, small chorus and string orchestra, piano, harp, and timpani (Latin text by Patrick Wilkinson), op. 69 — B. & H.
NIGHT PIECE (NOTTURNO): for piano solo — B. & H.

1964

CADENZAS TO HAYDN'S CELLO CONCERTO IN C — B. & H.
NOCTURNAL (AFTER JOHN DOWLAND): for guitar solo, op. 70 — F.M.
CURLEW RIVER: a parable for church performance (text by William Plomer after the Japanese Noh Play, *Sumidagawa*), op. 71 — F.M.

1965

SUITE NO. 1 IN G MAJOR: for cello (edited by Mstislav Rostropovich), op. 72 — F.M.
GEMINI VARIATIONS: for flute, violin, and piano (four hands), op. 73 — F.M.
SONGS AND PROVERBS OF WILLIAM BLAKE: for baritone and piano, op. 74 — F.M.
VOICES FOR TODAY: anthem for full choir and boys' chorus, with optional organ accompaniment, op. 75 — F.M.
THE POET'S ECHO: six poems of Pushkin for high voice and piano, op. 76 — F.M.

1966

THE BURNING FIERY FURNACE: second parable for church performance (text by William Plomer), op. 77 F.M.

THE GOLDEN VANITY: vaudeville for boys' voices and piano, words by Colin Graham after the old English ballad, op. 78 F.M.

CADENZAS FOR MOZART'S PIANO CONCERTO IN E FLAT MAJOR (K. 482) F.M.

HANKIN BOOBY: folk dance for wind and drums F.M.

1967

OVERTURE 'THE BUILDING OF THE HOUSE': for orchestra and chorus, op. 79 F.M.

THE OXEN: carol for women's voices and piano (text by Thomas Hardy) F.M.

SUITE NO. 2 IN D MAJOR: for cello (edited by Mstislav Rostropovich) F.M.

1968

THE PRODIGAL SON: third parable for church performance (text by William Plomer) op. 81 F.M.

1969

CHILDREN'S CRUSADE: ballad for children's choir and orchestra (text by Bertolt Brecht), op. 82 F.M.

SUITE IN C: for harp solo, op. 83 F.M.

1970

WHO ARE THESE CHILDREN? for tenor and piano (Lyrics, Rhymes and Riddles by William Soutar), op. 84 F.M.

1971

OWEN WINGRAVE: opera (text by Myfanwy Piper after the story by Henry James), op. 85 F.M.

CANTICLE IV—*Journey of the Magi*: for counter-tenor, tenor, baritone and piano (text by T. S. Eliot), op. 86 F.M.

SUITE NO. 3 for cello (edited by Mstislav Rostropovich), op. 87 F.M.

1973

DEATH IN VENICE: opera (text by Myfanwy Piper after Thomas Mann), op. 88 F.M.

1974

CANTICLE V—*The Death of Saint Narcissus*: for tenor and harp (text by T. S. Eliot), op. 89 F.M.

SUITE ON ENGLISH FOLK TUNES '*A time there was . . .*' for orchestra, op. 90 F.M.

1975

SACRED AND PROFANE: eight medieval lyrics for unaccompanied voices (SSATB), op. 91 F.M.

A BIRTHDAY HANSEL for voice and harp (texts by Robert Burns), op. 92 F.M.

PHAEDRA: dramatic cantata for mezzo-soprano and small orchestra (text from Robert Lowell's translation of Racine's *Phedre*), op. 93 F.M.

STRING QUARTET NO. 3, op. 94 F.M.

1976

EIGHT FOLKSONG ARRANGEMENTS with harp or piano F.M.

WELCOME ODE: for young people's chorus and orchestra, op. 95 F.M.

Works Published Posthumously by Faber Music

1928

QUATRE CHANSONS FRANÇAISES: for soprano and orchestra (texts by Paul Verlaine and Victor Hugo) published in 1982

1932

PHANTASY: for string quintet (edited by John Evans) published in 1983

CHRONOLOGICAL LIST OF PUBLISHED COMPOSITIONS

1936

THREE DIVERTIMENTI: for string quartet (I March II Waltz III Burlesque) revised by the composer from *Alla Quartetto Serioso: 'Go play, boy, play'* (1933) and published in 1983

RUSSIAN FUNERAL: march for brass and percussion, published in 1981

1937

REVEILLE: fanfare for violin and piano, published in 1983

1937–9

CABARET SONGS: for voice and piano (words by W. H. Auden): 1. Tell me the truth about love 2. Funeral Blues 3. Johnny 4. Calypso. Published in 1980

1939

YOUNG APOLLO: fanfare for pianoforte solo, string quartet and string orchestra, op. 16: withdrawn by the composer but published in 1982

1947

MEN OF GOODWILL: variations on 'God rest ye merry, Gentlemen', for orchestra: composed for a BBC radio feature broadcast on Christmas Day 1947: published in 1982

1962

THE TWELVE APOSTLES: for solo voice, unison chorus and piano: published in 1981

Appendix B
First Performances of the Operas

PAUL BUNYAN

5 May 1941	New York, Columbia University Brander Matthew Hall

Operetta in a prologue and two acts. Text by W. H. Auden

In the Prologue

OLD TREES	Chorus
YOUNG TREES	Ellen Huffmaster, Jane Weaver, Marlowe Jones, Ben Carpens
THREE WILD GEESE	Harriet Greene, Augusta Dorn, Pauline Kleinhesselink

In the Interludes

NARRATOR	Mordecai Bauman

In the Play

THE VOICE OF PAUL BUNYAN	Milton Warchoff
CROSS CROSSHAULSON	Walter Graf
JOHN SHEARS	Leonard Stocker
SAM SHARKEY	Clifford Jackson
BEN BENNY	Eugene Bonham
JEN JENSON	Ernest Holcombe
PETE PETERSON	Lewis Pierce
ANDY ANDERSON	Ben Carpens
OTHER LUMBERJACKS	Alan Adair, Elmer Barber, Arnold Jaffe, Marlowe Jones, Charles Snitow, Robert Zeller, W. Fredric Plette, Thomas Flynn, Joseph Harrow
WESTERN UNION BOY	Henry Bauman
HEL HELSON	Bliss Woodward

JOHNNY INKSLINGER	William Hess
FIDO	Pauline Kleinhesselink
MOPPET	Harriet Greene
POPPET	Augusta Dorn
THE DEFEATED	Ben Carpens, Eugene Bonham, Adelaide Van Wey, Ernest Holcombe
SLIM	Charles Cammock
TINY	Helen Marshall
THE FILM STARS AND MODELS	Eleanor Hutchings, Ellen Huffmaster, Ben Carpens, Lewis Pierce
FRONTIER WOMEN	Marie Bellejean, Eloise Calinger, Irma Commanday, Alice Gerstz Duschak, Marian Edwards, Elizabeth Flynn, Rose Harris, Ethel Madsen, Jean Phillips, Evelyn Ray, Irma Schocken, Adelaide Van Wey, Jane Weaver, Ida Weirich, Marjorie Williamson

Conductor: Hugh Ross
Producer: Milton Smith

PETER GRIMES

7 June 1945 London, Sadler's Wells Theatre
Opera in three acts and a prologue derived from the poem of George Crabbe. Text by Montagu Slater

PETER GRIMES	Peter Pears
ELLEN ORFORD	Joan Cross
AUNTIE	Edith Coates
NIECE I	Blanche Turner
NIECE II	Minnia Bower
BALSTRODE	Roderick Jones
MRS. SEDLEY	Valetta Iacopi
SWALLOW	Owen Brannigan
NED KEENE	Edmund Donlevy
BOB BOLES	Morgan Jones
THE RECTOR	Tom Culbert
HOBSON	Frank Vaughan
DOCTOR THORPE	Sasa Machov
A BOY (GRIMES'S APPRENTICE)	Leonard Thompson

Conductor: Reginald Goodall
Producer: Eric Crozier
Scenery and Costumes: Kenneth Green

THE RAPE OF LUCRETIA

12 July 1946 — Glyndebourne Opera House, Sussex

Opera in two acts. Text by Ronald Duncan, after *Le Viol de Lucrèce* by André Obey.

MALE CHORUS	Peter Pears
FEMALE CHORUS	Joan Cross
COLLATINUS	Owen Brannigan
JUNIUS	Edmund Donlevy
TARQUINIUS	Otakar Kraus
LUCRETIA	Kathleen Ferrier
BIANCA	Anna Pollak
LUCIA	Margaret Ritchie

Conductor: Ernest Ansermet
Producer: Eric Crozier
Designer: John Piper

ALBERT HERRING

20 June 1947 — Glyndebourne Opera House, Sussex (E.O.G. production)

Comic opera in three acts. Text by Eric Crozier, freely adapted from a short story by Guy de Maupassant.

LADY BILLOWS	Joan Cross
FLORENCE PIKE	Gladys Parr
MISS WORDSWORTH	Margaret Ritchie
THE VICAR	William Parsons
THE SUPERINTENDENT OF POLICE	Norman Lumsden
THE MAYOR	Roy Ashton
SID	Frederick Sharp
ALBERT HERRING	Peter Pears
NANCY	Nancy Evans
MRS HERRING	Betsy de la Porte

EMMIE	Lesley Duff
CIS	Anne Sharp
HARRY	David Spenser

Conductor: Benjamin Britten
Producer: Frederick Ashton
Scenery and costumes: John Piper

THE BEGGAR'S OPERA

24 May 1948 — Cambridge, Arts Theatre (E.O.G. production)

A new musical version of John Gay's ballad opera (1728), realized from the original airs, in three acts.

BEGGAR	Gladys Parr
MR. PEACHUM	George James
MRS. PEACHUM	Flora Nielsen
POLLY	Nancy Evans
CAPTAIN MACHEATH	Peter Pears
FILCH	Norman Platt
LOCKIT	Otakar Kraus
LUCY LOCKIT	Rose Hill
JENNY DIVER	Jennifer Vyvyan
MRS. VIXEN	Lesley Duff
SUKY TAWDRY	Lily Kettlewell
MRS. COAXER	Catherine Lawson
DOLLY TRULL	Gladys Parr
MRS. SLAMMEKIN	Elisabeth Parry
MOLLY BRAZEN	Anne Sharp
BETTY DOXY	Mildred Watson
HARRY PADDINGTON	Roy Ashton
BEN BUDGE	Denis Dowling
WAT DREARY	John Highcock
MAT OF THE MINT	Norman Lumsden
JEMMY TWITCHER	Norman Platt
NIMMING NED	Max Worthley

Conductor: Benjamin Britten
Producer: Tyrone Guthrie
Assistant Producer: Basil Coleman
Scenery and costumes: Tanya Moiseiwitsch

APPENDIX B

THE LITTLE SWEEP

14 June 1949 — Aldeburgh, Jubilee Hall (E.O.G. production)

The opera from *Let's Make an Opera!*, an entertainment for young people. Text by Eric Crozier. One act.

BLACK BOB	Norman Lumsden
CLEM	Max Worthley
SAM	John Moules
MISS BAGGOTT	Gladys Parr
JULIET BROOK	Anne Sharp
GAY BROOK	Bruce Hines
SOPHIE BROOK	Monica Garrod
ROWAN	Elisabeth Parry
JONNY CROME	Peter Cousins
HUGH CROME	Ralph Canham
TINA CROME	Mavis Gardiner

Conductor: Norman Del Mar
Producer: Basil Coleman
Scenery and costumes: John Lewis

BILLY BUDD

1 December 1951 — London, Covent Garden

Opera in a prologue, four acts,* and an epilogue. Test by E. M. Forster and Eric Crozier, after the story by Herman Melville.

CAPTAIN VERE	Peter Pears
BILLY BUDD	Theodor Uppman
CLAGGART	Frederick Dalberg
MR. REDBURN	Hervey Alan
MR. FLINT	Geraint Evans
LIEUTENANT RATCLIFFE	Michael Langdon
RED WHISKERS	Anthony Marlowe
DONALD	Bryan Drake
DANSKER	Inia Te Wiata
NOVICE	William McAlpine
SQUEAK	David Tree
BOSUN	Ronald Lewis

* In the 1960 revision, these four acts were reduced to two.

FIRST MATE	Rhydderch Davies
SECOND MATE	Hubert Littlewood
MAINTOP	Emlyn Jones
NOVICE'S FRIEND	John Cameron
ARTHUR JONES	Alan Hobson
FOUR MIDSHIPMEN	Brian Ethridge, Kenneth Nash, Peter Spencer, Colin Waller
CABIN BOY	Peter Flynn

Conductor: Benjamin Britten
Producer: Basil Coleman
Designer: John Piper

GLORIANA

8 June 1953 London, Covent Garden

Opera in three acts. Text by William Plomer. Composed in honour of the Coronation of HM Queen Elizabeth II, and first given at a gala performance in the presence of HM The Queen.

QUEEN ELIZABETH I	Joan Cross
EARL OF ESSEX	Peter Pears
LADY ESSEX	Monica Sinclair
LORD MOUNTJOY	Geraint Evans
PENELOPE LADY RICH	Jennifer Vyvyan
SIR ROBERT CECIL	Arnold Matters
SIR WALTER RALEIGH	Frederick Dalberg
HENRY CUFFE	Ronald Lewis
LADY-IN-WAITING	Adele Leigh
A BLIND BALLAD-SINGER	Inia Te Wiata
THE RECORDER OF NORWICH	Michael Langdon
A HOUSEWIFE	Edith Coates
SPIRIT OF THE MASQUE	William McAlpine
MASTER OF CEREMONIES	David Tree
CITY CRIER	Rhydderch Davies
TIME	Desmond Doyle
CONCORD	Svetlana Beriosova

Conductor: John Pritchard
Producer: Basil Coleman
Designer: John Piper
Choreographer: John Cranko

APPENDIX B

THE TURN OF THE SCREW

14 September 1954	Venice, Teatro la Fenice (E.O.G. production)

Opera in a prologue and two acts. Text by Myfanwy Piper, after the story by Henry James.

PROLOGUE	Peter Pears
THE GOVERNESS	Jennifer Vyvyan
MRS. GROSE	Joan Cross
QUINT	Peter Pears
MISS JESSEL	Arda Mandikian
FLORA	Olive Dyer
MILES	David Hemmings

Conductor: Benjamin Britten
Producer: Basil Coleman
Designer: John Piper

NOYE'S FLUDDE

18 June 1958	Orford Church, Suffolk (E.O.G. production)

The Chester Miracle Play set to music. One act.

THE VOICE OF GOD	Trevor Anthony
NOYE	Owen Brannigan
MRS. NOYE	Gladys Parr
SEM	Thomas Bevan
HAM	Marcus Norman
JAFFETT	Michael Crawford
MRS. SEM	Janette Miller
MRS. HAM	Katherine Dyson
MRS. JAFFETT	Marilyn Baker
THE RAVEN	David Bedwell
THE DOVE	Maria Spall
MRS. NOYE'S GOSSIPS	Penelope Allen, Doreen Metcalfe, Dawn Mendham, Beverley Newman
PROPERTY MEN	Andrew Birt, William Collard, John Day, Gerald Turner

Conductor: Charles Mackerras
Production and setting: Colin Graham
Costumes: Ceri Richards

A MIDSUMMER NIGHT'S DREAM

11 June 1960 — Aldeburgh, Jubilee Hall (E.O.G. production)

Opera in three acts. Text adapted from William Shakespeare's play by Benjamin Britten and Peter Pears.

OBERON	Alfred Deller
TYTANIA	Jennifer Vyvyan
PUCK	Leonide Massine II
PEASEBLOSSOM	Michael Bauer
COBWEB	Kevin Platts
MUSTARDSEED	Robert McCutcheon
MOTH	Barry Ferguson
FAIRIES	Thomas Bevan, Thomas Smyth
THESEUS	Forbes Robinson
HIPPOLYTA	Johanna Peters
LYSANDER	George Maran
DEMETRIUS	Thomas Hemsley
HERMIA	Marjorie Thomas
HELENA	April Cantelo
BOTTOM	Owen Brannigan
QUINCE	Norman Lumsden
FLUTE	Peter Pears
SNUG	David Kelly
SNOUT	Edward Byles
STARVELING	Joseph Ward
MASTER OF CEREMONIES	John Perry
ATTENDANT	Jeremy Cullum
PAGES	Robert Hodgson, Nicholas Cooper

Conductor: Benjamin Britten
Producer: John Cranko
Scenery and costumes: John Piper, assisted by Carl Toms

APPENDIX B

CURLEW RIVER

13 June 1964	Orford Church, Suffolk (E.O.G. production)

Parable for church performance in one act. Text by William Plomer, after the Japanese Noh-play *Sumidagawa* by Motomasa.

THE ABBOT	Don Garrard
THE FERRYMAN	John Shirley-Quirk
THE TRAVELLER	Bryan Drake
THE MADWOMAN	Peter Pears
THE SPIRIT OF THE BOY	Robert Carr
HIS VOICE	Bruce Webb
THE PILGRIMS	John Barrow, Bernard Dickerson, Brian Etheridge, Edward Evanko, John Kitchener, Peter Leeming, Philip May, Nigel Rogers

Production and setting: Colin Graham
Costumes: Annena Stubbs

THE BURNING FIERY FURNACE

9 June 1966	Orford Church, Suffolk (E.O.G. production)

Parable for church performance in one act. Text by William Plomer.

THE ASTROLOGER (THE ABBOT)	Bryan Drake
NEBUCHADNEZZAR	Peter Pears
ANANIAS	John Shirley-Quirk
MISAEL	Robert Tear
AZARIAS	Victor Godfrey
THE ANGEL	Philip Wait
ENTERTAINERS AND PAGES	Stephen Borton, Paul Copcutt, Paul Davies, Richard Jones, Philip Wait
THE HERALD AND CHORUS LEADER	Peter Leeming
CHORUS OF COURTIERS	Graham Allum, Peter Lehmann Bedford, Carl Duggan, John Harrod, William McKinney, Malcolm Rivers, Jacob Witkin

Production and setting: Colin Graham
Costumes and properties: Annena Stubbs

THE PRODIGAL SON

10 June 1968	Orford Church, Suffolk (E.O.G. production)

Parable for church performance in one act. Text by William Plomer.

THE TEMPTER (THE ABBOT)	Peter Pears
THE FATHER	John Shirley-Quirk
THE ELDER SON	Bryan Drake
THE YOUNGER SON	Robert Tear
CHORUS OF SERVANTS, PARASITES AND BEGGARS	Paschal Allen, Peter Bedford, Carl Duggan, David Hartley, Peter Leeming, John McKenzie, Clive Molloy, Paul Wade
YOUNG SERVANTS AND DISTANT VOICES	Robert Alder, John Harriman, Peter Heriot, Richard Kahn, David Morgan

Production and setting: Colin Graham
Costumes and properties: Annena Stubbs

OWEN WINGRAVE

18 May 1971	BBC 2

Opera for Television. Text by Myfanwy Piper based on the short story by Henry James.

OWEN WINGRAVE	Benjamin Luxon
SPENCER COYLE	John Shirley-Quirk
LECHMERE	Nigel Douglas
MISS WINGRAVE	Sylvia Fisher
MRS. COYLE	Heather Harper
MRS. JULIAN	Jennifer Vyvyan
KATE JULIAN	Janet Baker
GENERAL SIR PHILIP WINGRAVE	Peter Pears

COLONEL WINGRAVE AND GHOST	Peter Pears
YOUNG WINGRAVE AND GHOST	Stephen Hattersley
YOUNG WINGRAVE'S FRIEND	Geoffrey West
NARRATOR	Peter Pears

Conductor: Benjamin Britten
Producer: Brian Large and Colin Graham
Designer: David Myerscough Jones
Costumes: Charles Knode

DEATH IN VENICE

16 June 1973 — The Maltings, Snape (E.O.G. production)

Opera in two acts. Text by Myfanwy Piper, based on the short story by Thomas Mann.

GUSTAV VON ASCHENBACH	Peter Pears
THE TRAVELLER THE ELDERLY FOP THE OLD GONDOLIER THE HOTEL MANAGER THE HOTEL BARBER THE LEADER OF THE PLAYERS THE VOICE OF DIONYSUS	John Shirley-Quirk
THE VOICE OF APOLLO	James Bowman
THE POLISH MOTHER	Deanna Bergsma
TADZIO	Robert Huguenin

and members of the English Opera Group, the Royal Ballet, and children of the Royal Ballet School

Conductor: Steuart Bedford
Producer: Colin Graham
Designer: John Piper
Costumes: Charles Knode
Choreographer: Sir Frederick Ashton

Appendix C
Short Bibliography

This short bibliography is confined to books (and booklets) by Britten, and on him and his music. A useful list of articles in periodicals and books, and of special Britten issues of magazines, up to 1952, is given in the Mitchell/Keller symposium listed below.

ABBIATI, FRANCO. *Peter Grimes.* (A volume in the series 'Guide Musicali dell'Istituto d'Alta Cultura'.) Milan, n.d. [1949].

BRITTEN, BENJAMIN. *On Receiving the First Aspen Award.* London, Faber and Faber, 1964.

BRITTEN, BENJAMIN, AND IMOGEN HOLST. *The Story of Music.* London, Rathbone Books, 1958. Reissued as *The Wonderful World of Music,* London, Macdonald, 1968.

CROZIER, ERIC (ed.) *Peter Grimes.* (Sadler's Wells Opera Books, no. 3) London, The Bodley Head, 1945.

(ed.) *La Création de l'Opéra anglais et 'Peter Grimes'.* French translations of Sadler's Wells Opera Books nos. 1 and 3 by C. Ormore and Annie Brierre. Paris, Richard-Masse, 1947.

(ed.) *The Rape of Lucretia: a symposium.* London, The Bodley Head, 1948.

GISHFORD, ANTHONY (ed.) *Tribute to Benjamin Britten on his Fiftieth Birthday.* London, Faber and Faber, 1963.

HOLST, IMOGEN. *Britten.* (A volume in the 'Great Composers' series.) London, Faber and Faber, 1966. 2nd edition 1970, 3rd edition 1980. [See also under BENJAMIN BRITTEN]

HOWARD, PATRICIA. *The Operas of Benjamin Britten.* London, Barrie and Rockliff, 1969.

HURD, MICHAEL. *Benjamin Britten.* (A pamphlet in the 'Biographies of Great Composers' series.) London, Novello, 1966.

KELLER, HANS. *The Rape of Lucretia: Albert Herring.* (A booklet in the 'Covent Garden Operas' series.) London, Boosey and Hawkes, 1947. [See also under DONALD MITCHELL]

MITCHELL, DONALD, AND HANS KELLER (eds.) *Benjamin Britten: a Commentary on his works from a group of specialists.* London, Rockliff, 1952. (Also: Greenwood Press reprint, U.S.A., 1972.)

[MITCHELL, DONALD (ed.) and JOHN ANDREWES] *Benjamin Britten: A Complete Catalogue of his Works.* London, Boosey & Hawkes, 1963. Revised edition 1973 with supplement to 1976, Boosey & Hawkes and Faber Music Ltd.

[PEARS, PETER]. *Armenian Holiday: August 1965.* Privately printed. n.d. [1965].

STUART, CHARLES. *Peter Grimes.* (A booklet in the 'Covent Garden Operas' series.) London, Boosey & Hawkes, 1947.

WHITE, ERIC WALTER. *Benjamin Britten: a Sketch of his Life and Works.* London, Boosey & Hawkes, 1948.

Benjamin Britten: eine Skizze von Leben und Werk. German translation by Bettina and Martin Hürlimann. Zurich, Atlantis Verlag, 1948.

Benjamin Britten: a Sketch of his Life and Work. New edition, revised and enlarged. London, Boosey and Hawkes, 1954.

Benjamin Britten: His Life and Operas. London, Faber and Faber in association with Boosey & Hawkes, 1970.

YOUNG, PERCY M. *Benjamin Britten.* ('Masters of Music' series.) London, Benn, 1966.

Since this Bibliography was compiled in 1970, and particularly since Britten's death in 1976, a great number of books have been written about the composer. The Editor has included these for reference purposes, though they obviously have no bearing on Eric Walter White's text.

BLYTH, ALAN. *Remembering Britten* (with notable contributions from Britten's family, friends and colleagues). London, Hutchinson, 1981.

EVANS, PETER. *The Music of Benjamin Britten.* London, Dent, 1979.

HEADINGTON, CHRISTOPHER. *Britten.* (A volume in the series entitled 'The Composer as Contemporary'—General Editor: John Lade.) London, Eyre Methuen, 1981.

HERBERT, DAVID. *The Operas of Benjamin Britten.* London, Hamish Hamilton, 1979.

KENNEDY, MICHAEL. *Britten.* (A volume in the 'Master Musicians' series.) London, Dent, 1981.

MITCHELL, DONALD and JOHN EVANS. *Benjamin Britten: Pictures from a Life 1913–1976.* London, Faber and Faber, 1978.

MITCHELL, DONALD. *Britten and Auden in the Thirties: The Year 1936.* (The T. S. Eliot Memorial Lectures delivered at the University of Kent at Canterbury in November 1979.) London, Faber and Faber, 1981.

WHITTALL, ARNOLD. *The Music of Britten and Tippett: Studies in Themes and Techniques.* Cambridge University Press, 1982.

Appendix D
From **The Britten Estate Executors' Press Statement** (1977)

A.1 The Aldeburgh Festival has already celebrated its thirtieth year, and with the continuing artistic guidance of Peter Pears and the other Artistic Directors who will be joined next year as an Artistic Director by Mstislav Rostropovich, the world-famous cellist and long standing friend of Aldeburgh, the Executors are confident that the Festival's future is assured.

A.2 As for the development of the Britten–Pears Library at The Red House, where Britten lived and worked for twenty-five years, and which was already established by him and Peter Pears during the last years of Britten's life, the Executors are acutely aware of the unique opportunity which exists to keep together *in an integral collection* the contents of Britten's working library, his personal archives and papers and—most important of all—a major collection of his musical manuscripts and sketches which includes some of his most celebrated compositions, such as WAR REQUIEM, THE TURN OF THE SCREW, and DEATH IN VENICE. That the integrity of the collection should be preserved and that the manuscripts should remain at Aldeburgh are aims to which the Executors are vigorously committed, and these form the basis of their current negotiations in both the national and international interest—so they believe—with HM Treasury. The importance of Aldeburgh is central to the understanding of the composer, who himself said in 1964: 'I belong at home—there—in Aldeburgh. I have tried to bring music *to* it in the shape of our local Festival; and all the music I write comes *from* it. I believe in roots, associations, in backgrounds, in personal relationships. . . . I do not write for posterity. . . . I write music, now, in Aldeburgh, for people living there, and further afield, indeed for anyone who cares to play it or listen to it. But my music now has its roots in where I live and work.'

A.3 Britten's concern for the development of musicianship and musical understanding among young people scarcely needs stressing in view of such famous works as LET'S MAKE AN OPERA! and NOYE'S FLUDDE—which beguilingly 'educate' those participating in their performance—and the

YOUNG PERSON'S GUIDE which has educated successive generations of listeners. It is those primarily creative ideals, matched with the standards of excellence and musical insight embodied in the performances given by Peter Pears and Benjamin Britten throughout the long years they worked together as partners—not to speak of Britten's activities as a performer and conductor of many other composers' works beside his own—which the Britten–Pears School for Advanced Musical Studies will nourish, sustain and expand. The School, to which Britten devoted much thought before his death, is fortunate in having Peter Pears as its Director of Singing, and Cecil Aronowitz as Director of Strings. It is also planned to develop the area of Academic Studies, which will introduce specialist study and research in the Britten field as well as in those other musical territories especially associated with Aldeburgh. Imogen Holst has been closely associated with the planning of the School and its curriculum. The School will gradually evolve from its present part-time status into a full-time institution, and one which will not only fill a unique national need for a Music School post-graduate in character, but also constitute a permanent living memorial to Benjamin Britten and to his work as a performer with Peter Pears. His Executors intend to support the development of this project, which will further the challenging musical standards on which Britten insisted throughout his life. Public financial support on a substantial scale is needed now, and extensive preparations are being made for launching the Britten Memorial Appeal in the autumn.

A number of Britten's manuscripts, including the full score of the *War Requiem*, were presented to the Nation and received by HM Treasury in lieu of capital transfer tax. They are at present on loan from the British Library, together with the composer's other manuscripts, at the Britten–Pears Library in Aldeburgh.

The Benjamin Britten Memorial Appeal was launched in order to convert the south block of the Maltings complex for the Britten–Pears School for Advanced Musical Studies, as the national memorial to the composer. The School was officially opened by HM Queen Elizabeth, The Queen Mother (Patron of the Aldeburgh Festival) on 28 April 1979, and it continues to flourish under its Founder-Director, Sir Peter Pears, C.B.E.

J.E. 1982

Index

Figures in **bold** indicate major entries and figures in *italics* refer to illustrations. Works by Britten are indexed only under Britten, Edward Benjamin.

INDEX

INDEX

INDEX